Reflections on Risk
Volume V

ASA Institute for Risk and Innovation

Annie Searle & Associates LLC

Edited by Emily Hayes

Printed in the United States of America
First edition: September 2019
Tautegory Press, Seattle, Washington USA

Printing History
All research notes here were previously published as "ASA Research Notes" in ASA Newsletters ©Annie Searle & Associates LLC and at its website www.anniesearle.com, from August 2017 through July 2019.

Library of Congress Control Number: 2019912896
ISBN: 978-1-7334390-1-5

Cover design by Jesse Brown

CONTENTS

FORWARD

Just as technology has undergone remarkable transformation over the past ten years, ASA's Institute for Risk and Innovation has evolved to provide both immediate and longer-term access to research notes that reflect the most urgent issues of our time.

Early on, we focused on risks around our nation's critical infrastructure and public-private partnerships because those areas represented our advisory practice. More recently, we have published more research around the impact on society of social media and sophisticated cyber-tools. As a result, research has focused not only on critical infrastructure risks or public-private partnerships, but also around information ethics and policy, privacy, disinformation, artificial intelligence, surveillance and cryptocurrency. My own time is spent primarily in the classroom, but also working on policy issues around regulation, disaster recovery and advocacy for privacy regulation.

With this fifth volume of Reflections on Risk, we will have published 124 research notes by over 60 authors since 2012. Each research note is published first in our monthly publication, *ASA News & Notes*, then housed on the ASA website until we have 24 or so research notes to gather into a volume like this one. We have streamlined our processes for publication somewhat over the years, but the principles from which we publish remain the same.

The primary source of research notes is from courses I teach at the University of Washington's Information School, most of which focus on risk, cybersecurity and information ethics, policy and law. I read all the papers that my students submit, as does my assistant, so students get two sets of comments on their work. Papers that I offer to publish must meet a high bar: not only must they be well organized and well written, but they must contain original analysis and cutting-edge recommendations for managing the risks as well. The papers that become research notes are meant to provide executives and practitioners alike with a short but accurate lens through which to view increasingly complex issues driven by information and technology, such as privacy, ethics, artificial intelligence, the Internet of Things, cryptocurrency, disinformation, policy, and regulation.

I hope you find this fifth volume useful. Special thanks to Emily Hayes (formerly Oxenford), editor of this and three other volumes of Reflections on Risk. Emily is also the editor of our monthly newsletter, *ASA News & Notes*, where these research notes first appear.

Annie Searle
Seattle, 2019

THE CONTRIBUTORS

Catherine Bahn is a seasoned content and marketing business leader and producer. She has worked for Microsoft, managing teams and establishing partnerships with other content leaders and corporations worldwide such as CBS, Associated Press, and The New York Times. She received her Master of Science in Information Management degree from the University of Washington in 2019 and holds a Bachelor of Science degree in Biology from Pepperdine University.

Elizabeth Crooks is an associate security consultant for Coalfire, where she works as a part of their GDPR and Privacy team, performing readiness and compliance assessments, and helping clients execute data privacy plans. She holds a Master of Science in Information Management degree with a focus on information security from the University of Washington, and a Bachelor of Arts degree in History from Haverford College.

Blake Franzen graduated from the University of Washington in 2019, majoring in Informatics with a focus in information security and data science. He is currently working with Amazon Web Services as a technical apprentice in the hopes of becoming a solutions architect for the platform. Blake is also working with a small software engineering firm in Seattle as well as the city, to help develop an early warning system for earthquakes in the Greater Seattle area.

Alexander N. George is a graduate of the University of Washington holding a Master of Science in Information Management and a Bachelor of Arts in Business Administration with an Information Systems focus. Alex is a United States Marine Corps veteran, having served honorably from 2002 to 2006 including a deployment during Operation Iraqi Freedom. He currently works for the United States Department of Veterans Affairs as a Management Analyst where he strives to deliver value to veterans by improving processes and supporting compensation and pension operations.

Lukas Guericke received his Bachelor of Arts in Sociology with a minor in Informatics while completing the Interdisciplinary Honors Program from the University of Washington in 2019. He has interned at PSB Market Research where he worked on a reputation tracker for Amazon in 12 different countries. He hopes to enroll into an MSIM program after working for a couple years in the intersection of data science and social good.

Beth Hutchens is a data privacy and security professional in Seattle, Washington. She began her career as a privacy, technology, and intellectual property attorney. In 2017, she earned her LLM (Master of Laws) degree in privacy and public policy from the University of Washington School of Law. She currently runs her own consulting company where she assists clients with regulatory compliance, information governance, cyber risk management, and written policies and procedures.

Phoebe Keleman holds a 2019 Master of Science in Information Management degree from the University of Washington. Combined with her undergraduate degrees in Business and Theatre Arts from the University of Puget Sound, Keleman is committed to improving information fluency and the use of information technology in nonprofit organizations in the Pacific Northwest.

Bruno Langevin is a risk professional who has worked in the banking, manufacturing and pharmaceutical industries. He holds an associate degree in computer science from College Ste-Foy, and numerous industry certifications including the MBCI and CBCP designations.

Jeff Leonard received his Master of Science in Information Management degree and a Bachelor of Science degree in Physics, both earned at the University of Washington in 2018 and 1998, respectively. Jeff has been a professional software developer since the early 1980s and owner of Mentat Consulting from 1996 to 2017. Currently, Jeff works as an independent consultant at TopDevz.

Miranda Lin graduated Magna Cum Laude from the University of Washington with a Bachelor of Science degree in Informatics in 2019. Her professional experience includes interning as a UX designer at Holland America Line and at Kernel Labs.

Kyle McNulty is a cybersecurity consultant at KPMG where he has helped various Fortune 500 companies build out robust security tool sets and processes. He graduated from the University of Washington with a Bachelor of Science in Informatics with a focus in information security, and he has previously presented on the Internet of Things (IoT) in front of international groups.

Nicolas Montgomery is currently a cybersecurity consultant at Sila Solutions Group, where his current primary role is to threat model his client's applications as they migrate into different cloud vendors. Nick received his Bachelor of Science degree in Informatics from the University of Washington in 2017 with a focus on information security.

Malory Rose graduated from the University of Washington in 2019 with a Bachelor of Science in Informatics as a Division One athlete for the University of Washington Gymnastics team. She was a part of the top one percent chosen for a Nike summer internship in 2018, where she was able to use the skills achieved through the Informatics program. Malory was part of the Workplace Design and Connectivity division where she was placed on four projects, with roles ranging from research analysis to project management.

Zhuo Shan received his Bachelor of Science degree in Informatics with a focus in information assurance and cybersecurity from the University of Washington in 2019. His professional experience includes completing an internship with Transcend Academy, an education technology startup, where he developed educational platform "Lana". Currently Zhuo continues working as a full stack software engineer for Lana, helping the platform reach global customers.

Kyle Simpson received his Bachelor of Science in Informatics degree from the University of Washington in 2019. His professional experience includes completing an internship with Liberty Mutual Insurance's information security team, where he helped implement cloud-agnostic auto-remediation systems for enterprise container pipelines, in addition to serving as the director of the University of Washington's tour guide program in 2018-2019. Currently Kyle works as a data analyst at the Institute for Health Metrics and Evaluation, assisting multiple teams with their work on the Global Burden of Disease study.

Emily Ye received her Bachelor of Science in Informatics degree with a focus in information assurance and cybersecurity, as well as data science from the University of Washington in 2019. She is working at Boeing on a rotation program, currently as a full stack developer that helps to create analytic frameworks.

SECTION ONE

Information Infrastructure

PAPER	AUTHOR
Arrayent's Inherent Risks	Kyle Simpson
Life-Critical Applications and Serverless Computing	Kate Schenot
Risks with BYOD in Government Agencies	Beth Hutchens
Shadow IT and Organizational Risks	Nicholas Montgomery
Smart Homes: Evaluating Risks and Being Smart	Mikhail Victorovich Savvateev
The Airline Industry's IoT Risks	Kyle Simpson
The Internet of Things: A Dark Precursor	Kyle McNulty

Arrayent's Inherent Risks

Kyle Simpson

Written: Nov. 2017
Published: Dec. 2017

Abstract: Risk is an inherent part of every business, and in the ever-evolving global economy, managing risk effectively and appropriately is crucial to maintaining competitive advantage as a company. This paper examines Arrayent, an Internet of Things (IoT) cloud service company that manages dozens of large companies including Whirlpool, Maytag, Liftmaster, and Febreeze; and makes recommendations of risk mitigation paths given the company's potential control failures.

Arrayent is a third-party cloud service that partners with companies to help them connect their products to the Internet of Things (IoT). Arrayent's platform "transforms traditional products into connected devices, acquires and transmits usage and device data in formats that power business intelligence systems, and enables device interoperability through cloud-to-cloud integration with third-party ecosystems."1 This essentially boils down to Arrayent being a cloud connection service that offers consumers "a way to interact with their connected product," and allows companies to outsource their data collection and management.1 Using Whirlpool as an example, Arrayent uses the sensors in washing machines manufactured by Whirlpool, collects any and all data Whirlpool may be interested in, and presents this data in a portal that Whirlpool can use to make informed decisions based on insights from their own data. By outsourcing their data collection, Whirlpool can spend more time on the manufacturing and customer relations side of their business, freeing up resources they can dynamically allocate elsewhere.

Being a cloud-based company, and a company that works heavily with third-party businesses, there are inherent risks that are present. In a meeting with two House of Representatives subcommittees, Bruce Scheiner, a cybersecurity researcher, commented that there is a clear relationship between cost and vulnerability potential. Products that are frequently replaced (such as smartphones) are patched more often since these companies want to maintain a content, consistent customer base. Products that are infrequently replaced (like refrigerators) are patched less frequently since there is a longer life-cycle and less turn-around. Scheiner puts it simply, saying that, "If there is not a profit or cost benefit for the manufacturer to patch a less frequently replaced product, then there is no drive for the manufacturer to patch it regularly."2 Since Arrayent typically collaborates with businesses that specialize in the long-lasting category of product Scheiner references, there is already an inherent operational risk for Arrayent that is based on the partner company's willingness to provide long-term support for their products. In conjunction with this overarching operational risk, there are three specific risk areas to examine: 1) the risks associated with systematic failures, 2) the risks associated with external fraud, and 3) the risks associated with internal fraud.

Systematic Failure

The operational risk associated with systematic failures has two primary focuses: IT system failures and information security failures. With IT system failures, a number of things could go wrong. There is the obvious risk which is having company technology stolen and used for malicious purposes, but there is also the possibility where a system is not properly created and something as simple as an unexpected transaction tears apart the system. The point of faulty software also relates to the potential for an information security failure, and is where much of Arrayent's potential for risk lies. Being a cloud-based service that interacts with many third-party clouds, there is a strong potential for a hack in one of the third-party clouds that can then be used to hack Arrayent's cloud. This method is essentially how Equifax's data was breached, and is a common occurrence with large companies that employ third parties. Back in September when it was announced that Equifax was hacked, it was made clear that it was one of Equifax's subsidiaries that was breached, giving the hacker access to all the data in the Equifax network. The event of a third-party hack is a circumstance we can be sure Arrayent has considered, but it is currently unclear what their risk mitigation strategy looks like for this kind of event.

External Fraud

Second, the primary operational risk associated with external fraud is phishing. Phishing has become more and more of a problem, especially in relation to elderly communities. When you think about who is primarily buying expensive appliances, and who is often pressured into buying "industry leading" technology, it is mostly the elderly, who are then even more of a target for phishing scams. Eric Carson, a researcher who in 2006 published a paper on the frequency of phishing in elderly communities, noted, "up to five million seniors annually are victims of some type of financial fraud."3 In addition, those raised in earlier generations were often "taught to be polite and trusting," so when a scammer offers to fix their product, elderly are more willing to trust the scammer.3 Meanwhile, elderly tend to be relatively new to the internet, so these scams are more likely to be effective when those targeted are ignorant to what is occurring. All of these opportunities to be phished represent large potential risks for the company to be hacked from the inside. These risks are difficult for companies to proactively mitigate without specific customer training sessions, which for most businesses are out of the question, and become a strong factor in determining what users have access to in any customer portal. Ultimately, the potential for external fraud should be a large factor in the cybersecurity needs of any company, and Arrayent is one such company where external fraud should be a top priority.

Internal Fraud

Finally, there are two primary operational risks associated with internal fraud: misappropriation of assets in response to an event, and insiders aiding fraudsters. Insiders aiding fraudsters is relatively self-explanatory. This would be a scenario where an employee, or even a group of employees, knows some vulnerability within company procedures, and gives this information to someone outside the company who is looking to gain access to data or break the internal system. We see many instances of this risk in the banking world, where employees find ways to smuggle money between the lines of a ledger, or help to clean money, for an external organization. Misappropriation of assets in response to an event can also be an incredibly dangerous problem, and is one that could take up its own short paper. The way in which a business responds to an emergency is incredibly important, and any negligence within the company at this stage could spell disaster. For example, last week Equifax was hacked for a second time, and there are surely investigations looking into misappropriation of assets. The fact that one of the three big credit firms was hacked twice in the span of three months is to be of large concern for customers, and should be a concern for management of the company. It is important to note that this assertion is just speculation, and there is currently no proof that there was any form of misappropriation of assets within Equifax or any of its related companies. The use of Equifax's press release is simply an example for where misappropriation of assets could be investigated, and again, there is currently no evidence that misappropriation of assets is present anywhere within the company.

Best Practices

With all of these potential operational risks in mind, what are some best practices for companies who want to mitigate or avoid these risks? Starting with internal ways to mitigate risks, controls are a great way for companies to manage procedures and can be implemented at many different places within the company. A few tried and true controls include: directive controls where things like IT configuration settings and corporate policies are managed, recovery controls where data backups are performed in the event of system failure, and automated controls where access permissions and password requirements are managed.4 These are three basic controls to help prevent potential internal fraud, and there are many more ways companies can institute types of controls, so businesses should not feel limited by these three examples. If Arrayent were to implement a few of these techniques throughout their company, they would surely increase trust between themselves and their consumers.

Moving into ways to mitigate system failures, the best way to prevent IT issues and cyber threats is simply to design and implement risk mitigation strategies throughout the entire company, and not just in certain sectors. Again, system controls are a great way to manage some of the network activity, but the best way to avoid system failures is to design and implement a better system. Finally, external fraud. It is safe to say that there is no way to eliminate the potential for external fraud, and that the best way to handle the potential for external threats is, again, to have a robust internal structure capable of thwarting such intrusions Having strong internal software and procedures to manage risk are truly the best way for a company to handle threats from any front.

During the process of researching and writing this analysis, Arrayent was acquired by Prodea, an even larger cloud-based IoT service. Prodea's focus has been around creating "a generic framework with the ability to communicate with devices, move media, create interactive experiences for end users, execute service logic, and enable end-to-end service management and control."5 Essentially, this acquisition has placed Prodea/Arrayent in a strong position to control much of the IoT service platform that, as we have seen with other businesses controlling large parts of any market, can be fantastic for creating a strong industry standard, but can also be a large organizational risk if the company is breached. One would expect that Prodea and Arrayent are currently working diligently to create new frameworks to manage both repositories of data, and hope that both companies prioritize the safety of customer data when designing any new systems.

Conclusion

As we have now seen, operational risks thwart every part of a business. Often, there is no way to completely eliminate a risk, so the best strategy is to try to prevent it and develop risk mitigation strategies that will be implemented throughout the company to be deployed in response to a risk. One can hope that there will soon be greater regulations enforced to ensure that companies are following stricter risk mitigation practices, but it is also important to recognize that general regulations are never one-size-fits-all. One can likewise hope that Prodea and Arrayent are successful in the merging of their two companies, and that their customer base will ultimately benefit from a strengthened cloud platform with increased security precautions.

Life-Critical Applications and Serverless Computing

Developer Usability vs. Public Risk in AWS Lambda

Kate Schenot

Written: February 2018
Published: April 2018

Abstract: This paper discusses the risk arising from the emerging intersection of public safety, emergency response technology, the Internet of Things, and computerless servers such as Amazon Web Services' Lambda. The critical question is: When a product such as Lambda poses such powerful possibilities in the public sphere, at what point is developers' ease-of-use a liability for the people?

Public Safety Answering Points: Overview and Governance

The emergency services sector is one of 16 critical infrastructure sectors identified by the Department of Homeland Security (DHS) as integral to American national security.[1] While this sector covers multiple areas vital to public safety — law enforcement, fire and rescue services, emergency medical services, emergency management, and public works[2] — these services tend to be geographically-distributed and community-based, showing an overall pattern of local administration in first-response services.[3]

Public Safety Answering Points (or PSAPs) are, for most Americans, the single point of contact for these life-critical requests. PSAPs receive 911 calls and dispatch (or transfer requests to) the appropriate emergency services:[4] operating as twenty-four-hour emergency centers for areas in their jurisdiction. Although PSAPs are one of the most important entities in emergency management, their governance is — by design — also local.[5] While states hold regulatory power over PSAPs,[6] local authorities (such as cities and counties) hold responsibility for designing, implementing, and operating these services.[7] In the context of their importance to national security, this may seem surprising. However, with the diversity of cultures, challenges, and physical circumstances across the United States, local control is thought to be best-positioned for leveraging the strengths of community knowledge in emergency situations.[8]

The federal government's role in PSAPs, then, is limited. The DHS offers initiatives designed to lessen cyber risk for 911 services;[9] [10] and the Federal Communications Commission (FCC) monitors and makes limited rules supporting such services' reliability,[11] although its interstate jurisdiction constrains its power in local telecommunications infrastructure like PSAPs. While some have called for increased action by the FCC in regulating 911 services,[12] these complaints have typically been in response to internet or telephone network outages, rather than the structure or function of PSAPs themselves.

Perhaps the most direct standards across PSAPs nationwide, then, are those offered by professional organizations like the National Emergency Number Association (NENA). From a security standpoint, NENA offers detailed recommendations, best practices, and checklists for PSAP systems, activities, and audits.[13] [14] [15] NENA also offers comprehensive resources in regard to risk assessment.[16,] [17] However, all NENA standards and practices are voluntary[18], so they do not represent a

Mikhail Savvateev is a product manager at Intellasphere, a Seattle-area marketing technology startup. He holds a Master of Science degree in Technology Innovation, and a Bachelor of Science degree in Informatics, both from the University of Washington. Mikhail is originally from Moscow, Russia, and serves as Vice President of the Russian-American Cooperation Initiative.

Kate Schenot is a senior strategist at DEI Creative. She helps brands and organizations uncover insights about how people interact with their products, services, and culture; and then develops creative solutions to act on these learnings. She received her Master of Science degree in Human Centered Design and Engineering from the University of Washington in 2019, and her Bachelor of Fine Arts in Photography + History of Art from the Massachusetts College of Art and Design.

Lee Segal received her Bachelor of Science degree in Informatics, with a focus in information assurance and cybersecurity, from the University of Washington in 2018. Her professional experience includes completing internships at Starbucks, the Walt Disney Company, and Netscout, where she developed and improved on her Cyber Security skill set. Currently Lee works as an information security engineer at Starbucks on the identity and access management team. Within the year of working there she has become the lead on the firm's external identity platform and secondary on their interior access gateway aiding in smooth authentication for external and internal partners.

regulatory mandate across the 5,874 PSAPs in the United States.[19]

While calling 911 to access a dispatcher may be a common point of cultural reference for Americans, the reality of PSAP systems is far more complicated. In the age of the Internet of Things (IoT) — in which objects and devices are increasingly internet-connected and engaging in the collection and communication of data[20] — PSAPs are encountering many more technologies and processes for integration with first-response systems.[21] Some examples of such IoT devices include building sensors (like smart smoke detectors, security systems, and industrial controls), personal sensors (for health monitoring), and mobile sensors (such as drones for environmental sampling, or car components for crash detection) — any of which might be integrated with PSAPs for enhanced emergency response times following detection of life-critical circumstances.

With more IoT devices and software originating from both public and private sources, PSAPs increasingly face growing external data — and with it, growing vulnerability to external threats. As the DHS puts it: "*Because our nation is now dependent on properly functioning networks to drive so many life-sustaining activities, IoT security is now a matter of homeland security.*"[22] When it comes to the life-critical functions of PSAPs, the implications of this IoT risk become magnified and ethically significant.

Serverless Computing: A Platform for Life-Critical Functions

Serverless computing has achieved popularity on a timeline similar to IoT ubiquity.[23] While running code on these cloud systems is not literally "serverless" — servers still exist, handled by another party[24] — this type of service *functionally* frees the developer from the logistics of servers, enabling code handoffs that can run without any further infrastructure management.[25] The extreme implication of this is that organizations can transition to a "NoOps" model, in which enterprise IT becomes a thing of the past: developers could be the sole technical hires, deploying code at a faster clip without infrastructure knowledge or barriers.[26] [27] [28] [29] Indeed, serverless architectures are increasingly being adopted by developers because of the convenience that they offer.[30] Conceivably, this model could allow a single developer to manage all aspects of delivering an application.

Serverless computing is sometimes called a Function as a Service (FaaS). Within the FaaS realm, several platforms are currently competing for market share: among them Microsoft's Azure Functions,[31] Google Cloud Functions,[32] and IBM's Cloud Functions.[33] However, the market leader in serverless computing[34] is currently AWS Lambda (a product of Amazon Web Services).[35] In addition to serving massive customers like Netflix[36] and Expedia,[37] Lambda is also the compute platform that Amazon itself uses for Alexa[38] and its AWS IoT services.[39]

It is beyond the scope of this paper to assess risks in *all* serverless computing platforms. Given Lambda's market share, then, it will be our principal subject for the analysis that follows.

Lambda is already being used in emergency response contexts. Emergency services in the Australian state of Victoria are using AWS services, including Lambda, to manage alerts and responses to natural disasters.[40] Agero, out of Medford, Massachusetts, uses a similar stack (again including Lambda) to cue an emergency response following IoT detection of a severe auto crash.[41] Due to its IoT compatibility, pay-as-you-go-model, and scalability,[42] Lambda may be especially useful for emergency applications like these. When responding to unpredictable events that potentially involve extremely high user loads at irregular intervals, the flexible capacity and lack of fixed costs during downtime are particularly attractive from an emergency operations standpoint.[43]

Lambda is also becoming HIPAA-eligible,[44] a sign that Amazon believes that life-critical services (such as medical applications) can and should be run on the platform. Between this direction in policy and the existing use cases in emergency scenarios, it becomes clear that Lambda is a platform — and a product security standard — on which people's lives will depend.

Risks to PSAPs

Since Lambda is a major platform on which data may be delivered to/from PSAPs (as described in the previous examples), it follows that Lambda's attack vectors should be examined as part of an overall PSAP risk assessment. As PSAP infrastructure is a known target for terrorism,[45] [46] this becomes especially relevant in a discussion of critical infrastructure.

If life-critical technology running on Lambda is compromised by cyberterrorists, PSAP functions could also be compromised in multiple ways. PSAPs could be fed *false information* from a compromised IoT sensor network[47] running on Lambda, and rescuers could be dispatched to the wrong location during a simultaneous terrorist event elsewhere. Similarly, a sensor network could be completely disabled, thereby veiling an attack in progress. Digital emergency alert systems (running on Lambda, and relaying PSAP data) could also be disabled by a cyberterrorist, thus sending *no information* out to the community, leaving individuals vulnerable in an emergency scenario. Lastly, if PSAP systems *themselves* are running functions on Lambda, they are also directly vulnerable to Lambda's attack vectors.

While such attack vectors would also be possible on another platform (self-hosted or cloud-based), these types of attacks are particularly easy on Lambda for two reasons: The ease of mismanaging a single set of credentials, and the particular policies of Lambda's public code repository. Both of these factors can become vulnerabilities through a combination of lazy security policy and moderate social engineering, as will be described below.

Attack Vectors in Lambda

The AWS default (on account creation) is a single username/password combination that contains all administrative privileges to all services (of which Lambda is one). If a developer does not follow the best practice of creating users with limited permissions[48] — instead maintaining this default root user for all tasks — this single credential, if compromised, has the potential to take the entire Lambda application down. Compromising this credential could be as simple as calling up Craig in accounting and impersonating a need for the AWS password. Since AWS payment and Lambda code controls are locked behind the same credential, it's possible that well-meaning nontechnical employees could have access to the credentials for the root user without understanding the implications therein. In contrast to the days of multiple servers being physically located in somebody's basement, this single sign-on makes Lambda (and AWS as a whole)[49] an attractive target for nefarious remote access. Although this penetration scenario may seem elementary, the pattern of socially engineering a root credential is well-established in the hacking toolkit.[50] [51] [52] Interestingly, one publically-presented working prototype has already demonstrated Lambda exploits based partially on bad AWS identity + access management (IAM) setup.[53]

While the previous scenario is an opportunistic attack on a weak customer target, there is also a risk for more proactive compromises of the serverless ecosystem. As of February 21, 2018,[54] the AWS Serverless Application Repository[55] has been a public, unmoderated resource for sample Lambda code that anyone can run in a single click. Inherent in this is that anyone can engineer a vulnerability into code submitted to the repository — and engineer popularity of this code through manual downloads from different destinations — thereby making the insecure code spread to those who build a dependency on it. (Lambda offers no way to preview the actual source code of uploaded samples within the repository: the user is only offered an external GitHub link[56] to view the source, begging the question of whether a contributor could upload one thing to Lambda, but represent it as another in the supplied external link.) Through following forked code in this system, it becomes easy to reverse engineer who's using that code — and therefore, who has a particular security vulnerability. Although the Serverless Application Repository is undoubtedly a move by Amazon to make its serverless ecosystem more usable, "sticky" and developer-friendly, the tradeoff with security is nevertheless troubling when viewed through the lens of how easy this code is to access, versus how few security guardrails are mandated by the ecosystem.

Amazon's Stance on Security Practices

AWS has a shared responsibility model[57] for the security of all its cloud services: emphasizing individual customers' responsibility for the security of their own data, code, and access management, while AWS is responsible for infrastructure security. This offers the customer maximum flexibility for configuring and managing their projects, but it also leaves the customer vulnerable should they not take that responsibility seriously (i.e., in a mistaken belief that "the cloud is secure"). While AWS offers security measures to their customers, such as multi-factor authentication (MFA)[58] and resources on best practices,[59] all is optional and up to the customer.

Interestingly, AWS's most recent SOC3 specifically disclaims cybersecurity risk management in its scope, and notes "human error" and "circumvention of controls" as inherent limitations of the SOC3 assessment.[60] AWS management echoes this in an appendix to the SOC3, noting that "ineffective controls at a vendor or business partner" are inherently beyond the scope of AWS's security controls.[61] At a recent AWS Re:Invent presentation, a customer also echoed this division of responsibilities, noting that "good AWS IAM [identity and access management] account setup […] will be key to showing good governance" once an AWS customer moves into SOC2 compliance[62] — although, once again, this responsibility falls on the customer.

Who is Responsible?

Should a breach in a Lambda application affect a PSAP, as imagined in our scenario, who would be responsible? The federal government does not regulate the details of PSAPs or of Lambda; state regulations would likely not be granular enough to spell out technical security practices; NENA guidelines are strictly voluntary; and Amazon specifically disclaims responsibility for everything but infrastructure. Ultimately, it is the local PSAP authorities who are responsible for making all decisions about their own security and data policies — including the decision to trust a developer offering a useful integration. Similarly, it is the developer's responsibility to secure their application.

But from a practical perspective — with nearly six thousand independent PSAPs, and untold numbers of developers working on technology that could integrate with emergency response — expecting everyone to execute flawlessly on their responsibilities may be unrealistic.

What Needs to Change?

Although we may have a clear answer for *legal* accountability in the event of a breach, the answer on *ethical* accountability may be broader than this.

In supporting life-critical applications — indeed, in *seeking* them through HIPAA compliance — AWS Lambda has become a steward (no matter how reluctantly) of people's lives. Yet, rather than building policies and principles that reflect the gravity of this reality, Amazon continues its libertarian attitude toward its customer community: offering security resources, but not taking a strong stance on them. In the context of a peer group doing otherwise — Facebook building features to detect and counteract self-harm,[63] Twitter writing algorithms to counteract abusive users,[64] Google creating proactive responses to searches indicating at-risk status[65] — this is a disappointing response to an important burden.

Amazon has the opportunity to create a culture of security in its Lambda user community. Much like how it incentivizes its own employees to seek out training and expertise (via phone tool icons[i]), Amazon could incentivize its user community to become security experts through more visible and socially-enforced user education: promoting the existing AWS certification program (which includes a security component)[66] as a less-optional industry standard, and rewarding developers who complete it with discounts on AWS services. Amazon could similarly incentivize customer use of multi-factor authentication by offering discounts for those who use it, or even requiring that applications involving a life-critical component use MFA as a non-negotiable security measure. Amazon could evaluate code before adding it to the Serverless Application Repository — much like how Apple reviews all apps that are submitted to its App Store.[67] And Amazon could also allow the user to preview repository code directly, resolving the uncertainty of whether such code could be misrepresented by its originator. However, as it currently stands, Amazon's hands-off attitude on these issues sets a clear — yet indifferent — tone at the top.[68]

Although Amazon is not known for a strong stance on corporate social responsibility — only hiring a director for

---

[i] Flair on an employee's internal profile that functions like merit badges, received for completing certain tasks, education, or accomplishments.

this role in 2015,[69] twenty-one years into its existence — this history does not stand in the way of its potential future of proactively-responsible stewardship. As a market leader with Lambda, Amazon has the opportunity to set policy at the same time as they mitigate risks in their serverless computing ecosystem. The business value of such mitigation is directly expressed in their 2018 10-K filing:

> As a result of our services being web-based and the fact that we process, store, and transmit large amounts of data, including personal information, for our customers, failure to prevent or mitigate data loss or other security breaches, [...] could expose us or our customers to a risk of loss or misuse of such information, adversely affect our operating results, result in litigation or potential liability for us, and otherwise harm our business.[70]

A voluntary change in security tone and policy could be both a marketing tool, and a hedge against the risk (reputational and otherwise) inherent in being the site of a crisis, should a life-critical Lambda breach happen. Indeed, user security education ultimately aligns with Amazon's business, with citizens' interests, and with PSAPs' security needs. For a company touting "customer obsession"[71] as a core principle, this seems like an ethically- and financially-sound investment.

A Role for Government

While it can be argued that enhanced regulation of PSAPs could lead to stronger security standards and greater compliance, the original intention of PSAPs' independent governance holds some weight. Allowing local knowledge, priorities, and culture to inform emergency response gives individual PSAPs the freedom to allocate their resources in response to local trends; collaborate with individuals and community organizations which may assist in the overarching public safety mission; and nurture public/private partnerships with owners of infrastructure that holds importance to the community's overall wellbeing. Applying a set of standard rules, particularly in response to new technology, risks quashing progress and efforts of local importance. PSAPs may be the best judges of risk/reward equations in their jurisdictions, due to their authority on the area.

However, attainably-designed mandates may offer a realistic improvement in security, without compromising innovation significantly. States could require that any third-party software or device linked to PSAPs be developed by someone with the appropriate evidence of security-specific study: Perhaps, in this way, the AWS credential could gain some teeth (especially if Amazon partnered with government stakeholders in the credential's design). To use the metaphor of a pilot's license or a lawyer's bar admission: government has determined in the past that positions with the potential for harming others through their practice should be regulated by a credentialing process in which mastery is demonstrated. When it comes to platforms, software, and data that determines the course of human lives, this seems all too appropriate.

Technology — and Policy — Designed for Humans

AWS Lambda is undoubtedly designed with ease of use at the forefront. From streamlining developers' responsibilities, to managing everything from a single set of credentials, to offering crowdsourced off-the-shelf code: Lambda's ecosystem reflects the tremendous importance Amazon places on usability. However, it is exactly that degree of usability which catalyzes the vulnerabilities discussed above.

When a product such as Lambda poses such powerful possibilities in the public sphere, at what point is developers' ease-of-use a liability for the people? Within Lambda's design and defaults, it is easier to ignore security than it is to master it. And although this "frictionlessness" is attractive to software developers, the overall lack of security culture and incentives in Lambda creates an environment in which the actions (or inactions) of an ignorant or inexperienced developer may cause grave public consequences.

In this author's opinion, the key takeaway for future Lambda development is the idea of proportionality: an idea described by Sons, Jackson and Russell[72] as "*tailoring security strategies to the magnitude of the risks.*" If Lambda (and its Serverless Application Repository) were conceived as products for conventional business applications, the current evidence of life-critical use should provoke reflection on the human cost of disproportionate usability and insufficient security incentives. Although PSAPs are one downstream example of these implications, they are not the only one. In the context of Amazon's love for human-centered design, perhaps security policy *itself* can be factored into human-centeredness — when the end customer is all of us.

Risks with BYOD in Government Agencies

Beth Hutchens

Written: June 2017
Published: November 2017

Abstract: This research notes explores the practice of "bring your own device" (BYOD), specifically within the public sector. Permitting employees to use their personal technological devices (such as smartphones, laptop computers, and tablet PCs) has been an increasingly popular option within organizations as a means to cut costs, increase productivity, and provide better work-life flexibility. While BYOD is generally looked upon favorably, what is often overlooked or ignored, however, is the fact that there are significant risks associated with the practice, including legal liability, regulatory scrutiny, data exposure, increased costs and expenses, and potential brand and reputation damage.

Introduction

As the connectivity of society continues to trend upward, organizations and government agencies frequently look for new ways to increase productivity, give employees more flexibility, and cut costs. Permitting employees to use their personal devices for work purposes is one way to accomplish these goals. Commonly referred to "Bring Your Own Device" - or "BYOD" - it is a term that collectively refers to the related technologies, concepts, and policies in which employees are allowed to access internal corporate IT resources (such as databases and applications) while using their personal mobile devices like smartphones, laptop computers, and tablet PCs. Put simply, BYOD is a business practice in which employees of an organization are allowed to use their own electronic devices (as opposed to those supplied and controlled by the company) to access company information and applications.[1] It is not a practice that is well understood and many times BYOD is conducted under the radar without meaningful guidance or rules from managers, stakeholders, or even regulatory authorities.

BYOD is generally looked upon favorably by CEOs and the overarching attitude is that the increased productivity and reduced operating costs that BYOD facilitates by far outweigh the added risks for many organizations. For example, Cisco's 2016 annual report found that 66 percent of IT decision makers feel that BYOD is a good thing and that workers save an average of 81 minutes per week when permitted to use their own devices.[2] What is often overlooked or ignored, however, is the fact that there are significant risks associated with BYOD, including legal liability, regulatory scrutiny, data exposure, increased costs and expenses, and potential brand and reputation damage.

Operational Risks Accompanying BYOD

For the most part, the risks associated with BYOD in the public and private sectors are similar, if not identical. In addition, those risks are numerous, complex, continually changing, and occur in a regulatory environment that is still evolving. In fact, the practice is often jokingly referred to as "bring your own disaster" with good reason. [i] While the

---

[i] While this paper discusses risks in a negative context, the increased costs incident to creating and implementing a BYOD program and employing still-developing technologies such as mobile device management can also be thought of as positive risks in that they present tremendous opportunities for growth and efficiency.

cadre of risk factors that accompany these practices fit into traditionally defined categories -people, processes, systems, and external events- there is a uniqueness to BYOD that causes the risks and control failures involved to become increasingly intertwined.

For example, a single event- such as ransomware[ii]-involves an external force in the form of an individual or group of individuals hijacking a user's computer, a personnel failure at the hands of the person who unwittingly clicked a harmful link, a process failure in the form of a lack of education to help the employee identify suspicious emails, and a system failure in the form of an as yet unknown exploit. Broadly defined, the risk associated with BYOD leads back to leakage and / or exposure of sensitive data belonging to the public, the employee, or in some cases, both. Accordingly, while it is true that the "risk" associated with BYOD is nearly always the broad concept of data exposure, an analysis that only looks into technological ways to prevent or mitigate that (and only that) is incomplete and misses the big picture because it focuses too much on an IT solution as opposed to a companywide, systemic approach.

BYOD is also unique from a risk management standpoint because of the inherent insecurity of mobile devices. Not only are they easier to exploit, but also an important function of these devices is that they are always

---

[ii] Ransomware is a type of malware that prevents or limits users from accessing their system, either by locking the system's screen or by locking the users' files unless a ransom is paid. More modern ransomware families, collectively categorized as crypto-ransomware, encrypt certain file types on infected systems and forces users to pay the ransom through certain online payment methods to get a decrypt key.

connected wirelessly. Thus, vulnerability to malicious attacks is increased because the communication channels are more numerous and varied as opposed to traditional desktop machines relying on a wired connection. Further, unlike other types of computing devices, BYOD means that personal and company data are permitted to exist on the same device, which creates at least two conflicting interests when it comes to risk management. Among other things, this puts personal autonomy and privacy of the employee at odds with the controls necessary to safeguard company data. In addition to this, the opportunity for inadvertent exposure of sensitive information by, for example, mistakenly sending sensitive information to personal contacts is extraordinary high. These problems are compounded by the fact that BYOD involves devices that require a very high level of IT support, regardless of the make, model, age, or type of the device.[iii]

Moving beyond a purely technology-focused inquiry requires an assessment of a company or agency's internal protocols, culture, and approach to conducting business. Many of the risks associated with BYOD can be directly tied to personnel, or more specifically, to the ignorance and/or indifference of personnel. For example, it is quite common to have stakeholders and members of the management team who cannot or will not make the commitment of company

---

[iii] It is worth mentioning that the risks associated with BYOD are heightened with the instance of a disgruntled former employee or rogue current employee. In some cases, the control failures and risk mitigation associated with these types of events share some similarities with the actions of "innocent" personnel, but a thorough discussion of how to prevent these types of events is beyond the scope of this paper.

resources to create, implement, and/ or enforce BYOD protocols. Even if they could, personnel tend to push back on what they view as yet another set of hurdles that prevent them from being able to do their jobs efficiently and effectively. The result of this collective reluctance can be thought of as the cause of a level of ignorance that translates into an opportunity for an organization to virtually hemorrhage sensitive information, which can cause legal liability, federal scrutiny, reputational damage, and internal strife, or a combination of the four.

Current Controls Pertaining to BYOD in Government Agencies

Public records laws, data security and privacy regulations, accountability, and legal liability are more keenly felt in the public sector, and change is not easily accomplished for a variety of reasons. Thus, the state of BYOD remains inconsistent across state lines, differs between agencies depending on their function, and the practice is still in its infancy stages. This is not to suggest that BYOD does not exist at the state, federal, or even local level, but what has emerged is a practice that is largely unregulated, undeveloped, and more often than not, proper procedure and risk management are an afterthought (if ever). The result is an ad hoc business practice where the lines between professional and personal lives are blurred, employees have concerns that their privacy is at risk (either from a member of the public or a snooping employer), and serious issues associated with the public's personal information are created- all of which go unaddressed.

From a planning standpoint then, risk management with BYOD might not be feasible for agencies that are subject to higher information security standards such as state and federal law enforcement agencies. Those agencies might do well forbid BYOD and supply any and all mobile devices themselves, as the risks- no matter how remote in possibility- are simply too great to ignore.[iv] Thus far, the overwhelming attitude from the public sector is to ignore the existence of, rather than embrace, the complex issues that come with BYOD. The reality is that BYOD occurs in government agencies whether management knows it or not, which results in a general attitude of denial or willful ignorance when it comes to personal devices in the public workplace.

In 2015, mobile security company Lookout analyzed 20 federal agencies and discovered 14,622 Lookout-enabled devices associated with government networks, despite the lack of permission or a BYOD policy in place for that agency. In another survey of a thousand federal employees, Lookout found that 37 percent said they are willing to sacrifice government security to use a personal device at work despite understanding security concerns, and 40 percent of those working at agencies with policies preventing the use of personal smartphones admitted the rules have little to no impact on their behavior. Lookout's State of Federal BYOD report also found that 24 percent of employees install apps from places other than official app

---

[iv] Some states and companies do not permit employees to use their personal devices at all and opt for agency supplied and controlled devices. This is certainly the easiest way to reduce risks associated with personnel, but is reportedly the least popular option among employees.

stores, and that 18 percent reported encountering malware on their devices.[3]

Alarming as these numbers are, this is not to say that government agencies have no BYOD controls whatsoever. Though sporadic and imperfect, some state and local governments are beginning to address the growing BYOD issue and the federal government has identified some best practices.[4] Some agencies permit BYOD so long as the employee agrees to give the agency at least some control over the device. Known as mobile data management, or "MDM", this includes installing software that gives the agency the power to remote wipe the device in the event it is lost or stolen, limit access to certain kinds of apps and downloads, and sequester the device owner's personal data. Others have not embraced the practice yet, and are working on developing a program before allowing the use of personal devices. Still others have acknowledged that BYOD is happening regardless of a meaningful protocol and are using the "under the radar" approach as a way to shape and drive their program in a way that best meets their internal goals and needs.

It is an accepted truism that, when it comes to cyber incidents, it is not a question of *if* one will occur; it is a matter of *when*. With that in mind, external actors are a driving force that should be accepted as fact and while cyber security is always at the forefront, because a BYOD device necessarily and by definition involves people, the control factors that should have the greatest amount of attention are personnel and processes. ᵛ

The Private Sector's Approach to BYOD

Permitting employees to use their personal devices for work is well established in the private sector. Companies engaging in the practice typically have a robust policy in place that establishes rules, procedures, and polices relating to use of personal devices. Many times, employees must undergo extensive training and agree to company procedures before they are extended the privilege of using their personal device. A common theme in the private sector is to start with answering the general questions of who owns the device, who manages the device, and who secures the device. The answers to these questions help drive the company policy and establish the rights and responsibilities of both the employer and the employee.

In addition to employing innovative technology, the private sector has been implementing and adopting BYOD procedures for quite some time. This may be for any number of reasons, such as the fact that private industry has differing goals and concerns than public entities, is not hindered by public records laws, has more internal controls, and is in a better position to shoulder risks. For whatever reason, private companies have been honing and developing

---

ᵛ It is interesting to note that BYOD is not as prevalent in Europe and Canada. As cross border data transfers become more prevalent, and as the United States struggles to remain compliant with increasing security and privacy regulations, the question remains whether BYOD will decline in popularity for practical reasons. This is especially true when considering the European General Data Protection Regulation that goes into effect in 2018 and requires, among other things, Privacy by Design.

controls for BYOD that, at least in some cases, the public sector could learn from. For example, there is a litany of guidance from trade organizations and interest groups that routinely publish studies, guidance, templates, checklists, and all other manner of help a company wanting to develop a BYOD program might look to.[5]

A common approach is for a private sector company is to limit certain types of applications that may be installed on the device. For example, in 2012, IBM banned the Dropbox and Siri apps over concerns about data security.[6] In fact, some companies and agencies scrap BYOD altogether and do not permit commingled data on devices as a matter of course. Others use MDM or other types of software solutions that are still under development and still others create protocols and practices that are company-specific and tailored to their business needs. When it comes to device security, a collaborative and effective relationship with the IT department is common in the private sector and many times, the IT department is involved early and often.

Recommendations for Implementing a BYOD Program

As a threshold matter, a meaningful program must start with stakeholders and management and will require cooperation among departments, so the first step should be to obtain a commitment to dedicating the time, energy, and resources to such a large-scale endeavor. The next step in deciding whether to permit BYOD in an organization is to conduct a thorough privacy assessment and threat risk. This will determine if BYOD is feasible, possible, or desirable for the particular organization[vi]. In some cases, it may not be.

Then, operating under the premise that developing a workable BYOD program is wanted, needed, and possible, there are a few considerations that an agency can address to mitigate the risks. Of the utmost importance is to develop, communicate, implement, and enforce a BYOD policy. The parameters of this policy will be specific to each organization, but at a minimum, the policy should: 1) identify the information collected, used, and disclosed; 2) clarify the user's rights and responsibilities; 3) discuss how the devices will be monitored and / or controlled by the company (including software application management); 4) identify what privacy rules, regulations, and practices come into play; 5) develop an incident response team and a clear chain of command in the event employee or public data becomes compromised; and 6) provide a clear set of protocols, tasks, and guidelines to help them manage the risk.

Naturally, before the program is implemented, there must be thorough employee training that includes a discussion of safety and security protocols, but also their rights and obligations when it comes to using their personal device for work purposes. There should be an employee handbook that details their rights, responsibilities, and

---

[vi] In some cases, depending on the type of data collected, used, disclosed, and retained BYOD is not an option. This is especially true where federal or state regulations that may be implicated such as for example, health information or information pertaining to persons under the age of 13. *See e.g.,* HIPAA, COPPA, and GLBA, state data breach notification laws, and the like.

obligations and a detailed incident response protocol that is routinely tested, analyzed, and perfected. Finally, regular audits of the incident response protocol, reviews of the program's regulatory compliance, and tests for the efficacy of the program should be conducted frequently to make sure the program remains viable in a rapidly evolving environment.

Conclusion

Permitting employees to use their personal devices for work purposes is not the right solution for every company or every government agency. The risks related to commingled data on such devices are high, nuanced, and will vary depending on the type of data the organization collects, hosts, and shares. They include legal liability, enhanced regulatory scrutiny, and reputational damage. The benefits include time and cost savings, happier employees, and increased efficiency in the work place.

There is some guidance from the federal government and a smattering of state and local governments are beginning to create policies when it comes to BYOD best practices. Government agencies can learn much from the private sector's approach to BYOD. From the outset, developing, implementing, enforcing, and monitoring an effective BYOD policy requires a commitment to early involvement from senior management and stakeholders. Moreover, agencies and private companies will do well to be cognizant of, and adhere to, applicable state and federal data security and privacy regulations in developing their programs. Then, using known risk assessment and privacy impact tools, the decision can be made whether or not to permit employees to use their personal devices according to the agency's goals and the regulatory environment. By starting with asking the right questions and involving stakeholders and the IT department in the process, a collaborative approach can be fostered and a meaningful program can be developed that accommodates and mitigates those risks to the extent possible. Though the private sector perhaps has more flexibility to embrace BYOD as much or as little as they choose, the public sector need not eschew the practice entirely. By adopting established practices and protocols, and by engaging in Privacy by Design practices, state and local governments can establish themselves as thought leaders with respect to BYOD.

Shadow IT and Organizational Risks

Nicholas Montgomery

Written: December 2016
Published: August 2017

Abstract: This paper discusses the rising prevalence of and risks associate with shadow IT - the use of unauthorized devices, software, and services - on organizations. After examining these risks, the author goes on to identify recommendations to help prevent shadow IT and allow organizations to enable business units to be able to make smarter purchases.

Gartner defines shadow IT as "IT devices, software, and services outside the ownership or control of IT organizations."[1] Essentially, any device or software being used inside of an organization that the IT department has not approved the use of can be categorized as shadow IT. Shadow IT can be happening in different ways, including the use of social media without the approval of IT. Employees may not even know that they are conducting shadow IT because they are either unaware of what it is or unaware of the current policies that an organization has in place with the usage of non-approved applications. However, these employees are potentially putting both an organization and any sensitive information that they are handling at risk if the proper measures are not taken. This paper will explore the risks associated with shadow IT and make recommendations to an organization for ways to combat them.

The rise of cloud technologies has been one of the main driving forces behind enabling shadow IT in an organization, specifically Software as a Service (SaaS). Although cloud technologies are not the reason for why shadow IT first started, it is one of the major reasons for its rapid growth.[2] SaaS is one of the three cloud services that are offered, the others being Infrastructure as a Service (IaaS) and Platform as a Service (PaaS). SaaS gives the least amount of responsibility and ownership to the organization or user, having ownership of the application and the maintenance left to the responsibility of the service provider. SaaS also makes it easy for users to be able to access it from anywhere with an Internet connection and all the user does is use their own data to put inside of the application. This makes the use of these applications extremely convenient for the user to begin using and will often come at a low, or even no, cost.

There are multiple reasons why employees are using these non-approved SaaS applications, from people simply wanting to do their jobs to the employee not knowing that an application needed to be approved by IT. Frost & Sullivan conducted a survey from a range of different sized companies that made many discoveries about the usage of non-approved SaaS applications. Of the respondents, 80 percent of which admitted to using applications that were not approved by the IT organization inside of their company. A very surprising discovery was that more IT professionals admitted to using shadow IT than the line of business users were, with 83 percent of IT professionals and only 81 percent of line of business users admitting to using the non-approved applications. There are many implications for why this is happening, including that the IT professionals believe that because they understand the risk that they are confident with knowing how to mitigate it.

Whether the ability for them to mitigate the risks is true or not, it is still leaving an organization at risk.[3]

There are four risks associate with shadow IT for businesses that will be discussed in this paper. The first is vendor or third-party risk, or the risk that arises when an organization relies upon outside sources to preform services on their own behalf.[4] The second is the legal risk of shadow IT, or risk that comes when failing to be compliant with government statutory or regulatory obligations.[5] The third risk is the financial risk that an organization will face, or the risk that a company may not be able to meets its financial obligations.[6] Finally, the last risk that will be discussed is reputational risk, or the threat to the name and standing of an organization.[7]

The first of the risks that will be discussed is the vendor or third-party risk. This deals with the risk behind the vendor not properly keeping either the sensitive information or their own systems secure. This can also be an issue if the proper research on the vendor has not been conducted in advance. Some vendors may be more prone to having security flaws or breaches and can be a liability for the organization. If the employee decides to place sensitive information onto the applications that the vendor is hosting and the vendor was to experience a breach, the sensitive information may be accessed by unauthorized users or potentially stolen. This can have some serious implications on an organization that trusted the vendor with this information, especially because an organization might not even know that the vendor is housing this information unless the employee reports it. If the information is intellectual property or trade secrets, this can lead to another business using the information for their own use and potentially reducing advantages that an organization previously had.

There is also the risk that the user is using the same account name and password on the vendor's application that they are using inside of their own business. It is common for users to recycle the same username and password across multiple different applications, posing large risk if the credentials are taken. A study from Ofcom, a communications watch dog in UK, suggested that 55 percent of users used password for most or all websites, making the risk of credentials being repeated reasonably high.[8] If the user with the stolen credentials had access to sensitive information and proper measures are not taken, such as regular password resets, the hackers may use those credentials to infiltrate an organization. This could then lead to a hack of an organization because of the vendor, but all comes down to the employee who originally used a vendor without the IT department's approval.

The second risk is the legal risk that comes with shadow IT. With the use of non-approved applications by the user, the user may be using applications that will make the organization no longer compliant with certain compliances. An example of this in the past is the use of Dropbox with sensitive information. There have been cases of nurses using Dropbox to share patient information back and forth with each other because the file sizes were too large for emails and the internal IT had not supplied a file sharing application that the nurses were using. The problem with this is that the use of Dropbox would make the hospital no longer compliant with HIPAA, and the survey conducted by Frost & Sullivan showed that of the 36 percent of respondents who were using Dropbox unapproved, 16 percent of those have experienced a security event.[9] If the sensitive information is stolen from an organization, this has the potential for heavy fines to be placed.

Shadow IT also brings a financial risk to an organization. Without approval from IT for applications or cloud services, the purchases being made may already be owned by the organization or people may be purchasing more than what they will need for their usage. Without the approval or consultation of the IT organization, business units may not be aware of all the options that are available to them and may not have educated staff making the purchasing decision to know how much of that service they will need. This can also lead to multiple business units purchasing the same service without the IT department even knowing. Cisco had found that 28 percent of the total amount of IT spend a company does is completely outside of the IT department.[10] Of that 28 percent, there is the potential that funds are being spent inefficiently and may have a significant impact on the amount of revenue that an organization will make.

Finally, the last risk is the possible damages to the organization reputation from Shadow IT. The use of non-approved applications has been shown to lead to a higher risk of having a security event with sensitive data. If sensitive information is stolen from an organization, consumer trust of an organization can decrease and it can have an impact on customer loyalty if not properly handled. This can also double as a financial risk because the decrease in loyalty may influence the amount of money that an organization will make. If consumers do not trust an organization with their sensitive information or are worried that the information may be stolen, there is a possibility that the consumer will make the decision to support a competitor's business instead of their own.

Shadow IT may have many potential risks that can have a serious impact on an organization, however there are multiple different ways to combat shadow IT. The following will discuss five recommendations to help prevent shadow IT and allow an organization to make smarter purchases. These five recommendations are that an organization should have a well-educated IT/Cloud Broker; proper software should be implemented in an organization; the IT approval process for applications should be streamlined; the policies for applications should be inclusive instead of exclusive; and finally that an organization needs to communicate with and educate its employees on its policies and shadow IT.

The first recommendation is for an organization to enable the purchasing ability of business units by having a well-educated IT/Cloud Broker on hand to consult for IT purchases. This is someone who will be knowledgeable on the current business and what it can offer its employees, as well as knowing the market and knowing which tools are available with the right vendors. This will enable business owners to be able to make swift purchasing decisions with the help of the broker. It will also provide the IT department with information on what is being purchased and used inside of an organization. This will give business units the ability to quickly determine what the current available options to use are within an organization, and then make a swift purchasing decisions if none of the available options are a right fit for them. Business owners might not be aware of the available options to them are, but the broker will allow a quick way to learn them. This will also help to build a stronger relationship between the IT department and the rest of an organization. Without a strong relationship, business units may not listen to the advice or policies that are implemented by the IT department; having shadow IT continued to be conducted inside of an organization.

The second recommendation is for an organization to implement software to help the IT department detect when shadow IT is going on, as well as secure the use of applications. This is a way to help automate the discovery process by monitoring the network and being able to see when non-approved applications are being used in the work place.[11] When non-approved applications are being used, this gives the IT department a chance to act upon the situation and for them to be able to seek out the answer to why this application is being used. If an application is being used because IT does not currently have an application approved that can fill that specific need, this gives an opportunity for the IT department to act upon the situation by understanding the behavior of employees, as well as allowing them to work towards approving an application for that need. This will enable the IT department to consistently tackle shadow IT as it is detected in an organization.[12]

Implementing software that will secure the use of these applications will also help an organization stay secure when these applications are being used. If an application sends its packets unencrypted, this leaves open the opportunity for someone to dive into the packets and see the information inside. An attack like a man-in-the-middle attack would benefit from unencrypted traffic. The man-in-the-middle attack is when a person has traffic diverted to a device that allows them to monitor and see all the packets, which would allow them to look inside certain packets and steal any important information. By having software that will encrypt the traffic, this will allow users to use applications that originally did not encrypt the traffic that it sends.[12]

Third, the IT department should redesign and streamline the approval process of applications inside of an organization. This will allow people to stay true their want of doing their jobs, while also allowing for people to complete their tasks in a secure way. The ability for the IT department to continuously deliver solutions swiftly will help decrease the likelihood that an employee will totally skip the process and use an application that is not currently approved. This will also help increase the amount of applications that are approved for usage by employees. A speedy approval process allows for the ability for employees to look at the IT department as a tool for helping them use applications, instead of a deterrence.[12]

Fourth, an organization needs to create a policy that is inclusive to new applications instead of being exclusive. You do not want to try to force your employees into using only one application, because this can lead employees back into their habits of using applications that are not approved by the IT department. As previously stated, people just want to do their jobs and get their tasks done in a timely manner. By having a policy that is inclusive to these new applications, the IT department will be able to better recognize the risks of using all the additional applications and create plans on how to handle security events that are to arise. This will also allow employees to be more comfortable reporting security events that are to occur. Employees should not be punished for committing shadow IT because this will lead to them not wanting to report anything to the IT department to save themselves. Having an inclusive policy will include protecting the employee if an event is to occur. This will help an organization because the sooner that a security event is reported, the sooner an organization can work towards mitigating any further damages that are to occur.[12]

Finally, the last recommendation is that there needs to be communication on the policies and solutions that a company offers, as well as employees needing to be educated on these policies and processes. When new policies and processes are implemented into an organization, employees need to understand them and be aware, especially inside the IT department itself. Employees should also understand the proper actions to take if a security event is to arise, as well as understand the need for quick reporting. Employees who do not know what to do if they are to perceive that an event is happening may report it for fear of the repercussions. However, an employee who has been trained on what to do will know the process of reporting an event and can potentially save the company a lot of trouble and money in the future.[12]

Overall, shadow IT is currently affecting businesses in a significant way, and there is not a whole lot of options to stop employees from wanting access to other applications in addition to what an organization currently offers. With the vendor, legal, financial, and reputational risks that come along with shadow IT an organization needs to be able to adapt and change its policies to work with its employees, not against them. To accomplish this, an organization should implement multiple different strategies, including: Having a IT/cloud broker, implementing the right software to detect shadow IT and help improve applications, redesigning and streamlining their application approval process, having policies that are inclusive instead of exclusive to new applications, and finally to communicate and educate their employees. All the recommendations mentioned in this paper will allow for an organization to enable employees and business units to be able to use or buy applications, however it enable them in a way that will also keep an organization aware of these purchases and protect sensitive information from being accessed.

Smart Homes: Evaluating Risks and Being Smart

Mikhail Victorovich Savvateev

Written: December 2016
Published: September 2017

Abstract: This paper discusses the emerging risks associated with the "Smart Home" technological advances that are becoming increasingly ubiquitous across the human experience. "Smart Home" is the term commonly used to define a residence that has appliances, lighting, thermostats, electronics, and other systems that are capable of communicating with one another and can be controlled remotely via the Internet. The author examines how these new technologies have created new security and other technological system risks, and provides some suggestions for industry participants.

Introduction

The Smart Home revolution, which has recently been gaining momentum in the markets, is the first major change in decades affecting how we live and interact with our dwellings. Because of this movement, many novel technologies will finally make it into the average household, and the next several years will show both the benefits and potential dangers of this shift. A new and rapidly growing market of this kind is prone to many internal and external risks, and it is imperative that the industry's key players and up-and-comers alike consider these risks, ensuring market and the innovations it inspires reach their full potential.

Background

Smart Home technology is the household application of the Internet of Things (IoT), which is a major technical trend spanning many industries worldwide. The IoT is the principle of giving devices connectivity capabilities. This allows devices to form networks which record, process, and share data in order to improve their utility and optimize their operation, linking them together for coordinated execution. Ultimately, by linking the functionalities and data streams of multiple devices, and tapping into processing capabilities (which can be located remotely or within one of these devices), the goal of the technology is to learn about people's habits, and adapting how each device functions in order to meet each user's unique needs.[1] This means that in the future, Smart Home solutions might be able to automate complex tasks involving learning and predicting customers' preferences, such as controlling house heating or cooling systems to maintain optimal temperatures while saving power, or taking care of pets in accordance with the animals' preferences and habits. As a result, we could reach what might be considered the ultimate level of convenience, since household tasks will be handled automatically without needing the user to program instructions, operate triggers, or even think about the task being done.

The Market

Though consumers are some time away from being able to purchase fully automated homes, there is already a lot of excitement surrounding devices and appliances with networking capabilities. A 2015 report by Icontrol Networks, a leading Smart Home developer, cites a global study by the Gartner research company showing that 50 percent of consumers planned to purchase a connected device within a year.[2] Analysts expect sharp growth across the industry, predicting that in contrast to the 15 billion IoT devices active worldwide in 2015, by 2020 there could be as many as 200 billion devices across the globe.[3] Gartner expects that by 2022, a typical family house could contain over 500 smart devices.[4] While the exact magnitude of growth is difficult to predict, these figures paint a very optimistic future for the sector and tell us of the massive potential in Smart Home development.

Not only are these devices very prevalent and continuing to spread, but they also touch on nearly every aspect of the modern home. Market research shows that the most common reasons given for purchasing household smart devices are: home security, cost-saving potential, convenience, environmental friendliness, productivity, entertainment system enhancement, and access to advanced communication functionality.[5] These span nearly everything relating to one's house, and as time goes on, more and more devices and systems will crop up seeking to fill these needs. From existing products like connected thermostats, light systems, and cameras, to futuristic systems like independent cooking or cleaning automatons, soon these devices will control every element of the home.

While the possibilities presented by this sector are exciting for both consumers and businesses, the staggering magnitude of these devices' spread, pervasiveness, and variability drives home the point of how important it is to ensure that the companies behind these devices do everything to mitigate any relevant risks. Possible pitfalls and dangers surround every young technology, and failure to manage them can have huge repercussions as that technology develops. At this scale, even seemingly minor issues and risks can be catastrophic for businesses and whole segments of the market. Therefore, as excitement surrounding Smart Homes persists, the only way ahead is to avoid potential risk and to ensure proper measures are in place at every step of the technology's development.

The Sector

Smart Home technologies, and the Internet of Things as a whole, have evolved very rapidly in recent years. As such, the producers' market remains largely decentralized: examination of popular products and lists of market leaders reveals that major players are a mixture of companies of many different sizes and focuses.[6] While large tech firms (e.g. Google, Amazon, GE, etc.) are starting to invest in and consolidate Smart Home solutions, many winning products continue to come from startups or small companies focused solely on IoT device production. Smart lighting is a good example: network-connected lights are set to generate global revenue of roughly 17 billion dollars in 2016, which is distributed across brands that vary greatly in size.[7] Leaders come from giants in the standard lighting market like GE and Philips, as well as segment-specific startups such as LiFi, whose LIFX bulbs are very popular with American consumers even though the company is a newcomer on the tech scene with humble beginnings coming out of a 2013-2014 Kickstarter crowdfunding campaign.[8] Therefore, the industry also has to deal with mass decentralization while trying to tackle the aforementioned boom in demand. On one side, the prospect that any company can participate is good for innovation and controlling prices, however, when considering how to ensure these eclectic networks of devices are compatible and secure, the lack of clear leaders in the market makes piloting solutions or industry standards an arduous procedure at best. This of course further complicates the business' abilities to manage risk and react to problems, making early risk analysis all the more crucial.

Risk Analysis

The Smart Home concept, like any novel field, has its fair share of risks. New technologies being pioneered often create security and other technological system risks, while the initial dive by companies big and small to seize a slice of the fresh market often breeds process risks as this high-urgency development tends to leave any talk of procedures or standards in the dust. Finally, no market boom goes unnoticed from the outside, and external risks spring up as everyone from criminals to government actors attempt to either exploit or control the young industry for their own needs. It is important to investigate these risks in depth, as failure to resolve them can kill a growing new sector as fast as it was created in the first place.

System Risks

As was demonstrated in the discussion of Smart Homes' market, the industry as it stands must deal with a largely disjointed set of products. Because of being such a decentralized market with a very strong startup presence, a consumer today will likely purchase every element of a Smart Home system from a different manufacturer. Combined with a lack of industry standards, this leads to a dismal state of security and standardization across the board.

A major source of problems as Smart Homes evolve is the fact that the industry has not created a universal standard for connections. Different devices use a variety of protocols and technologies, such as Bluetooth, Wi-Fi, RFID, and others, to form connections and transmit data. Issues arise when mismatches in these technologies create either connection problems for customers, or worse, create security gaps which can make systems vulnerable to attack.[9]

If companies do not take care to select the right connection methods, it is quite apparent that customers may run into either connectivity problems, or interference if different devices attempt to use the same channels, or wavelengths to simultaneously send information. For example, RFID tags are cheap, low-energy connectivity chips that allow data transfer between nearby devices, and work through a setup of readers and tags able to transmit signals. They are often used in IoT due to their low cost and energy efficiency. While these chips are undoubtedly useful, they fall short on many of the factors needed for sound Smart Home system design. For example, RFID readers are not very good at handling multiple connections, so a lot of work must go into collision resolution fail-safes, which prevent malfunctions if several tags contact one reader at the same time.[10] Because there are no established guidelines for designating uses for the range of RFID tag signals, companies have much more difficulty and must dedicate additional resources to developing anti-collision algorithms. If a logical system was in place for assigning ranges of RFID frequencies, filtering out extraneous signals would be much simpler, and consumers would be safer from technical failures resulting from programming oversights or coincidental frequency collisions.[11] This correctable oversight is a possible source of reputation and financial risk for manufacturers (since regular technical issues will lead to a poor customer experience, an image of a buggy product, and ultimately loss of sales), and there is even potential legal risk if inadvertent signal collisions cause damage or injury through the failure of vital systems like health monitors or home security devices. These problems are present (to varying extents) in all connectivity protocols which are in use today, so it is certainly a considerable risk all IoT manufacturers must deal with.

Additionally, experts predict that soon many of the current connectivity technologies will face the problem of bandwidth oversaturation. In the last few years, network traffic has grown considerably, and with IoT development leading in a new influx of connected devices, continuity will be a growing problem as time goes on.[12] Unless new tech is introduced to expand the available bandwidth range, providing all devices access to the data streams that they need will be more and more difficult. Even if local collisions (like those common with RFID devices) are avoided, increasingly large and bandwidth-hungry systems will have to learn to share progressively more crowded networks. If congestion on networks becomes too extreme, customers may start to ditch IoT in favor of higher-priority Internet use. To avoid being labeled an industry of network vampires capable of slowing users' connections to a snail's pace, Smart Home companies must work together to find a solution.

In general, connectivity options are not a main consideration in device design, typically playing into other questions like hardware costs. But to avoid pushing home networking into a state of battle over resources and forcing consumers to choose which of their devices are most deserving of a connection, IoT manufacturers must work together to optimize their bandwidth use and protocol selection. As convenient as connected Smart technologies are, most consumers will not sacrifice internet speeds or the smooth operation of vital systems (e.g. health monitors) for some added comforts.

Security and privacy worries are at the forefront of the concerns people have about the Smart Home sector. The Smart Home movement is seeking to place an unprecedented number of network-connected devices capable of data collection and given control over physical processes in consumers' homes—a traditionally private and intimate place for most people. So, there is no surprise that fears of breaches prevail, even among early adopters.[13] High profile cases bringing up the possibility of IoT hacking, such as the 2015 experiment where researchers were able to access internet-connected baby monitor feeds[14] often make rounds in the news and heighten consumer fears of the technology. New markets are especially sensitive to sector-wide reputation risks as mass fear over the new tech can seriously harm sales and set back pioneering firms. On top of this, financial and legal risks can be a considerable problem for companies if a breach is to occur and customers seek damages for failure to protect their data.

There is a number of security-related oversights in how most Smart Home systems are designed, and it is an unfortunate reality that such new and rapidly-growing markets tend to lead to a culture of brushing off best practices (most notably in security) in a rush to release products sooner. In a recent survey by online authentication provider Auth0, 85 percent of IoT developers admitted to being pressured to get a product to market even though the implementation of adequate security software was not yet completed. This abysmal statistic shows how critical (but fixable) the problem is, and outlines a prisoner's dilemma for the Smart-Home sector: unless all the market participants put their competitive drives on hold and focus their attentions on dealing with these issues and rectifying their security-averse practices, soon enough there might not be a market to compete over.

Studies point out some of the most severe problems with the way security is implemented in IoT devices today. A very serious one is the lack of connection protocols. Going back to the RFID example from earlier, consider that RFID tags have very low processing capabilities and thus can only use lightweight authentication solutions, which can be less secure. As there are no established industry-wide standards, devices that can tolerate the risks of low-strength authentication are able to connect to high-risk devices such as medical equipment, thus exposing the more vital machine to unauthorized access. Another problem is the deficiency of encryption in communication between devices, with some devices even failing to encrypt key data like passwords or security certificates[15]. While encryption can be hard to maintain when working with embedded devices not powerful enough to run standard encryption algorithms,[16] consumers' focus on the security and privacy warrants favoring secure solutions over more lightweight or energy-efficient ones. Unencrypted information is easy to intercept from a network, so it is imperative IoT device makers follow basic procedure for their own data, and respect the security of information received from other systems. Other issues, such as the lack of password strength rules or account-locking defenses (to fend off automated attacks) are reported to be just as prevalent. There is also a surprising lack of support for functionality for the manufacturer to be able to remotely send out firmware updates or patches to devices as a way to resolve security problems.[17] HP ran a study last year on ten popular IoT security systems, and found rampant failure to either properly configure or even to attempt to implement minimal security basics like encryption, proper authentication, or the capacity for remote updates. A hundred percent of the tested devices failed at least one basic check.[18]

Following initial IoT trends, Smart Home developers tend to focus on low-power systems, minimal local processing, and the simplest overall solutions in order to reduce cost and energy consumption of devices. This is now a big concern for the industry: to earn consumers' trust and lay a framework for future growth, some of the current minimalism must be traded in for stronger security before consumers are scared off for good.

Process Risk

As was briefly mentioned in the discussion of Smart Home security risks, part of the problem with IoT today is that industry-wide oversight and coordination on security and privacy issues is largely absent. Not only does this make it harder to maintain a secure system when multiple products and manufacturers are involved, but it leaves a control vacuum which—in the case of a major breach or public outcry—might lead to increased government regulation. However, government regulation may either solve some of the security issues or hamper furutre innovation with overcomplicated policies and burdensome auditing procedures.[19]

LACK OF CONSUMER EDUCATION INITIATIVES

A common sentiment in the computational security industry is that the biggest vulnerability is the user. After all, the strongest password encryption methodologies are powerless if the user leaves the password on a sticky note by the keyboard. Therefore, vendors of Smart Home systems should ensure customers are instructed and guided to make sure that the defenses that are in place on their devices are being utilized fully.

A key example is relating to the use of default passwords on connected devices. When purchasing an internet-connected device, customers are typically given a default username and password, which they are theoretically expected to change during setup. This is often not the case, which largely defeats the purpose of a password. There already exist copious online databases listing varying IoT devices and their default login information, meaning hackers trying to access a device can automatically try the default information with little difficulty.[20] The magnitude of the problem is exhibited in the Dyn cyberattack of October 2016. The hackers involved built a bot network by compromising IoT devices worldwide, and used them in a massive DDoS attack. When the code used in the attack was examined, security analysts found that the botnet, which at its peak was made up of roughly 400,000 devices, was created by simply attempting to use a list of 61 passwords on each encountered device. Therefore, hackers could harness almost half a million devices by trying a few dozen passwords (many of which were standard defaults like "admin" and "root").[21] If the owners of these devices were given a few pointers on the creation of strong passwords, and perhaps guided with simple authentication system enhancements such as password strength or double authentication requirements and the implementation of one-time first-use credentials,[22] Dyn Inc. would not be looking at the aftermath of the biggest DDoS attack recorded in history.[23]

ABSENCE OF INDUSTRY STANDARDS

Also tying closely to system risk is the industry's failure to formulate any kind of standards or best-practices to date. Unless the industry forms some sort of accepted protocol to be used across the Smart Home market, manufacturers will continue to face connectivity, compatibility, and security risks. There will be immediate benefits from industry-wide oversight, which will greatly reduce the third-party risk of a company allowing a connection to any other manufacturer's devices.

Due to their interconnectivity, Smart-Home Systems follow the principle that "a chain is only as strong as the weakest link," so the breaching of any element can allow a lithe hacker to access any other part of the network. For instance, while the manufacturer of a smart toaster oven might have little concern for security (what sensitive data can be stolen from a toaster?), if that toaster is hooked up to the same network as important devices containing sensitive data, suddenly that toaster is a liability. This can hurt both the toaster's manufacturer for being at fault for the penetration, as well as the company behind the more sensitive devices for failure to prevent the attack. Therefore, it is in the interest of every developer of Smart Home technology to ensure that they and the other players in the sector follow the same security procedures.

External Risk
HACKING AND LOSS OF PRIVACY

The issue of the possibility of malicious or unwanted access to IoT devices and data in the home is a repeating theme in examining possible risks within the industry, and likely poses the gravest threat to Smart Home sales.

Privacy concerns are especially big among potential consumers, given how much the technology can be embedded in every element of the home. With this massive capacity for generating data, consumers worry about the disclosure of information ranging from embarrassing (such as fitness tracking weight data) all the way to highly important and personal, like "the user's residence location, income, lifestyle, behaviors, heath status and other sensitive information."[24] At that, users are concerned about different levels of data leakage, from malevolent, forced entry by hackers, to unwanted data collection by companies for marketing and research, all the way to fears of government surveillance. As put by the *Wall Street Daily*, "without privacy assurances, wide-scale consumer adoption simply won't happen."[25]

Additionally, the hijacking of devices by hackers for use in major cyber-attacks is a growing concern. Even though, according to chief research officer of F-Secure Mikko Hypponen, consumers mostly do not care about their devices' possible involvement in cybercrimes (especially if the operation of the device is unaffected),[26] other risks will affect the industry if the threat is not dealt with. Due to the sheer scale and spread of the IoT device market, botnets targeting these devices can quickly acquire thousands of nodes, which form a formidable threat to any server or network they are used to target. Like the aforementioned Dyn hack, which utilized almost half a million IoT devices to take down a major DNS server and thus forced several major websites offline in parts of the US for several hours, this vulnerability poses a massive threat which is very hard to combat due to the decentralized and complex nature of such cyber-attacks.[27]

Attacks of this scale can cause huge finance losses, physical infrastructure damage, or even loss of life if certain vital utilities or centers are targeted. As a result, failure to react to these threats results in a big risk of government involvement in the industry, which can hurt startups, increase manufacturing costs, and in general bog down any drive for innovation with audits, checks, and bureaucratic procedures.[28] This would especially threaten IoT manufacturers in countries that do implement government control, since delays and costs induced by regulation can give the advantage to regulation-free foreign firms, all while failing to do much about the problem if international manufacturers do not need to comply with these rules and their products remain vulnerable.[29] Even with these downsides to regulating the sector, the government may feel its hand forced in light some major incident, so proactivity is key to preserving the industry's freedom.

REPUTATION

Another repeating theme that ties to a number of the other risks is the impact certain problems can have on the reputation of IoT technology, which can directly affect sales. As the industry stands on the cusp of being able to offer full Smart Home solutions that cover all elements of the household to the average consumer, a make-or-break element is how people feel about the technology. The media has been happy to publicize breaches and research into security problems in popular devices, so even a single major event can turn off the masses to the idea of IoT-powered homes.

Customers' (often well-justified) concerns with privacy and security are major barriers to adoption of the technology, with a survey run by Auth0 showing that 52 percent of consumers and a shocking 90 percent of developers do not feel that IoT is secure enough.[30] So as was stated above, unless the industry comes together to handle these problems and invests in marketing to reassure buyers, the initial excitement over the potential of Smart Homes can sizzle out, forcing IoT tech vendors back to peddling their wares in fringe markets.

MITIGATION

As Smart Homes have not been a part of mainstream markets very long, their sector seems surrounded by threats, and the prospect of having to counter them all is daunting even to already-established tech companies, and can be downright terrifying to startups. So how can the industry retain its youthful vigor and vibrant startup and innovation scene while resolving the risks that look to be forming an existential threat to the whole market?

The ray of light in the darkness might be the collaborative environment in the hi-tech sector. If competing Smart Home companies can come together (as they already do to some extent in allowing their devices to interface with other companies'), they can cooperatively resolve the above risks and help their market grow into a much more stable and expansive segment of the technology and household appliance sectors. Here are some major recommendations:

Industry Consortium

An organization of sector leaders and major players is a key first step to resolving much of the industry's fragmented nature. By working together, companies can come up with standards for technologies used, connection and transfer protocols, and security requirements. This will resolve the major system and process risks faced by each company thus saving time, simplifying development, and ensuring consumes get the best experience. Additionally, this will mitigate reputation and legal risks across the sector since the consortium can guarantee products that it produces are compliant and secure, thus upping the security level across the industry and reassuring consumers in a highly visible and easily marketable way. Plus, the formation of an institution where industry stakeholders can resolve common issues can improve response rates to threats and breaches, helping enterprises of all sizes to respond to new vulnerabilities, counter ongoing crises, and recover from any incidents. Finally, an established collective of key market players will be a better platform to negotiate with governments and simplify the discussion of any reform or action as needed, as well as a unified channel for communicating with the media and other organizations. Augmenting the companies' outreach abilities is a good way to improve consumer relations and build trust as well, further buffering the industry from reputation risk.

Security Improvements

Each company in the Smart Home market should also take individual steps to strengthen their security protocols, perhaps with enforcement from the aforementioned consortium where needed. Relatively simple steps like implementing improved and expanded encryption, enforcing strong passwords and multi-step authentication, adding the framework for rapid firmware and security update deployment, and strengthening the security and general architecture of digital user interfaces do not add too much bulk to IoT devices or require much work. These are all common practices in other branches of software development, but can make a huge difference in improving device security.[31] Even something as seemingly trivial as forcing a password reset when setting up a device can help prevent massive breaches like the Dyn hack.

In general, companies should maintain a focus on eliminating vulnerabilities and following best practices during development of their hardware and programs. This approach is taken in much of the software industry, and helps ensure that the system is as impenetrable as possible. This cannot be done if security is added as an afterthought. While there are other drivers, like the desire for energy-efficiency, each manufacturer and the industry as a whole will benefit from secure design that and If these principles are outlined and accepted by an association of sector players, companies will be assured of their partners' compliance, and thus will have an easier time in development since they can focus on external threats, without having to worry about vulnerabilities within the system.

Changes in Approach

If the industry lags in adopting the two previous recommendations, a few major players might take the initiative and redirect the market to otherwise resolve the market's problems.

THE FULL PACKAGE

One possible direction for the market is a large corporation developing a single packaged solution for the Smart Home. With one manufacturer making all of the components, there will be no concern for compatibility. Security risks can be dealt with by building safeguards throughout the system, and since one company manages the whole system and has full control of its peripheries, security can be further improved by surrounding the system with a single firewall. Again, problems with standards, protocols, and resource sharing will be made irrelevant by the single company's full authority over the system.

This grab-and-go solution, though likely more expensive and coming at the cost of customizability, will make Smart Homes quicker to establish since consumers pick a package as opposed to selecting individual devices. The full control and security focus will also make accessing the market much tougher for small companies; the resources needed to put together a wholesome, pre-packaged system exceeds those available to startups, and a large corporation managing such an ecosystem will certainly make it difficult to access its systems and integrate any third-party devices. Almost like the Apple Inc. approach to Smart Homes, this solution has a number of tradeoffs, and though a major win for the one or two enterprises that manage to push it into the mainstream, it will be a huge blow to the innovation of the technology and the freedom of the market as a whole.

THE CONTROL CENTER

Another possibility is a more liberal version of the above where a corporation creates a central hub to which a user can connect other devices. This corporation essentially takes on the role of an industry consortium, and will have to vet third-party manufacturers and enforce certain levels of security and mutual rules in order to overcome the general sector's problems. Potentially, these hubs can become much more secure by changing to an intranet configuration and doing all processing locally, without the need for external Internet connectivity. Of course, closing the system to all outside connection will make it much more secure. Though a little less monopolistic, this approach also places a lot of power in the hands of one-two market leaders and complicates the process for new devices to get to the market. Though a sound solution, the optimal route is of course a more free-market-based approach.

Conclusion

Today, there is a lot of excitement around the application of the Internet of Things within the home. The collective human fantasy has long run wild with images of automated houses that take the effort out of household maintenance and provide its residents with a multitude of benefits in every category of home living. Being a staple of science fiction works for many decades, Smart Homes have at some point entered the daydreams of almost every person, painting tantalizing pictures of delicious meals ready at the click of a button, chores taken care of with a wave of the hand, and every whim fulfilled with but a flicker of thought. Now, for the first time ever, one does not need to be a king or sultan to command such powers. With a few purchases, any household task can be bent to one's will.

However, in this age of constant security fears and technological growth, customers cannot be kept with just offerings of neat shortcuts and household optimizations. Customers will not give up privacy, risk security breaches, or compromise the functionality of their other gadgets just to say they live in a "smart" home. Therefore, every player seeking to capitalize on the opportunities the Smart Home market entails must think about sustaining the interest and enthusiasm amongst consumers with truly beneficial products oriented towards meeting all of the purchasers' needs. If the products end up causing users more headaches than they resolve, the market's excitement will quickly fade into nothing more than a passing fancy.

As difficult as it is to put aside competitiveness in such a fresh, ripe market, the best chance businesses entering this sector have to ensure their developments persist and avoid becoming a dying fad is a collaborative approach to solving the primary problems facing the industry. By taking steps that seems counter-intuitive in a free market and putting off the instant gratifications of cashing in on quick product releases, the Smart Home sector can ensure it has a bright, fruitful future and will see its key players usher in a future where fully automated Smart Homes pass from humanity's reveries into every household's reality.

The Airline Industry's IoT Risks

Kyle Simpson

Written: November 2017
Published: March 2018

Abstract: There is not sector left untouched by the creeping application and presence of the Internet of Things (IoT). Despite its historic reputation for driving innovation in its sector, the airline industry has been unusually slow to implement widespread use of devices connected to the Internet to drive business needs. In defense of this caution, this research paper outlines some potential areas of innovation leveraging the IoT for the airline industry, while highlighting the corresponding risks.

Introduction

The broad aviation industry has long been absorbed in innovation, from jet manufacturers working tirelessly to produce top quality and efficiency airbuses, to airline companies constantly reworking customer experiences and interactions. The industry consistently adopts new technologies and methodologies to improve user experience, but where does it stop? At what point do industry operators slow innovation in order to ensure customer safety, rather than releasing new, potentially insecure technology? Lately, the answer to this question has come to focus on the area of the Internet of Things (IoT). The Internet of Things Global Standards Initiative defines IoT as "the network of physical objects or 'things' embedded with electronics, software, sensors, and network connectivity, which enables these objects to collect and exchange data."[1] There has been noticeable hesitation on the part of airlines when it comes to implementing sensors and other small devices to collect user data; at the same time, impatient industry experts have increasingly demanded progress in this space. One such industry expert, Raj Dalal, wrote in October 2016 heavily pressuring the aviation industry to roll out more connections to the IoT in order to improve passenger experience; however, the argument completely avoided the subjects of passenger information security and cloud integration.[2] This research paper outlines some of the possible implementations of the IoT in the airline industry, and highlight some risks associated with each implementation in defense of the airline industry's hesitations.

The Internet of Things

The definition of what the IoT encompasses is incredibly broad, leaving a lot of room for innovation and potential risks. The Online Trust Alliance (OTA) recognizes the incredible breadth IoT has the potential to manifest itself in, and seeks to understand best practices companies can follow to maximize customer satisfaction. In short, the OTA outlines "security, privacy, and sustainability" as the three pillars upon which businesses should build their IoT platform.[3] Meanwhile, for the purposes of this research paper, the definition of IoT will be restricted to include only physical electronics and sensors that collect and exchange data, in order to narrow the field of view and give opportunity to focus more on the OTA's pillars. It will also be necessary to distinguish the two categories for which IoT could be applied within the airline industry – airline employees and consumers. When examining use cases for both groups, it becomes evident each have very different needs which would equate to very different solutions. As a brief example, an airline employee might be interested in a piece of physical technology that could track a passenger through check-in and TSA to consider delaying a flight; while a passenger might be interested in a piece of software they could integrate into their existing hardware that could look up on-flight menus or track their luggage on the way to the baggage claim. Each of these solutions would require a different IoT device and measurement, and would have varying security access controls, entailing nuanced risks for each service. Keeping this in mind, it is important to delineate which category a service would fall under to fairly consider the risk involved and to be able to recommend appropriate controls and procedures.

Airline Employees

From the perspective of an airline employee in the role of checking passengers in for flights, they use a physical computer and a scanner to read passenger's QR codes and check them into the system. From the employee's perspective, this can be a slow and clunky process since they are connected to large, physical hardware and must always be in the same place, often causing congestion for other passengers trying to move through a space. A potential innovation for this role could be a small, handheld scanner to replace the physical computer, similar to devices many retail stores have adopted. These small devices would only be accessible to airline employees, and as such would need to consider the following controls in implementation. First, they would need appropriate access to passenger data, primarily needing flight numbers, seat numbers, passenger names. This information would provide enough for airline employees to efficiently check-in passengers, while also not providing access to passenger payment information. Having the mobile handheld devices may also allow for increased efficiency and decreased cost. Since the smaller hardware would be cheaper than a typical computer, airline companies could afford to have more of them, speeding up the check-in process, while also allowing for the existing mobile check-in systems.

Although having a more efficient and dynamic check-in system seems nice, it is important to consider the risks associated with new, smaller hardware. The primary risk associated with this potential implementation would be the information security risk.[4] The potential of a passenger with malicious intents stealing one of these readers is moderate-to-high considering the number of passengers traveling through an airport at any given time. Given this risk, it would be incredibly important for the handheld device to have automated controls built in, only granting access to airline employees who are registered with a username and password.[5] In addition to automated controls, it would be import to only provide necessary information about passengers on the device so that even if a malicious party got access to the device, they would not get highly protected information about every passenger.

Since this implementation of IoT relates to aviation employees, rather than passengers, there is greater feasibility for preventative control establishment.[6] In this case, a preventative control could look like an employee training on how to use the new device, a training on what passenger data they have access to and what data they should not have access to, or registration of usernames and passwords. Whatever the form the preventative control takes, the main point is to inform employees of the functions of their new hardware, and train them on proper uses and access.

Flight Attendants

Moving on to the role of the flight attendant. The place of highest probability for innovation would be food and drink service. Currently, flight attendants slowly move through the aisle with large, clunky carts, asking each passenger if they would like to purchase anything, so to innovate in this position, one idea would be another small handheld device distributed to each passenger or built into each seat that performs a similar function. This device would need a small display, most likely a touch pad, along with a card reader so passengers could look through options and purchase what they want. On the receiving end, there could be a panel for flight attendants to see what passengers order, and distribute individual orders, rather than blocking the aisle for 20-30 minutes at a time. Similar to the check-in handheld device, the devices passengers use would need very specific access to items available on-flight, and restrict access to items on other flights, or access to other passengers' information. Meanwhile, the panel for flight attendants would need automated controls to access only seat and order information, to prevent similar malicious passengers from stealing passenger's private data while attendants were away from the panel. In this case, preventative controls would be appropriate for the flight attendants, but inappropriate for passengers, since having some form of training for each passenger is not typically a feasible option for most airlines.[7]

Airline Passengers

Transitioning to the consumer side of airline industry IoT, this is the category of aviation IoT where there is the most opportunity for innovation, and the most opportunity for risk. Consumers of IoT products can be wildly unpredictable in what they accidentally access, so it is very important to heavily structure access to data. Meanwhile, hackers are notorious for wanting to breach important databases, and any database related to aviation would be a high target. There are three primary implementations the industry could develop: 1) sensors to track traffic conditions around airport and in parking garages, 2) sensors to track luggage from the airplane to baggage claims, and 3) sensors and trackers to locate lost luggage. For each, it is critical to note the potential control failures in implementation, as well as the associated risks, beginning with traffic conditions and parking garages.

Traffic Conditions

Cameras noting traffic conditions have been sparsely implemented in and around large metropolitan areas. These existing cameras are used primarily for news sources to report on conditions for television and radio listeners to get an idea of what their morning commute looks like. This system has been effective in the past, but relies on qualitative measures, and is open for interpretation from whomever is reporting. A new system that could be implemented is a system where sensors track motion, in this case around airports, and use quantitative measures to more accurately report the traffic conditions. A similar system could be used in parking garages, tracking the number of open parking spaces and congestion in parts of the garage, and reporting this information in a similar manner. The most probable form of reporting would be some mobile application users could download to receive the information, primarily allowing them to better plan for their trip.

The primary risks associated with sensors tracking traffic are system failures, information security, and processing errors.[8] A system failure has the potential to occur when a sensor improperly categorizes data and causes a data center failure. An easy solution to this problem would be to instantiate automated controls, and test the device thoroughly enough to ensure that a miscategorization would not occur. An information security failure could occur if a hacker tried to breach the network where the sensors transmitted data, or if someone damaged or stole the sensor itself. To prevent hackers from breaching the system, automated controls and strong firewall protection would be the best solutions, doing everything possible to protect and segment the system. A processing error would look very similar to a system failure, in that a miscategorization of data has the highest potential of causing such an event. Similarly, automated controls could solve this problem, ensuring that data would not be miscategorized.[9]

Another issue to bring up surrounding the implementation of sensors is the potential for users to be tracked over long periods of time. If the sensor system used some form of machine learning to track cars, there is the potential for the system to begin noticing long-term patterns and accidentally track someone's long-term behaviors. If this were the case, the network would become a larger target for hackers since it has the power to track users and note patterns. To address this issue, whoever operates the sensor system would need to implement strong directive and corrective controls, in the case of a breach.[10]

Luggage Tracking

Switching over to the two IoT implementations regarding luggage, these are the two most feasible IoT innovations the aviation industry could make, since both are already currently in existence in other applications. Small GPS tags already exist in the realm of tracking cell phones and car keys, so transferring this feature into aviation is entirely probable. The brand Tile already sells such a product, so the industry could very easily integrate Tile's hardware into their software.[11] Both locating lost luggage, and tracking luggage progress towards a baggage claim could be achieved with the integration of Tile or a similar product, and the most challenging task for airlines would be third-party coordination. The highest risk associated with third-party integration is the opportunity for hackers to breach either system. If airlines chose to create their own system and simply partner with Tile, rather than relying entirely on Tile's service, then the opportunity for hackers to breach the system is doubled. The Equifax breach in June 2017 demonstrated the challenges associated with third-party cloud integration, and the importance of having proper controls in place to restrict access to data is crucial. Consequently, cloud integration would need to be a major consideration for any airline planning to make third-party partnerships.

Conclusion

To summarize the potential implementations of consumer IoT in the aviation industry, the most probable form of information synthesis would be a mobile application. The traffic and parking garage sensors, and the luggage tracking would all have to be aggregated somewhere, and for current consumers, mobile applications tend to be the best option. Mobile applications of course have their own risks and control needs, namely information security and system failure risks and automated controls, so these applications would need frequent monitoring and updates.[12] Many airlines already have their own mobile applications for passengers to check-in, get boarding passes, and pay for checked bags, so adding these features to their current systems seems like a feasible goal.

The final area to address in implementing IoT within the airline industry is how everything will actually be developed. When it comes to creating a system as complex as the one described, there needs to be an appropriate amount of time dedicated to ensuring the system is designed well and will not bring about too many negative risks. When in development, the tone at the top will heavily influence the developer's priorities, and will dictate whether they focus on speed of implementation, or strength of the system. A study conducted by the Ponemon Institute found that "the tone at the top … has a trickle-down effect on all employees of the organization," and as a results "risks such as insider negligence and third party risk are minimized."[13] If executives are more focused on spitting out a flimsy system that only works some of the time, then developers will respond with mediocre work. However, if the executives truly want the system to be effective, efficient, and durable, then they must take the time to emphasize the importance of secure networks. The hope is that the current caution of the airline industry to implement IoT is due to executives demanding strong networks, and that when the industry is ready to deploy IoT features, that these be well-developed, secure and highly functional. Assuming that a positive tone at the top is the reason why the industry has been slow in implementing IoT, industry experts should reduce their pressure on airlines as this may encourage sloppiness over dependability. "Security, privacy, and sustainability," should continue to be top priorities for any company looking to integrate IoT into their business and the airline industry is no exception.[14]

The Internet of Things: A Dark Precursor

Kyle McNulty

Written: September 2017
Published: October 2018

Abstract: This paper explores the growing risks associated with the spreading web of internet-enabled devices across consumers' lives. The explosive proliferation of Internet-connected devices has resulted from rapid progress in technology and expanding demand for internet-connected capabilities from consumers. However, this technological advancement and consumer behavior has also created a significant vulnerability: cybersecurity. The current risks associated with the Internet of Things will only have more serious consequences if left unaddressed.

The number of Internet-connected devices reached a count of 13 billion in 2017, estimates research firm Gartner. That number is projected to double by 2020 and reach global revenues of $1.7 trillion for the ecosystem.[1] The idea of the "Internet of Things" (IoT) refers to the collective whole of Internet-enabled devices. Included in this collection are devices that range from personal laptops and mobile phones, to household appliances such as refrigerators, coffee makers, and lamps. These so-called "smart" devices are penetrating households across the world, and the industry as a whole is rapidly expanding as technology miniaturizes, and consumers increasingly demand connectivity and convenience in their everyday lives.

This explosive proliferation of Internet-connected devices has lead to incredible technological progress, but has also created a significant and gaping hole: security. A pair of researchers from Trend Micro discovered more than 178 million vulnerable and exposed IoT devices in 10 major U.S. cities. These included webcams, medical devices, databases, and routers.[2] Simple tools such as Shodan, a free database and search engine for identifying IoT devices, serve as reconnaissance tools for hackers allowing them to easily access and take control of these devices.

We have already seen hackers capitalizing on these exposed and vulnerable devices. "Mirai" is malware that turns Linux and Windows devices into "bots" that can be used at the infector's command in DDoS (Distributed Denial of Service) attacks. These attacks leverage the "botnet" to send out a deluge of requests to overwhelm a target device and cause it to crash. One of the most prominent cases of the Mirai botnet was in September 2016 against the popular security blog site Krebs on Security. The site was receiving traffic at a rate of 620 Gbit/s, the largest in history up to that point. Then a month later, the French cloud computing company OVH was the victim of a 1Tbit/s Mirai attack, 61 percent larger than the previous attack.[3]

The growing prevalence of these attacks is attributed not only to the rapid increase in the number of devices that exist, but also to the carelessness of implementing sound cybersecurity practices when these devices reach consumers and end-users of the devices. The apparent apathy towards cybersecurity stems from lack of awareness, the fuel of competition in cutthroat markets, and the inevitability of human error.

Cybersecurity has only recently been acknowledged as noteworthy of attention within organizations. Many companies now have policies to prevent cyber-attacks, but these policies are often outdated or ignored. According to a survey of medical device manufacturers done by Ponemon Institute, only 17 percent of the individuals surveyed say their organization takes significant measures to prevent attacks.[4] In May of 2017, the "Wannacry" ransomware, an attack that locks users out of their systems until the attackers receive money, struck hospitals around the world. The vulnerability exploited in these attacks was disclosed with a patch in March, but the hospitals declined to patch their affected devices. Hospitals are often reluctant to patch devices because of the potential impact on patient care, but the resulting security environment leads to issues of its own. Because of these lackluster policies and procedures, vulnerabilities can remain in production systems for years after their disclosure, which ultimately leads to a larger host of vulnerable devices on the Internet.

Additionally, competition and the feature-centric attitude of the modern consumer dissuades manufacturers from concerning themselves with security. There are hundreds of companies competing for IoT market share. In 2015, technology giant Amazon jumped into the IoT market with offerings for cloud compatibility between IoT devices and other Amazon Web Services. Other major players include Microsoft, Oracle, and Siemens.[5] With fierce competition comes pressure from executives to meet quotas and get products to market. As a result, small and large companies alike are forced to forgo product changes they see as optional like security, in favor of features more tangible to consumers such as computing speed. While the average consumer remains impartial to the security of the product he/she purchases, companies will continue to omit security under pressure to compete and finish projects on budget.

Finally, even if consumers and producers alike recognize the importance of security, insecurity is inevitable. Humans are imperfect. Vulnerabilities stem from errors on behalf of humans. Whether the developer lazily coded and failed to remove a backdoor, an entry point to a system that bypasses authentication procedures, or the product security team failed to identify a vulnerability; these mistakes happen. Additionally, software developers are often content after shipping a product, whereas attackers are constantly looking for workarounds. Vulnerabilities will continue to occur because humans will continue to make mistakes, and as technology gains an increasingly important role in society the stakes of these vulnerabilities will rise exponentially.

Humans have all sorts of dreams for technology: self-driving cars, virtual reality, and jetpacks. The list may sound far-fetched, but we are making tangible progress towards all of the above. In 2016, technology accounted for 7.1% of the total U.S gross domestic product.[6] Because of the funding and investment in the industry, large companies like Amazon and Google have the freedom to experiment on technology that seems dreamlike. Elon Musk announced his new venture, Neuralink, earlier this year. Neuralink is centered on creating chips to place in the human brain in order to keep pace with advances in artificial intelligence. With the crucial impact these chips would play in the lives of their beholders, the security implications of these devices will become a major concern for the safety and wellbeing of the users.

The ability to impact the physical world through malware has been seen before. In 2009, an American-Israeli built virus dubbed Stuxnet was deployed in Iran to curb their growing nuclear program. Stuxnet is malware that targets programmable logic controllers, which are used in the automation of electromechanical processes in factories around the world.[7] Stuxnet was used to cause Iranian nuclear centrifuges to spin out of control and explode. Between 2009 and 2010, Stuxnet is estimated to have destroyed approximately a fifth of the nuclear centrifuges in the Natanz plant.[8] And cyber warfare is playing an ever-increasing role in government tactics today.

In President Trump's budget for 2018, he allotted over $1 billion for cybersecurity for the Department of Homeland Security.[9] In 2014, the FBI launched a cyber-hiring initiative aimed at recruiting talented cybersecurity individuals into the Bureau. This focus on cyber reinforces the role it is expected to play in the future of the US government, both on offense and on defense.

The combination of focus on research and growth of the industry, with a goal of enhancing convenience for human consumers in every aspect of life, can lead to catastrophe in the coming years. As self-driving cars become a thing of reality, the possibility of manipulating the driving system and causing a fatal wreck also materializes. In 2015, Security Innovation, a Seattle-based cybersecurity-consulting firm, hacked autonomous cars by simply shining a laser pointer at the camera and effectively blinding the sensors.[10]

Cybersecurity threats also affect industries that are not directly technology focused. In 2013, two researchers for the security company Cylance reported a hard-coded password vulnerability affecting roughly 300 medical devices across approximately 40 vendors.[11] Affected devices included surgical devices, infusion pumps, defibrillators, and others. The ability to access infusion pumps using hardcoded credentials could lead to cases as extreme as murder through patient overdose.

With companies like Neuralink and Google working on next generation technology for products such as brain chips and self-driving cars, it is easy to get swept away with thoughts of technological progress and only consider security as an afterthought. However, due to the lack of consistent adhere to cybersecurity best practices, intense competition, and the simple imperfections of human-created device, the next generation of IoT devices will still be prone to the same issues that have plagued the IoT industry. Nevertheless, the stakes are increasingly becoming life or death.

SECTION TWO

Information Integrity and Privacy

An Open Letter to Librarians: Ethical Imperatives in Post-Truth America

Alexander N. George

Written:
Published:

Abstract: This paper discusses the growing challenge that librarians face due to inaccurate, misleading, and flat-out false news ("fake news"), which is also creating new issues for our democratic societies in the age of 24-hour, instantly accessible, and always-changing news. The author explores the question of a librarian's ethical responsibilities related to fake news, and the implications for our society. However, this growing problem of fake news presents a unique opportunity for librarians to combine the job's information-related expertise and new technologies to evolve the role of librarian into information curator.

Do libraries and librarians have ethical responsibilities within American society given the predominance of fake news and the categorization of real news as being fake? What are those responsibilities and how can they have an impact in shaping the future of information literacy? These are questions, amongst others, I will explore in this paper. I will seek to build a case that librarians have a central role to play in solving this endemic problem. My goal is to show how a well-educated, functional, liberal democracy is, in-part, resultant of libraries, how the principles of librarianship could offer remedy to the post-truth campaigns of misinformation in America, and the ethical obligation I believe librarians carry in this environment.

Many have written on the topic of fake news. The Internet is teeming with accounts of fake news, poor journalism, and claims of outright lies. Who, and what, is to be believed? No longer are the days when a few major news outlets were available on cable television for the day's news, nor is it primarily consumed via print from trusted, well-known newspapers. The rise of the Internet has given way to the decline of traditional media sources. In a recent fact sheet, the Pew Research Center cites the, "newspaper workforce has shrunk by about 20,000 positions, or 39 percent, in the last 20 years."[1] Meanwhile, online media continues to grow. The same fact sheet shows 28 percent of adults consume news digitally, whereas only a decade ago the primary source of news was in print. *The Wall Street Journal* reports that its "average monthly unique visitors for the third quarter of 2015 was anywhere from two to 78 times greater than average Sunday circulation for the same period."

However, not all media comes from such reputable sources. "The digital revolution drastically lowers the costs of copying and distributing information."[2] What was once the domain of institutional media has transformed and is now available for the masses to contribute. In other words, any person with an Internet connection, and some modicum of skill, can put together a "real" looking "news" website or blog and it is left to the consumer to interpret the truth. Websites such as Facebook also make it very easy for stories such as these to be circulated quickly, especially when clever authors use catchy, provocative words and imagery. Tom Regan tells us that while individual thoughts and feelings may not settle moral issues, neither can the feelings of the masses.[3] "Questions of right and wrong cannot be answered just by counting heads." This is one, of many, dangers of questionable stories being shared rapidly via social media. The number of likes and shares a story gets may be good for Facebook advertising dollars, but it is not necessarily a good thing for public consumption. Just because a story becomes popular does not make it true. In the face of such constant, viral information flows, the necessity for information literacy becomes paramount to one's understanding of the world around them.

Nevertheless, let us take a moment to examine a couple of key pieces of information. At the outset, I said I am going to show how we need librarians to maintain our democratic culture and how they can help (and are morally obligated to help) with the problem of fake news. First, we need to understand what fake news is all about. What is news? Merriam-Webster defines it as, "a report of recent events," or, "previously unknown information," and, "material reported in a newspaper or news periodical or on a newscast."[4] What about fake? The same dictionary defines it as, noun, "one that is not what it purports to be," or, adjective, "not true or real." Therefore, by these definitions, fake news would be a report or previously unknown information that is not what it purports to be, or descriptively is not true, and it appears in news media in some form, in our case, online.

What about truth? From a philosophical perspective, can anything really be true? There are numerous theories regarding truth, of which I will present a few of the leading ones. The Correspondence Theory states that, "for any proposition p, p is true if and only if it corresponds to fact."[5] Later came Tarski's Semantic Theory, which asks the question, "Under which condition is that proposition true?" By contrast, there is the Redundancy Theory, which does not require a proposition to bear relation to something else to be true; instead, it suggests the concept of truth allows for indirect reference. For example, if we say something "is true," then truth is revealed by way of recognizing it would be redundant to add this phrase to the proposition. While there may be conflicting philosophical perspectives about truth, a common theme appears to be that truth is a property that through logical reasoning can be obtained. This brings us back to the concept of the fakeness of the news. I would argue then, to claim a published report of information is not true rests on an assertion that through logical reasoning the propositions contained within it cannot obtain truth either through relation to fact, nor conditionally, nor implicitly. This is to say the information contained within a fake news report is wholly false.

Is every fake news story necessarily entirely false though? A commonly coined phrase as of late is the "alternate fact." (As an aside, from the philosophical arguments above, there can be no such thing as an alternate fact, unless defined as an additional, optional piece of information as opposed to its mainstream application in which it is used to describe a difference of opinion on the matter of whether or not something is factually true.) I will submit that perhaps some news categorized as fake contains some factually true information and some factually false information. The lines are often blurred. Again, it is left to the consumer to interpret the information one reads or hears. This is where I think it is important we, and I mean we as information consumers and as American citizens, need to attempt to understand if the information presented in fake news stories is really misinformation or disinformation. Floridi defines a proposition as factual semantic information, "if and only if p is (constituted by) well-formed, meaningful, and veridical data."[6] He goes on to say this definition, "clarifies the fact that false information is not a genuine type of information." When semantic content is false, he says, it is classified as misinformation. However, he makes an important distinction that if the source of the information is aware that it is not true, and then it becomes disinformation. This is otherwise known as a lie. I will note here Floridi also comments that both misinformation and disinformation are "ethically censurable." The point is that fake news comes in many flavors, from the mildly annoying to the deeply troubling as measured in degrees of how serious we should be paying attention and how much effort should be put forth to challenge the sources of the information. This leads to a natural question then, what can or should be done about it?

Before I launch headfirst into a call to arms on the American Library Association (ALA) to rally the librarian troops and formalize a new charter of activism against the fake news engine, I would like to outline another concept as background for the assault. What is it about libraries that is tied to our functioning democracy? They are inextricably connected to our Constitutional protection afforded in the First Amendment of the Bill of Rights, that our government cannot abridge our freedom of speech. Libraries are centers for information, places where free speech is exercised and shared. As stated by President Franklin D. Roosevelt, "Libraries are... essential to the functioning of a democratic society... libraries are the great symbols of the freedom of the mind." They are centers for knowledge, and as great custodians of our rights, they ensure the public has access to varying perspectives. More importantly, this access is free to all citizens, enabling "the resources to develop the information literacy skills necessary to participate in the democratic process" and "discourse among informed citizens [to assure] civil society."[7] Look at the Seattle Public Library, for example, whose purpose, as stated within its selection and withdrawal of materials policy, is to enlighten, empower, and inform the people within our community. [8] "The Library and its board of trustees uphold the democratic right to freely express their thoughts and ideas, both popular and unpopular. We support the right of each individual to privately read, listen, and view the full range of published thought and ideas." Further, the library's collection objectives, which come at the direction of the Librarian, aim to be, "an unbiased and diverse source of information" and its selection policy includes goals to "develop the social awareness and knowledge needed for self-government and successful participation in a diverse community" and to "educate and inform." Lastly, while the library seeks to build a diverse collection, it does not endorse any particular viewpoint expressed in those materials.

Ostensibly, a primary function of libraries is to foment information literacy amongst the public. As seen with the Seattle Public Library, a key tool in a library's arsenal is its collection, the actual content in which it provides for the development of well-rounded literacy skills. Moreover, the key person behind the collection is the librarian, who carries the burden and discretion for adding or removing items from it. So, what is the guiding force that helps the librarian in his or her quest of building a collection that will assist in holding up to the lofty standard of maintaining our democratic and free society? It is a code of ethics. The ALA codified a guiding set of ethical principles by which all

American librarians are to follow. In this code, the ALA acknowledges librarians, "significantly influence, or control the selection, organization, preservation, and dissemination of information."[9] An important feature of the librarians' code of ethics is that it does not set forth to cover all possible situations, but instead serves as a framework within which ethical decision-making should occur throughout the profession. I ask then, in the current environment of politically motivated misinformation and disinformation campaigns that presumably aim to manipulate many for the benefit of the few, what obligations, if any, do librarians have? Professionally, there appear to be clear opportunities present, such as striving for excellence to be leaders in shaping public opinion in a rapidly evolving information environment. In my opinion, this opportunity has significant upward potential. In a separate report by the Pew Research Center, 37 percent of people surveyed felt libraries help "a lot" when it comes to helping them decide what information they can trust, and another 37 percent believed libraries helped "somewhat" in this regard.[10] Sentiment amongst Americans already points towards libraries being sources of trusted and respected information leaders. This should be leveraged further, particularly now when this service is in such great demand. But from an ethical standpoint, this isn't just an example of what libraries could be doing a better job at, I believe it's an example of something libraries are ethically responsible to tackle head on. The stakes are too high. The very fabric of our democracy is at risk. The ALAs very own code of ethics outline their responsibilities within "a political system grounded in and informed citizenry," including their "special obligation to ensure the free flow of information and ideas to present and future generations."[11]

The role of American academic librarians in developing information literacy dates back to the 19th century, according to Donald Barclay, a deputy university librarian at the University of California—Merced.[i] "Evidence exists of library instruction dating back to the 1820s at Harvard University."[ii] As time progressed, the phrase "information literacy" became synonymous with the duties of academic librarians. "Rather than being limited to locating items in a given library, information literacy recognized that students needed to be equipped with skills required to identify, organize and cite information. More than that, it focused on the ability to critically evaluate the credibility and appropriateness of information sources." He goes on to say how the challenges faced by students in today's information environment are much more difficult given the vastness of information availability. He points towards a revised Framework for Information Literacy for Higher Education released by the Association of College & Research Libraries (ACRL) that includes the concept that "authority is constructed and contextual."[12] This framework suggests it is the responsibility of the researcher to understand the context within which information is presented, from which the level of authority or veracity can be drawn. This bears striking resemblances to the semantic theory of truth, which burdens us with determining the conditions in which truth can be obtained, and Floridi's definition of factual semantic

---

[i] http://theconversation.com/institutions/university-of-california-merced-2056
[ii] http://www.tandfonline.com/doi/pdf/10.1300/J120v24n51_06?needAccess=true

information requiring meaningful and veridical data. While I agree an informed citizenry presupposes citizens bear an equivalent share of responsibility to actively seek out and validate information sources before making decisions and drawing conclusions, I think Barclay's claim that putting all of the resources of information literacy development in the hands of higher, secondary, and primary education alone will not be the panacea for "a future of election results and public policies based on whatever information – credible or not – bubbles to the top of the social media noise machine."[13] No, I believe the answer involves another layer, a technological layer that brings to the forefront the expertise and diligence of the community of librarians.

What can we expect rational, economically focused, technology corporations will do in the face of the fake news threat? I say threat because the core engine Facebook uses to bubble up stories based on how many clicks they can extract is the same engine that rapidly and widely distributes many of the fake news stories. Are customers going to leave? Are advertising dollars going to shrink? Naturally, we can expect Facebook will react in a way that will best serve its self-interests. We can also expect the solution will be a technological one. I will not speculate as to what exactly Facebook plans to do, but Mark Zuckerberg has alluded to some possibilities including, stronger detection, easy reporting, third party verification, and disrupting fake news economics.[14] As positive as his message appears to be, I cannot help but raise an eyebrow because none of these are reasons why Facebook is in business. Facebook's mission statement says its goal "is to give people the power to share."[15] The bottom line is this: the more people sharing things, the more clicks, the more money Facebook the business makes. That said, I believe there is potential in the concept of third party verification. I do not mean Facebook's selected "fact checking organizations" of which Zuckerberg lists none. Specifically, I mean librarians. What if partnerships between libraries and social media companies existed and a technological gateway were developed that enabled the entire American community of librarians to tag and archive social media news stories in localized collections? An algorithm could be imagined that leverages concepts from natural language processing, such as sentiment analysis, and flags social media news stories based on a level of sensitivity:

$$\text{Sensitivity} = D \times (L + E_1 + E_t) \times (S_1 + S_n)$$

Where D equals the total distribution, or number of times a social media story has been shared, L equals the number of "likes," E equals the number of "emojis" by type, and S equals the number of instances of sentiments captured in comment threads by type. Stories flagged in such a manner could be sent to a national queue where any librarian could opt to review a story, prioritized by the perceived level of attention, and the type of attention it is actively receiving on a social media platform. Librarians could then choose whether they would include the story in their library's collection, and the story itself could be tagged on the social media platform with some type of notification such as "reviewed and (excluded, or) included in the collections of the following public libraries: [names]." The alternatives include letting social media giants such as Facebook write the rules for what they want to allow people to share and what is viewed, or even noble sounding projects such as fakenewschallenge.org. This project's published goal "is to address the problem of fake news by organizing a competition to foster development of tools to help human fact checkers identify hoaxes and deliberate misinformation in news stories using machine learning, natural language processing and artificial intelligence."[16] Outside of the challenge of engineering such artificial intelligence technologies, I can only imagine the challenge of coding ethics into a robot is a monumental task that doesn't even appear to be one of the criteria posed by this fact-checking project.

While I propose one possible avenue for librarians to consider, I concede it likely is not a silver bullet solution to the problem. If anything, it is an example of a way of thinking that does not appear to currently be presently employed by libraries. This is not to say libraries in this country are technologically deficient *en masse*. Again, my point is that I see what appears to be a looming opportunity for librarians to re-engage with us all and to take our information literacy skills as a nation to the 21st century. Indeed, I believe I have shown that it is their ethical responsibility both professionally and as information leaders.

Facebook and Google Data, Privacy and Transparency

Catherine Bahn

Written: February 2018
Published: December 2018

Abstract: Facebook and Google are preparing for compliance with the European Union's General Data Protection Regulation, as are all other global companies, which will begin to be enforced in May 2018. The purpose of this new legislation is to "harmonize data privacy laws across Europe"; however, the implications are likely to reach beyond the geopolitical borders of Europe and change the direction of corporate transparency. Facebook and Google have the opportunity to be leaders in building dynamic corporate transparency and considering new economic models with the vast amount of customer data they have and will continue to gather.

Introduction

Introduction

Facebook and Google's current dominance in the digital advertising marketplace should come as no surprise. In 2017, total U.S. digital advertising spending reached $83 billion with Google and Facebook making up most of the market at 42.2% and 20.9%, respectively.[1] According to the *Financial Times*, this "digital duopoly" makes up 84% of the global digital advertising market, excluding China.[2] This growth came despite both companies having been questioned by the U.S. Congress last year about Russian operatives using their respective platforms to meddle in the 2016 U.S. presidential election.[3] Due to this market dominance, this paper argues for Facebook and Google to proactively take more responsibility for data and user privacy through transparency efforts. Advertising regulation is out of scope of this discussion, as much of the regulation that exists today is about protecting the consumer against dishonest claims and what kind of products can be advertised, and the U.S., the Federal Trade Commission (FTC) drives this regulation. Instead, the conversation here concerns the contemporary issues of data, privacy, and transparency.

Based on their dominance in the market, Facebook and Google are powerful institutional gatekeepers. Nahon and Hemsley define gatekeepers as "people, collectives, companies, or governments that…can promote or suppress the movement of information from one part of a network to another."[4] As consumers, using these platforms for their variety of services, we agree to their terms of use policy. These policies are to encourage proper use of their products and services, but also benefit the company more than the consumer[5]. In terms of privacy, not much has changed federally in the U.S., but the European Union (EU) Parliament is forcing private institutions to take responsibility with a new directive known as the General Data Protection Regulation (GDPR). This will be covered more in the privacy section of the essay. The potential impact of this regulation on Facebook and Google businesses has been considered seriously, with both companies identifying the GDPR as a risk factor in their annual *Form 10-K* filings with the U.S. Securities and Exchange Commission (SEC).[6,7] The impact of this regulation on Facebook and Google's advertising business model - and other global corporations – will begin to show once GDPR enforcement begins on May 25, 2018. The ripple effects go beyond businesses – the GDPR will likely impact governments, law, technology solutions, and ultimately human interaction with technology and online communities and services.

Data

The formats and business model of digital advertising has come a long way as has the amount of data and information now available to target and to customize for optimal return on investment. The first banner advertisement appeared in 1994 sold for a $30,000 12-week placement, and the Internet increasingly grew as an attractive medium to advertisers for its global reach and lower cost[8]. With Facebook's over 2 billion monthly active users[9] and Google's search engine dominance,[10] the products, services and reach offered by Facebook and Google are global and rich in the amount of data and information collected.

Lawrence Lessig states in *Code, v2.0*, "Everything you do on the Net produces data. That data is, in aggregate, extremely valuable, more valuable to commerce than it is to the government."[11] The rich data sets that Facebook and Google services collect and have allow for flexible and customizable advertising products that make them specifically attractive to advertisers of all categories and budget sizes.[12,13] The majority of revenue for Facebook and Google is driven by their business in advertising making it their primary business model. Based on the information in their 2017 10-K forms submitted to the Securities and Exchange Commission (SEC), 86% of total revenues for Google came from advertising.[14] For Facebook, 98% of total revenues came from advertising.[15] This makes their businesses highly dependent and vulnerable to their relationship with their users, advertisers, and market conditions, among other things.[16] Examining data in just two companies does not over exaggerate the value of information. Looking at information as value economics, Birchler and Butler state, "Knowledge itself is power." They argue, "In economic terms, knowledge or information has a value. By reducing uncertainty it helps us to take the right action."[17]

The legal enforceability of different electronic terms is something not covered in this essay; however, what follows is a summary of "terms of use." When users visit many of the web sites online today, they will find "terms" or "terms of use" linked to, often in the footer. What today is called "terms" or "terms of use" online actually predates the Internet. Companies put contract terms on the back of purchase orders or shipment invoices; when software was boxed, you agreed to terms once you opened the box.[18] Pause to think of how you or those you know use Facebook and Google products and services today: the likes, posts, shares, friends, searches, life moments, voice commands, signing into another service with a Facebook or Google account – the list goes on and on. Facebook and Google - and to a certain extent their partners – track, record, and analyze the accumulation of uncountable online actions.

Facebook and Google do provide users some mechanisms to control select types of data and implement privacy restrictions for accounts and profiles. Much of this is stated in the terms of use, so it should become good practice to know what your terms are. After all, "…in the long run, terms of use may have their most significant impact not on customers, but on businesses."[19] While defining appropriate usage behavior and content guidelines, at the core of Facebook and Google terms, you are allowing them to gather data in exchange for the usage of their collection of products and services.[20],[21] This kind of barter has become a customary practice on the Internet. As online users become more aware, research by Rapp et al. suggest that consumers do not do this blindly; consumers leverage a decision-making calculus to weigh personal exposure with the perceived value of the service.[22].

Privacy

Referring specifically to marketing on the Internet, Jef Richards states, "Never before has a medium been the catalyst of such a wide range of criticisms regarding privacy invasion."[23] Digital technologies and companies will continue creating a complex relationship with information and privacy as technology around products and services continue to advance, e.g. artificial intelligence, mixes/virtual/augmented reality, etc. The U.S. and the EU have differing approaches to privacy and has become part of the technology conversation today. After years of preparation, the EU Parliament passed the GDPR in 2016 to "harmonize data privacy laws across Europe" that will begin enforcement May 25, 2018.[24] Unlike the EU, the U.S. does not have a central governing law-defining privacy. Instead, we have separate legislation and policies across federal and state agencies and businesses.[25]

Bennett believes there is a path forward to the EU and U.S. to reconcile perspective and states, "Regulators and legal theoreticians on both sides of the Atlantic…recognize that harmonizing international data protection laws may be key to maintaining the health of the world's Internet-based economy."[26] Anderson argues that in legal circles, "[privacy's] vexatious nature is due to the inconsistent comparisons that are sometimes drawn between the various flavors of privacy in the public discourse."[27] What does this mean for Facebook and Google, not to mention all other U.S. companies doing business in European nations? They must all have systems in place to honor the EU GDPR by May 25, 2108 or face heavy fines. Both companies have mentioned the impact of the EU GDPR and other foreign and domestic laws as risks to their business in their 2017 Form 10-K SEC filing.[28,29] Essentially, the EU GDPR directive is putting the onus on businesses and corporations to comply to protect EU citizens regardless of where the data servers live or how the information is passed; if the information belongs to an EU citizen, they have the right to be forgotten.[30]

Personal privacy and the right to be forgotten are also distinctly different from some current cases regarding email and search and seizure. Zittrain refers to a person's "reasonable expectation of privacy for e-mail stored on their behalf"[31] and he points to a 2007 case *Warshak v U.S.* that upholds personal privacy search and seizure based on the Fourth Amendment that authorities violated by going directly to the ISP. Interestingly, the outcome of the current case of *U.S. v Microsoft*[32] will be compelling as it is a comparable situation where authorities want Microsoft to provide email content of U.S. citizen; however, the email content of this user is hosted on a server based in Ireland.

There are those who also feel Europe is leading the way with the GDPR as "a starting point for international standards and a trustworthy digital market."[33] Steven Bennett argues the tensional perspectives of the EU and

U.S. encouraging an inevitable convergence.[34] However, Bamberger and Mulligan present an argument against the common critique that "...the existing patchwork of privacy statues as weak, incomplete, and fractured."[35] To clarify, they agree that the privacy policies in the U.S. are incongruent "on the books," but in this study, they found U.S. corporations taking the initiative to prioritize and build consumer privacy protection frameworks "on the ground." They conclude, "If privacy is to be protected in an increasingly connected world, debates over its formal regulation must increasingly be informed by the ways that today's frameworks operate on the ground."[36]

Transparency

To be open and transparent is the antonym of being private. Yet, these opposing views are what society wants from ICTs. Evgeny Morozov states, "Our Internet debates...tend to be dominated by a form of openness and fundamentalism, whereby 'openness' is seen as a fail-safe solution to virtually any problem."[37] However, the ideas of openness and transparency have become conflated in the technology discussion. To simply say that for Facebook and Google or any company to become open and transparent about their practices and what they do with our data would suddenly resolve data privacy issues would be presumptuous.

In Morozov's book, *To Save Everything, Click Here: The Folly of Technological Solutionism*, he refers to the danger of this conflation with "open government." He argues that governments claiming they release and re open with data - even if it is just a train schedule – are not suddenly fully transparent that allows them to be held accountable.

Morozov states, "...both 'transparency' and 'openness' have their limits, and taken too far, can easily reduce the democratic process to a sham.[38] Further clarifying his argument, he is not against information being collection and shared, but that it should be done "...in full awareness of the social and cultural complexity of the institutional environment in which it is gathered." Researchers have studied the impact of ICTs and social media on e-government initiatives to foster transparency and accountability.[39] By leveraging social media tool sets such as Facebook, blogs, and wikis, they found this combination of transparency and social collaboration to be "...an essential element of the primary approaches that governments have employed to promote openness and reduce corruption."[40] However, thinking of Nahon and Hemsley's work in *Going Viral*, the governments in this case are the gatekeepers and still have power and control over the narrative.[41]

Other research take the idea of transparency a little deeper and introduce the concept of dynamic corporate transparency whereby there is a two-way exchange between the company and their constituents that accrue to their right to know about activities that "...affect their quality of life."[42] The researchers theorize that by applying a dynamic corporate transparency strategy will force others in the market to also put this into practice and produce "...a new conceptualization of corporate transparency as an ICT-driven, dynamic process of dialogue and co-evolution between firm and its socio-economic environment."[43]

Facebook and Google are doing a few things that can be perceived as transparency. First, they offer transparency reports.[44,45] Facebook offers transparency reports for government requests and intellectual property that began in

2013.[46] Google offers transparency reports in the following three areas – security and privacy, content removal and service disruptions that began in 2010.[47] Facebook further provides you control over your activity log[48] and you can download a copy of all your data.[49] Google also offers activity tools to view and manage.[50] While they are providing ways for users to get a report on their personal usage and content, what seems to be lacking and may be useful for improved accountability is overall easier access to these toolsets and for Facebook and Google to offer more precise reporting and control tools for user data they share with advertisers and partners.

It is common for modern businesses today to also have some codes of conduct to provide a public level of transparency, accountability, and expectation for users. Some argue the efficacy of businesses having codes of conduct, and it can have a wide range of definition.[51] Kaptein and Schwartz define a business code, aka. code of conduct, as follows, "…a distinct and formal document containing a set of prescriptions developed by and for a company to guide present and future behavior on multiple issues of at least its managers and employees toward one another, the company, external stakeholders and/or society in general"[52] and examined existing empirical studies with a variety of mixed results. Of the 79 studies examined, 35% found codes effective and 33% found no significance; they do conclude codes are not effective in isolation but how it has developed and implemented is significant. Table 1 below provides the current company mission and tagline that captures the essence of the code of conduct for Facebook and Google, respectively. Some questions that arise from these include: Do these give you, as a user, more confidence in the company? Do you have a more meaningful perception of transparency, accountability, and value for their products and services?

Table 1: Company Mission Statements

Company	Mission	Code of Conduct tagline
Facebook	"To give people the power to build community and bring the world closer together"[53]	"...expected to act lawfully, honestly, ethically, and in the best interests of the company while performing duties on behalf of Facebook"[54]
Google	"To organize the world's information and make it universally accessible and useful"[55]	"Don't be evil"[56]

Conclusion

Talking about data from a digital advertising and privacy perspective does not even capture the complexity of the relationship of technology companies like Facebook and Google and their users. Nahon and Hemsley capture modern digital activity well by stating, "Every activity we engage in while we are online – every link we follow, every page we download, every video we watch – has passed through some sort of gatekeepers."[57] These gatekeepers have a lot of data and knowledge that have implications on the economy[58] and it will continue to build upon itself as we are out in the world consuming. Balkin states that "the production and distribution of information [is] a key source of wealth... [creating] a new set of conflicts over capital and property rights that concern who has the right to distribute and gain access to information."[59] Facebook's main products and services are based on social media content and networks. This model is dependent on content users post and share amongst their network and network extensions thereof. Based on the information Facebook collects about you, the deeper you are, the more they know – not just about you but about your network, and their network and so on.[60] Google's main services are productivity based - email, search, document – so they collect information based on your Google account activity.[61] For both corporations, their primary business model is based on digital advertising from the wealth of data they have on us as individuals and our extended networks and their extensive properties and partnerships.

Facebook and Google are preparing for compliance with the EU GDPR, as are all other global companies. Facebook and Google have the opportunity to be leaders in building dynamic corporate transparency and considering new economic models with the vast amount of customer data they have and will continue to gather.[62] They are certainly motivated by their profits and dominance in the marketplace to be innovative with their transparency, accountability and expanding their corporate social responsibility portfolio, respectively. It will certainly get more interesting with privacy when compliance with the EU GDPR activates in just a few months. According to July 2017 data from the Pew Research Center, the American public still remains split on government regulation on business; however, Democrats are 35 points higher in favor of government regulation than Republicans.[63] Time will tell sooner rather than later what the next moves for U.S. regulation might be and how corporations and private citizens can participate.

Healthcare IT's Insider and Outsider Threats

Elizabeth Crooks

Written: May 2018
Published: July 2019

Abstract: This paper discusses the operational risks related to information technology (IT) within the Healthcare and Public Health sector. This critical infrastructure sector's faces particularly challenging risks due to its size, its diversity of organizations, and its inherently open-to-the-public nature. The analysis examines common operational risks that face both the public and private sides of the healthcare IT subsector across all dimensions of operational risk - people, processes, systems, and external events.

The Healthcare and Public Health Sector

The U.S. Department of Homeland Security (DHS) designates the Healthcare and Public Health (HPH) sector as one of the sixteen critical infrastructure sectors, charged with protecting "all sectors of the economy from hazards such as terrorism, infectious disease outbreaks, and natural disasters" and ensuring the health of the general population.[1] Managing the operational risks inherent in the HPH sector are particularly challenging due to how large it is, how diverse its mandate is, and from its inherent need to be open to the public, all of which has to happen at federal, state, local, territorial, and tribal levels.[2] Included in this sector are direct care for patients, mass fatality services, health information technology, medical materials, health plans and payers, public health, federal programs and response, and laboratories, blood and pharmacies. The Health and Human Services - as the Sector-Specific Agency for this sector - must work to manage these subsectors alongside the numerous private sector partners, which include a wide range of organizations including private insurers, medical equipment and pharmacy manufacturers, funeral homes, medical record software publishers, and other organizations involved in providing, maintaining, and governing healthcare across the country.[3]

Healthcare Sector Information Technology

One of the biggest risks facing the HPH sector overall stems from the possibility of healthcare information technology (IT) systems being compromised, resulting in the exfiltration or exposure of protected health information (PHI) and electronic health records (EHR). This risk is extremely salient as there continues to be a constant stream of very public data breach events in the healthcare sector, including 20 breach events in March of 2018 alone.[4] Verizon's 2018 *Data Breach Investigations Report* found that the healthcare sector had the largest number of breaches across all industries studied.[5] The steady pattern of healthcare organizations being a popular target for cybersecurity attacks shows no sign of slowing down. In 2017, the healthcare sector suffered 58 percent of all cyber-attacks that year, rising from 34 percent in 2016.[6]

The management of data in the healthcare industry is both a vast and complex job: data must be immediately available for timely service delivery while the majority of data is highly sensitive (and valuable). Additionally, there are strict legal requirements and regulations surrounding the protection of personal health data (HIPAA and HITECH, among others). This risk is faced by both the public and the private sides of the healthcare and public health sector and encompasses financial risk (through identity loss at an individual level and operational disruption) as well as loss of life risk if critical services are unavailable due to a lack of data. The risk of data breaches across the board in this sector is present across all dimensions of operational risk - people, processes, systems, and external event risks.

People Risks

Although people risks are present in every critical infrastructure sector to some degree, it is particularly salient in the healthcare sector. Healthcare was the only sector in the 2018 Verizon Data Breach Investigation report where there were more internal actors responsible for breaches than external actors.[7] The Verizon Report also noted that of the breaches that they received data on, the breaches most often happened due to error or misuse of privileges (although phishing is still certainly present as a risk as well).[8] A step away from outright error (which itself comes in many varieties, from disposal errors to publishing errors), even being careless about transmission methods also contributes to the risk of breaches. A 2018 survey of healthcare workers found that 87 percent admitted to using non-secure email to send PHI, and a majority said "when it comes to transferring data, documents, or information, they do whatever is easiest" – some even using cloud storage services like Dropbox.[9] The misuse of privileges is particularly egregious, as healthcare insiders were found to be "most likely to snoop on their family members" followed closely by looking up information about their co-workers and then VIPs.[10] The greater number of internal actors responsible for breaches, and misuse and error as the primary causes suggest that the internal controls around data security are not as strong as they could be in healthcare environments.

Some of the strongest internal controls to prevent employee ignorance or malfeasance (that would likely result in breaches) are strong codes of conduct and senior management 'tone at the top' to demonstrate ethical behaviors for the organization.[11] Without these two important components of governance, efforts to improve the number of breaches are likely to fail. The healthcare sector is no stranger to codes of conduct, but it is possible that they view the sanctity of private healthcare records as paling in comparison to their duties under the Hippocratic Oath. A stronger code of conduct regarding how data should be handled and modeling that behavior from leaders within the organization is one possible way to mitigate the tendencies of those working in healthcare to send documents via an insecure method, or to sneak a look at a celebrity's medical records in their database.

Process Risks

Inadequate processes create significant risks for protected health information on both the public and private sides of the sector. Those inadequate processes range from not having procedures in place at all, processes not being followed correctly (as seen with the risks created when employees chose to not use secure file transmission tools at their disposal), and either the lack of individuals managing these cybersecurity risks in the organization or those individuals are without appropriate authority to enact controls. In the private sector, organizational processes are still fluid in terms of reporting structure – the Chief Information Security Officer (CISO) does not necessarily report straight to the Board or the CEO, giving them less authority to work with. These process failures are larger indicators of internal controls not being in place that would otherwise "help ensure that actions identified to address risks are carried out."[12]

On the public-sector side, the risk stems more often from processes being either ineffective or not being reliably in place across different agencies. The Inspector General for the Department of Defense found in a 2018 report that "officials from DHA [Defense Health Agency], Navy, and Air Force did not consistently implement security protocols to protect systems that stored, processed and transmitted EHRs and PHI at the locations tested."[13] The report even warned that the locations visited by the Inspector General, which had HIPAA violations due to their lax security protocols "could cost up to 1.5 million dollars in penalties for each category of violation."[14] At the facilities the Inspector General visited, there were not reliable protocols in place for, among other things, compliance with password complexity requirements, multifactor authentication, access control based on duties, standard operating procedures for system access, and privacy impact assessments were not updated or did not exist at all.[15] The Office of Management and Budget (OMB) also found that across the federal agencies it looked at, "only 16 percent of agencies achieved the target for encrypting data at rest" – this problem of process is certainly not unique to healthcare.[16]

It is impossible to fully manage risks that are not well understood, and in the case of health record data, risk is introduced because those charged with its care are not fully aware of the assets they held. The audit by the Inspector General found that there was no requirement for the identification of systems that contained patient health information, so officials did not know about all the systems with that kind of vulnerable information.[17] Even when there are appropriate hierarchical structures in place and individuals within those pivotal roles, risk is still present if leadership does not prioritize the implementation of changes. The DHS and OMB's report *Federal Cybersecurity Risk Determination Report and Action Plan* found that across federal agencies "assessments show that CIOs and CISOs often lack the authority necessary to make organization-wide decisions despite direction to centralize authority in statutes such as FITARA and FISMA."[18] As Moeller adeptly says, the tone set at the top matters a great deal to the overall effectiveness of a control environment, and right now at the highest level of our government the position of cybersecurity coordinator has been eliminated from the National Security Council by the White House. This move signals that the current administration does not rank cybersecurity as a high priority, slowing momentum for government agencies to implement cyber directives.[19,20] The OMB report emphasizes how crucial senior leadership is to mitigating risk, as "OMB and the Inspector General have repeatedly found that senior-level visibility and authority is necessary to drive consistent improvement in agency cybersecurity."[21]

On the private-sector side, the exact same risks are present, both from a lack of adequate processes and from a lack of people that can put those processes in place and enforce them. As Moeller points out, "The control environment is greatly influenced by the extent to which individuals recognize they will be held accountable."[22] Many private healthcare organizations lack an authority that can drive policy around information technology risk and push for greater accountability. The Ponemon Institute's 2018 *Impact of Cyber Insecurity on Healthcare Organizations* study found that of the organizations surveyed, only 51 percent had a dedicated CISO, and a large percentage felt that their in-house cybersecurity skills were lacking.[23] The insufficient number of personnel overseeing data security increases the likelihood of risks stemming from little oversight and even a lack of processes. That same report found that only half of those surveyed had incident response plans in place.[24]

SYSTEM RISKS

The healthcare sector experiences increased systems risk when aging IT infrastructures are not updated in a timely fashion, third-party vendors have access to systems, and organizations introduce new medical devices without adequate security measures built in. Any of these circumstances increases operational risks and the vulnerability of personal health data. Aging IT infrastructure (of all kinds) inherently increases systems risk, particularly if an organization is not actively planning to update and replace this infrastructure in a timely manner. However, if an organization does not address known, existing vulnerabilities in their systems, this introduces a far higher degree of risk, as those systems then become 'low-hanging fruit' ready to be exploited.[25] This IT infrastructure may include x-rays or MRI machines running legacy software that has been overlooked for patching or may not be included in the process of systems being actively monitored. Legacy systems often have "hardcoded passwords that can be found with a simple Google search."[26] A hospital bed will have on average between 10 and 15 devices connected to it, which means the risk quickly multiplies, especially with different manufacturers and standards.[27] Even if all of the systems are relatively up to date, the healthcare sector must grapple with an enormous volume of devices connected to their networks and systems.

The systems risk that comes along with the sheer size of healthcare's mandate, as well as infrastructure not being updated, the risk is compounded by the addition of Internet of Things (IOT) capabilities being added to medical devices. In recent years, there has been movement towards imposing standards on IOT systems, but the market is currently being flooded with devices that do not always come with security built in mind. Without strong incentives, vendors have little reason to take the time and expense to build in the necessary security that would mitigate system risks from connecting these devices to healthcare environments. The FDA has starting issuing non-binding guidance and recommendations with regard to medical device security, but there are not yet mandatory requirements that would allow for security reliability and interoperability.[28] It is also possible (however unlikely it may currently seem) that legislation addressing the standards for IOT devices and systems could be passed by Congress. In the fall of 2017, Senators Warner, Gardner, Wyden, and Daines proposed the Cybersecurity Improvement Act, which would require "minimum security standards for federal procurements of connected devices."[29] Imposing federal standards would greatly simplify things on the public sector side, as there would be a consistent baseline to follow, and the private sector would soon follow, having incentives to be compliant for federal contracts, and because ensuring the interoperability of systems would also reduce risk.

External Event Risks

Risks from external events in the healthcare IT sub-sector stem from the public facing nature of most organizations, the crucial nature of services provided by operations, and the profitable nature of personal healthcare data which incentivizes bad actors to try obtaining it. The DHS's Sector-Specific Plan for healthcare that the "HPH sector is inherently more vulnerable than many of the other critical infrastructure sectors" due to their community focus, service ethos, and public access.[30] The risks created by the inherent nature of the sector will never be able to be fully mitigated, but the risks created are in fact exacerbated by other external factors. The incentive to target healthcare information technology with malware and phishing attacks is in fact doubled. There is the higher profit to be had from healthcare records. One estimate from The Ponemon Institute puts a healthcare record (including name, date of birth, and social security number) as worth about fifty dollars on the black market, compared to a credit card being worth about three dollars.[31] No matter which type of malicious actor is at work, from criminal syndicates to foreign nation-states, there is a strong financial motivation to target healthcare IT on both the public and private sides.

Additionally, the reality is that within the healthcare sector, critical systems support the delivery of emergency (acute) as well as persistent medical care to people. Hospitals and other organizations within the sector are far more likely to pay a ransom to get sensitive data back, and quickly, because that information may be needed in order to provide treatment. In January 2018, a hospital in Indiana paid a ransom of $55,000 (in bitcoin) to bad actors holding their IT system hostage, even though they had backups in place.[32] The administration of the hospital felt that restoring from the backup would have been too expensive and taken too long, in comparison to paying the ransom. In that particular case, no patient information appeared to have been compromised, but there is little guarantee of that in other circumstances.[33] These incentives for bad actors creates lots of external risk, and which is reflected in the amount of malware present in the healthcare industry – Verizon's 2018 *Data Breach Investigation Report* estimates that ransomware to get personal health data accounts for 85 percent of all the malware in the healthcare sector.[34] The sector is hard pressed to keep up with the volume of attacks, as even a single strain of malware can wreak havoc. The Department of Health and Humans Services issued a warning in March of this year that as of that time, there had been "at least eight separate cyber-attacks on healthcare and government organizations utilizing a form of ransomware known as SamSam."[35]

Recommendations

In order for there to be greater alignment and partnership between the public and private sectors, there should be better user experience design in healthcare tools and products, facilitated information sharing within the sector regarding emerging cyber threats, and legislation passed with cybersecurity requirements for both medical devices and IOT devices. To strengthen these efforts, organizations should provide regular training for those working with PHI and EHR data to increase awareness of the multiple areas of risks. Ultimately, senior leadership positions in healthcare and public health organizations will need to clearly and regularly communicate the high priority of implementing these risk mitigation efforts.

Improved user experience in healthcare tools and products would ease the burden of security fatigue on the end user and help to 'nudge' people in the right direction, mitigating the risk of internal actors causing breaches. Legislation putting cybersecurity standards in place for medical and IOT devices would not only show that our government is taking the risk presented by those devices seriously, it would also force the vendors creating those devices to incorporate security into their entire approach. Continuous training and tone at the top are the kinds of mitigations that seem obvious, but are still missing in too many places, where there is a lack of will or budget, or both in order to more effectively reduce data breach risks. Facilitated information sharing does already occur within the sector, due to DHS and ISAC coordination, and healthcare as a sector is still consistently facing threats to data that were not seen in other environments, suggesting that there is far more work to be done for threat environment awareness and risk mitigation.

Information Security in the Rise of E-Commerce

Miranda Lin

Written: November 2017
Published: February 2018

Abstract: This paper examines the growing e-commerce market within the U.S.; specifically, e-commerce companies with operations in the U.S., and some of the inherent risks that come with the model of conducting retail transactions online. These companies are exposed to higher levels of risk in the occurrence of a security breach, and the author discusses some potential recommendations for e-commerce operations to improve their information security through internal controls.

E-commerce activity – commercial transactions conducted electronically on the Internet – has been growing at a substantial rate around the world, connecting merchants and consumers across countries. Traditional "brick and mortar" – physical – stores are increasing their online presence to offer customers increasingly more convenient ways to shop, eliminating the to travel to a physical store. Inherently, businesses that operate solely online are important players of e-commerce as well. Companies like Amazon and eBay provide online platforms that enable almost anyone to sell products and services, practically anywhere in the world. As systems become more interconnected, however, the risks to merchants and consumers alike have increased. Consumers provide personal and financial data to e-commerce companies, which is then stored in company databases. Consider Amazon, whose number of active customers in 2016 was reportedly 310 million; the significant amount of sensitive data stored for the customers makes Amazon's databases a natural target for hackers.[1] Overall, any security or data-breach incident for online retailers leaves its customers' personal identifiable information exposed, and places the company's operations and reputation at risk. Laws and regulations in the U.S. pertaining to security of e-commerce operations are limited, complicated, and vary depending on location.[2] Regardless of whether there are laws in place that force companies to abide by best practices, it is certainly in a company's best interest to protect their assets and earn the trust and loyalty of customers.

The growth of e-commerce both in the U.S. and on the international level has been an area of exponential growth. The number of e-commerce sales in the U.S. reached 291.8 billion in 2016; this is approximately a 57 percent increase from 2012, when the sales were at 186 billion.[3] Globally, e-commerce sales in 2016 totaled 1.9 trillion; experts forecast global e-commerce sales will increase 21 percent by the end of 2017 to reach 2.3 trillion. By 2021, sales are predicted to grow an estimated 96 percent to come in at 4.5 trillion. This would mean that sales are expected to more than triple in a range of seven years, from 2014 to 2021. The largest e-commerce market in the world is currently China, with its e-commerce sales at approximately $672 billion. Other countries with prominent markets include the U.S., U.K., Japan, and Germany.[4] According to the Nielsen Global Connected Commerce Survey from 2016 that collected responses from 26 countries, 57 percent of the respondents "who made an online purchase in the past six months say they bought from an overseas retailer." Evidently, shoppers are increasingly looking outside their country's borders when shopping.[5] Though e-commerce operates across borders, governmental agencies have very limited powers to regulate processes that reach beyond its national jurisdiction. Thus, e-commerce companies themselves need to be deliberate in taking all the necessary precautions to protect its customers' sensitive data. This paper will focus on e-commerce companies' operations in the U.S., the risks these companies are exposed to in the occurrence of a security breach, and recommendations for them to manage their information security.

Managing information security is critical for online retailers to prevent security breaches and to keep their internal informational assets safe, especially with the proliferation of cybersecurity attacks in the e-commerce industry. Over 100 million attacks occurred between July and September of 2017, which is a 100% growth compared to the same period from 2015. Additionally, we can expect to see the "return of the 'Cybercrime Christmas'", when more attacks will occur with the increase in online transactions for the upcoming holiday shopping season.[6] The most common types of cyber-attacks against e-commerce sites include, but are not limited to, denial of service attacks, cross-site scripting, and SQL injections. Denial of service attacks occur when the attacker, often using botnets, floods the e-commerce website with fake traffic to overwhelm the network. This causes the e-commerce site to be extremely slow, and may even bring the whole site down to failure.[7] A successful denial of service attack would be especially detrimental in the holiday shopping season, when interruptions could cause the e-commerce company a substantial loss in revenue. Take e-commerce giant, Amazon, for example; a 20-minute outage on its online store in March of 2016 costed them an estimated $3.75 million.[8] The other two common types of cyber-attacks mentioned, cross-site scripting and SQL injections, both involve the attacker inserting malicious code into the legitimate website. In cross-site scripting, or XSS, the code injected can trick the user's browser into believing that the script is from the website and can be trusted, which allows the script to be executed. Depending on the type of malicious code inserted, consequences vary. For example, a specific script could allow the attacker to access the user's session cookies and use that to impersonate them.[9] Whereas cross-site scripting focuses on obtaining information from the user, SQL injection attacks focus on obtaining information from the company. In inserting SQL commands on a vulnerable website, the attacker can read information from the company's database. For example, a specific SQL command could allow consumers' name, birthday, and postal address to be displayed to the attacker.[7] XSS and SQL injection attacks are well-known and can be prevented by running penetration tests, but, there remains a countless number of other attacks that are more difficult to know beforehand.

Being prominent e-commerce players in the U.S that have also established an apparent presence in the international e-commerce industry, Amazon and eBay have both unfortunately experienced cyber security incidents that are concerning to their operations. Founded in 1995 in San Francisco, eBay is thriving as an e-commerce company with 168 million active buyers from 190 markets.[10] In May of 2014, they informed the public of a cybersecurity breach that occurred sometime between late February and early March, which had only been detected by the company two weeks before disclosing to the public. In the incident, attackers gained access to three corporate employees' account to obtain 145 million users' information contained in eBay's database. The information retrieved by the hackers include users' name, email address, postal address, phone number, birthday, as well as the encrypted password associated with the eBay account. eBay claimed that they used "proprietary hashing and salting technology to protect the passwords"; assuming this is true, hackers would undeniably have an extremely difficult time in unencrypting the passwords, thus this is less of a concern compared to the other unencrypted data.[11] The unencrypted personal identifiable data is concerning because it could easily be used by hackers to commit fraud outside of eBay, such as registering for various fake accounts online. Now three years after the security breach, there is still a lack of news on how the hackers were able to gain access to the three corporate employees' account. However, some individuals, such as Liron Damri, a former security technologist at PayPal and the current chief operations officer of the security company, Forter, believe that "the breach was likely the result of some form of 'social engineering'", where the employees were "tricked into handing over critical information to a cybercrook posing as a trusted person or party within eBay".[12]

Besides massive data breaches like the one eBay experienced in 2014, there are also countless smaller scale cyber-attacks against online retailers that we can expect to be constantly happening. For instance, in April of 2017, news regarding an increase in attacks on Amazon's third-party merchants surfaced. These third-party merchants, numbering roughly two million, account for more than half the sales on Amazon's e-commerce website. Some of the fraudulent activities executed by hackers include changing "the bank-deposit information on Amazon accounts of active sellers to steal tens of thousands of dollars from each", and posting "nonexistent merchandise for sale at steep discounts in an attempt to pocket the cash". The hackers were able to gain access to sellers' account through the dark web, where hackers trade and obtain "email and password credentials stolen from previously hacked accounts".[13] It would be unsurprising to also see some of the information hacked from eBay revealed on the dark web and be used for similar purposes as the attacks on Amazon's third-party sellers.

E-commerce companies share many similar processes and technologies in their operations, making them all susceptible to similar threats. Thankfully, there are some regulations enforced on the companies. One of the well-known regulations enforced is the Federal Trade Commission Act. The FTC Act serves to protect consumers, and it has been "applied to...online privacy and data security policies". For example, the Commission has "brought many enforcement actions against companies failing to comply with posted privacy policies". Other than federal regulations, states have also enacted their own laws involving information security. As of April 2017, every state except Alabama and South Dakota passed laws requiring companies to notify the public of all security breaches that involve the exposure of personal information.[2] Another regulation is the Payment Card Industry Data Security Standard (PCI DSS), which relates to online payment systems. All businesses accepting payment cards such as credit and debit cards, must follow this standard, which includes requirements such as maintaining a firewall and testing security network and systems on a regular basis. In enforcing compliance with the PCI DSS, individual payment brands, such as Visa, determine their own non-compliance penalties.[14] Though these regulations exist, there isn't a federally enforced set of cybersecurity practices that online retailers are required to follow. This makes it possible for companies to lack implementation of even the most basic security practices, such as data encryption. Therefore, it is up to the company itself to research for and embed appropriate security practices in their information security systems. Luckily, numerous guidelines developed by governmental agencies and private parties exist for e-commerce companies to consider. Guidelines specifically for online retailers include the Organization for Economic Co-operation and Development (OECD)'s "Consumer Protection in E-commerce" guideline which was "designed to address the newest developments in e-commerce, such as...mobile transactions and payments, and new platforms that enable consumer-to-consumer transaction".[15] The Federal Trade Commission also has a "Electronic Commerce: Selling Internationally" guideline that provides broad guidance on e-commerce security and consumer protection.[16] The National Institute of Standards and Technology (NIST)'s Cybersecurity Framework also provides a comprehensive set of "cybersecurity activities, outcomes, and informative references" to help organizations "align its cybersecurity activities with its business requirements, risk tolerances, and resources". The Framework was designed for critical infrastructure systems, but e-commerce companies can certainly find value in this document too.[17] From a public perspective, it's difficult to know whether an e-commerce company follows the guidelines mentioned, unless the company itself claims so. However, it's important to note that these guidelines cannot positively impact the company unless it's adopted. When a company chooses not to follow a guideline, these valuable guidelines remain just another piece of document.

Though each e-commerce company operates differently and vary in size of their business, the risks they face in the event of cyber-attacks are similar. One of the major risk is the company's information security. Risks in this area increase when unauthorized individual(s) gain access to a company's informational assets, which may include customer and employee's sensitive data, as well as the company's intellectual property. With data exposed, the likelihood of reputational risks occurring increases, because the public loses trust in the affected e-commerce company. This causes a direct loss for the company because people are less likely to purchase products from them. Stock price may also fall as the public deem the untrustworthy company's stocks to be less valuable. Reputational risks may also occur when an online retailer experiences system failure, which could occur from internal inadequacies or external attacks. Internally, if the company uses weak hardware and/or software filled with bugs, it may cause their web applications to crash. For operations that depends on those systems and are intolerant of interruptions, consequences could be extremely destructive. Externally, when hackers successfully carry out a denial of service attack and slows down or brings down the e-commerce website, customers are unable to shop when they want to. If the system is down for a long period, the online retailer will certainly be labeled with a bad reputation, causing them to lose customers. Lastly, for any of the risks mentioned, whether information security, reputational, or system failure risks, the increased likelihood of them occurring can result from third-party's negligence. E-commerce companies are engaged in close-knit relationships with various third parties, such as manufacturers, payment processing companies, or third-party merchants using the company's e-commerce platform. Each third-party introduces operational risks if they can't deliver their part of the service or if they experience cyber-attacks that puts the information shared between them and the e-commerce company in compromise.

Though it's impossible for e-commerce companies to prevent all cyber-attacks, there are various practices companies need to follow to reduce the likelihood of attacks, and thus reduce their exposure to the risks mentioned. Regarding third party risks, e-commerce companies need to establish clear communication with all third-party vendors to address both parties' concerns. In a study done by Ponemon Institute and sponsored by Shared Assessments, of the 617 individuals involved in the "risk management process in their organizations", only 18% "say they assess the cyber security risks of most third parties". This is concerning, considering that the organizations behind these respondents "spent an average of approximately $10 million to respond to a security incident as a result of negligent or malicious third parties". Thus, it's necessary for e-commerce companies to ensure that third parties are following best security practices, such as embedding up to date anti-virus and intrusion detection technology in their network.[18] If necessary, online retailers need to bind third parties in contract.

Next, strong tone at the top is also of vital importance to e-commerce companies. To build an influencing culture around risk management, companies need to first and foremost, educate employees on the most common types of cyber-attacks and what behaviors they need to avoid to prevent security incidents from happening. For instance, employees need to be aware of phishing scams and the various social engineering techniques used so they can be cautious around suspicious emails or phone calls.

To address system failure risks, e-commerce companies need to establish redundancy. One way this can be achieved is by contracting with a secondary DNS provider. This allows "a domain's query traffic" to be distributed between providers so that if one is unavailable, the other takes over and serves "with virtually no effects to end-users".[19] As for protecting informational assets, e-commerce companies need to have a comprehensive understanding of their assets. This should be done through careful identification, prioritization, and documentation of all data and databases, so companies are aware of what to monitor for suspicious activity. For instance, after identifying a sensitive database, companies should closely monitor that database's logs to detect abnormal logins from unauthorized personnel or authorized personnel who stay logged in to the database for an abnormal duration. Then, to actively protect these assets, basic preventative controls need to be implemented. This includes encrypting all data and salting and hashing any passwords that are stored. The principle of least privilege should also be applied so only those who need to access sensitive databases for job purposes are authorized. Furthermore, to detect if the assets are vulnerable to attacks, companies need to behave like the adversary and run comprehensive vulnerability scans and penetration tests on a regular basis.

There are also various detective controls specific to the e-commerce industry to protect consumers. Online retailers need to closely monitor all "devices and accounts that have a history of fraudulent activity" and "block these devices from transactions" if necessary. Retailers also need to "screen transactions using previous transaction data" so abnormalities can be detected early. Transactions "originating from a different country or IP address than where the [customer's] account was created" would also require additional monitoring.[20] Lastly, companies need to keep up to date with all the latest cybersecurity breaches by allocating time and resource to research cyber-attacks and preventative methods, as well as time to attend cybersecurity related conferences to discuss current events and collaborate with others in the industry.

In the rise of e-commerce, online retailers are storing more consumers' data than ever, making them targets for hackers. As a result, effective management of information security becomes increasingly important to prevent cyber-attacks to reduce the likelihood of operational risks occurring. Various cybersecurity guidelines are available for retailers to implement, but there are still a handful of companies that are not extracting value from these guidelines. E-commerce companies need to realize that the effects of not adhering to best security practices can be detrimental as cyber-attacks and security breaches result in lost revenue, customers, and a bad reputation. Though no laws in the U.S. force these private companies to follow a predetermined set of controls, it is in the best interest of these online retailers to take the initiative in carefully managing their information security to stay in business.

Operational Risk Challenges to the U.S. Election Infrastructure

Jeff Leonard

Written: May 2018
Published: September 2018

Abstract: This paper discusses the risks to the most recently identified critical infrastructure sector, election infrastructure (the facilities, technologies, people, processes, political parties, and legal frameworks required to conduct elections). This paper examines the risks, and identifies a system design, the technologies, and an operational architecture that would mitigates the risks to which modern election processes are currently exposed.

Introduction

In 2001, after butterfly ballots, pregnant and hanging chads, the "Brooks Brothers riot"[1] and a five to four Supreme Court decision, awarding George W. Bush the presidency, the U.S. population at large became aware, as never before, of the imperfect technology used in its voting infrastructure.[2] And in 2002, the Help America Vote Act (HAVA) was passed which mandated improving voting systems and addressed issues with voter access that were identified following the 2000 election.[3] At that, time the state of the art was first generation hand marked optical scan systems, but the more typical systems were lever action hole punch systems, while many smaller locales still used hand processed paper ballots. During the last eighteen years, new technologies have been created and deployed that were ostensibly intended to address the deficiencies of the old systems that were problematic during the 2000 election. Yet arguably, from a risk perspective, the U.S. election infrastructure is in a worse place than it was before the turn of the century. While new technologies addressed deficiencies such as confusing placement of candidate names and eliminated the potential of "pregnant" or "hanging chads," they introduced much greater systemic risks from lack of auditability and the potential for undetectable widespread manipulation of the results. Those old paper based systems are, from an operational risk point of view, superior in many ways to the electronic systems that replaced them in the aftermath of the election. They generated paper artifacts that allowed for independent audits. They had reasonable error rates. They were not susceptible to large-scale manipulation. However, as we saw in the 2000 election, they have their own drawbacks and those error rates were large enough to make a difference in a close race.

What is Critical Election Infrastructure?

When considering the risks related to the voting systems, it is necessary to examine the environment in which they operate. Today, critical infrastructure is defined by Presidential Policy Directive 21, which recognizes 16 critical infrastructure sectors.[4] If this paper had been written just 18 months earlier, election infrastructure would not have been considered critical infrastructure.

"On January 6, 2017 DHS Secretary Jeh Johnson designated U.S. election systems as part of the nation's critical infrastructure... Critical infrastructure is a DHS designation established by the Patriot Act and given to systems and assets whether physical or virtual, so vital to the United States that the incapacity or destruction of such systems and assets would have a debilitating impact on the security, national economic security, national public health or safety, or any combination of those matters."[5]

In this context, critical election infrastructure is defined as the facilities, technologies, people, processes, political parties, and legal frameworks required to conduct elections. More specifically, these are polling centers (schools, fire stations, city halls, shopping centers, malls and other places where people vote), tabulation centers where ballots are collected and counted, storage locations where equipment is stored between elections, data centers where results are stored or processed, post offices where mail-in and absentee ballots are transmitted. Technologies including voting machines, communication networks, voter registration databases, result-tabulation systems, paper ballots used for mail-in and absentee voting, and electronic systems.

After the Bush v. Gore decision, many states opted to update their voting rights laws at the same time the Help America Vote Act was being legislated. Many of these states issued Requests for Comments (RFC) on the topic of how to prevent another Bush v Gore from occurring and recommendations going forward. Though not a California resident, I submitted a comment[i] to the State of California RFC pursuant to their revised voting rights act of 2001.[6] In that letter, I laid out a systems design, technologies, and an operational architecture that would impart desirable properties to the election processes. Systems built according

---

[i] I lived in northern Virginia, in what are considered suburbs of Washington, DC, a place hostile to HAVA. Unfortunately, I no longer have access to this White Paper; it is on a hard drive in an old dead computer system.

to my recommendations would produce a transparent, tamper evident and auditable election infrastructure. Such a system could not be tampered with without producing tangible evidence of the tampering. It could be trusted by voters to produce measurable and accurate results; the accuracy of the results could be verified by both the voter and by audits. If the system failed it would fail in a predictable and visible way. These suggestions are still timely and will be revisited in greater-detail and updated when discussing recommendations going forward. I believe, but I am not positive that my comment to the state of California predates the "Computer Technologists' Statement on Internet Voting,"[7] which is undated but appears to have been published in 2004 at the earliest and from which I will subsequently quote profusely. The signatories are all share tremendous expertise on the subject.

The Election Assistance Commission (EAC) was created in 2005 under the auspices of the Help America Vote Act of 2002 but was not brought under the umbrella of DHS until the January 6, 2017 declaration by Jeh Johnson.

HAVA and the New Types of Voting Equipment

HAVA mandated replacing outdated election technology like lever-action systems and punched-card-based technology and so a new generation of voting equipment was manufactured in the early 2000s. These new systems can be classified into three general categories. Optical scanning devices, Ballot marking devices and Direct Recording Electronic devices.

"Optical or Digital Scanning devices are systems that tabulate paper ballots. Ballots are marked by the voter, and may either be scanned on precinct-based optical scan systems in the polling place or collected in a ballot box to be scanned at a central location."[8] These systems have the risk mitigating benefits of producing an auditable paper artifact and depending on the polling station, the voter may be able to scan the ballot before submission to ensure it reflects the correct intent. This type of system also allows for deduction of voter intent during recounts and audits.

A Direct Recording Electronic (DRE) voting system is a:

"Voting machine that is designed to allow a direct vote on the machine by the manual touch of a screen, monitor, wheel, or other device. A DRE records the individual votes and vote totals directly into computer memory and does not use a paper ballot. Some DREs come with a Voter-Verified Paper Audit Trail, a permanent paper record showing all votes cast by the elector. Voters who use DRE voting machines with paper trails have the opportunity to review a paper record of their vote before casting it."[9]

These systems are not auditable in any meaningful way unless they have an option of producing a paper trail at the kiosk so the voter can verify intent. However, this paper trail is, in my opinion, insufficient to verify that the correct vote is ultimately tabulated. I rate these as the riskiest systems to use. With no paper trail, the voter cannot verify the vote was recorded correctly. There is no artifact from which to deduce voter intent or to audit. A precinct's results may not be auditable at all. Diebold Systems of this type used in the 2004 election stored data in an unencrypted database and their laughable idea of auditability was reprinting a report of what was stored in the database. One of these systems was hacked as a demo during a recent DefCon.[10]

A Ballot Marking Device (BMD) is a technology that marks a paper ballot for the voter:

"A voter's choices are usually presented on a screen in a similar manner to a DRE, or perhaps on a tablet. However, a BMD does not record the voter's choices into its memory. Instead, it allows the voter to mark the choices on-screen and, when the voter is done, prints the ballot selections. The resulting printed-paper ballot is then either hand counted or counted using an optical scan machine. BMDs are useful for people with disabilities, but can be used by any voter. Some systems produced printouts with bar codes or QR codes instead of a traditional paper ballot. Security experts have pointed out that there are risks associated[11] with these types of systems since the bar code itself is not human readable."

In my opinion, these are the best systems from a risk mitigation point of view as long as the marked ballot is user readable. They are auditable, voter verifiable and the voter intent can be deduced from the ballots. Additionally, these systems have the potential to allow for voter audits that verify how their vote was counted.

Finally, the important category of the mail-in paper and absentee ballots. These ballots are user marked and delivered via the postal service. They are difficult to tamper with at scale but they are susceptible to interception in transit (especially for foreign cast ballots). Paper ballots allow for deduction of intent as well as auditability. They are also user verifiable but not third party verified.

Risks, Themes and Challenges

All electronic systems are vulnerable to being hacked, potentially allowing for misrepresentation of votes at a massive scale. However, systems following the recommendations in the letter, "Computer Technologists' Statement on Internet Voting"[12] can mitigate this risk to great extent through implementing systems with the properties described. These include producing auditable artifacts. Their audit trails must be reliable, strongly unforgeable, and unchangeable. The system must be resilient to disruption at scale. Votes must be recorded in a way that ensures the data's availability, integrity, authentication, confidentiality, and nonrepudiation. The entire system must be reliable and verifiable. Vulnerabilities inherent to particular voting systems (paper ballots, mail-in ballots, absentee ballots, scanning based systems, electronic systems) make this difficult if not impossible. In particular, DRE systems with no paper trail are completely vulnerable to undetectable electronic manipulation by both insiders and third parties. However, vote by mail and absentee ballots have their own drawbacks, possibility of interception, voter coercion, and bias introduced variations in the quality and timeliness of mail delivery being foremost among them.

Risks from technology are not the only risks to the voting systems. There are also risks from political interference. Politicians pass laws to disadvantage classes of voter like students and minorities.[13] Election officials shut down polling places before everyone in line has voted. Legislatures create obstacles to registration; disenfranchise classes of citizens such as convicted felons and Census reapportionments can be gerrymandered to render votes irrelevant. There are issues of fairness and bias that come from fairness of treatment like treating one area differently to another when the area correlates with a demographic. There are risks from solutions that introduce larger risks than the perceived problems they are solving. Like solutions to fraudulent in person voting that prevent more legitimate votes than they prevent fraudulent ones. Not to mention how ties are handled.

- There are risks to disruption of facilities. Polling places are generally government or civic facilities like schools, fire houses, libraries, city halls, churches, court houses that can be soft targets vulnerable to attack.

- There are risks from illegal behavior. Poll taxes, knowledge tests, intimidation, and dissemination of false information such as was prevalent during Jim Crow fall into this category.

- There are risks inherent in a constitutional system that does not weigh votes equally, of which the U.S. Electoral College system is an example. In three of the last five elections, the candidate with the most votes did not win.

- There are risks from foreign interference. Foreign governments have used big data to run micro-targeted PR campaigns seeking to influence populations. State sponsored entities have executed large-scale attacks on election systems. Both foreign and domestic entities have funded candidates in order to disrupt local elections.[14]

Current Mitigations

The biggest operational mitigation of the risk of widespread manipulation is the decentralized nature of the U.S. voting system. It is comprised of 527 independent voting districts that compartmentalizes the risk into 527 chunks that must be manipulated separately. However, each district has its own unique risks. The next big operational mitigation is the diversity of systems and control. Five companies produce the certified voting systems in use today.

The U.S. Department of Homeland Security (DHS) Government Facilities Sector-Specific Plan[15] lays out guidelines for understanding and mitigating risks to facilities. It also specifies a COSO-like Governance, Risk and Compliance (GRC) process for monitoring operational risks. This is based on industry best practices (though the G, R and C are voluntary). The EAC certifies voting machine integrity, maintains a glossary of critical infrastructure.[ii] EAC can assist state and local government in performing Gap Analysis, implementing best practices and can run tabletop exercises to help train personnel. EAC maintains voluntary processes for evaluating processes and systems, maintains an internal task force with the capacity to perform cybersecurity Assessments and provide Cyber Emergency Response Team services. Finally, EAC has the authority to grant secret clearance to state and local election officials so they can receive classified cyber threat briefings. Note that this is by no means a complete detailing of their capabilities.

[ii] Or at least it says it does, I was unable to track it down.

Recommendations

- *Add Election Infrastructure as a 17th DHS Critical Infrastructure Sector.* The fact that Election Infrastructure was designated in January 2017 as critical infrastructure under the government facilities sector is a good start but the election infrastructure is so cross-sector and deals with so much more than just facilities that it merits designation as a sector in its own right. It is also worth noting that this designation occurred during the transition period. It was not widely publicized, and it is unknown what level of support it has within the current administration. Given the current administration's propensity to undo everything accomplished by the previous administration, it is an open question whether even the current designation will survive to the next presidential election.

- *States and localities should implement the Government Facilities sector specific plan as appropriate.* In particular, storage facilities, information systems, and communication networks should be fortified and made resilient in the face of disruption.

- *States and localities should also implement a COSO-like framework for managing risk.*[16] In general, the sector specific plan recommends best practices that are harmonious with COSO and GRC (although the C is voluntary).

- *Increase the diversity of certified systems across all voting districts.* Only five companies currently produce all of the certified machines. A more diverse set of compliant products will increase the resiliency of the electoral systems overall.

- *Decertify the DRE type systems.* These systems do not implement two of the most important properties in the "Computer Technologists' Statement on Internet Voting,"[17] verifiable accuracy and resistance to large-scale disruption. DRE systems are used in about twenty percent of the systems certified by the EAC and in five percent of districts overall (counting mail-in states and non-certified states).

- *Implement dedicated infrastructure to minimize attack surface and protect data in transit.*[18] Election infrastructure must be capable of undergoing independent validation and verification and audits of all hardware and software. These requirements put it above the level of the public infrastructure upon which it currently relies.

- *Investigate the use of block chain as a way to implement a robust audit trail of system activity.* That being reliable, unforgeable, unchangeable voter-verified records. Votes need provenance proving the path they took from the voter to tabulator, to compilation to announcement of results. This is almost a canonical problem solved by the block chain ledger.[19]

- *Investigate e-coins as means of implementing voter audits of their own votes.* The coin plus the provenance should be sufficient to prove the vote was tabulated as cast.

- Finally, *implement Trustworthy Voting System Guidelines*, which is a superset of the guidelines in "Computer Technologists' Statement on Internet Voting."[20] Namely, voters should be authenticated. Votes should be recorded in a manner to ensure the data's availability, integrity, authentication, confidentiality, and nonrepudiation. Votes should be verifiable by both the voter and an auditor. Privacy of the voter should be protected in that user identifiable data should not be captured in the voting process. Additionally, there should be a stronger guarantee that votes should be confidential. Third parties should not be able to reverse engineer the identity of individual voters. Voters should receive a token after voting that they can use to prove that they voted and that they can use to self-audit and verify that their vote was counted as intended. This could be an e-coin. Systems should produce tangible artifacts with integrity and provenance. This again is could be a canonical implementation of the blockchain ledger. Results should be independently verifiable and auditable from the tangible artifacts.

The voting process should be transparent. There should be no black boxes in any of the operational systems involved in voting. The processes should be capable of undergoing government independent validation and verification audits. Additionally, hardware designs should be public, verifiable, and auditable. Systems and processes should be tamper evident. It must not be possible to tamper with any part of the system without creating evidence of the tampering. For, example ATM machine keypads are internally encrypted and built to self-destruct if taken apart.[21]

Conclusion

Since the passing of HAVA in 2002, voting systems and processes have migrated to IT based systems. These voting systems fall into three categories: optical scanning systems, ballot marking systems and paperless direct recording systems with related back end IT systems. These systems have introduced systemic risks that make them arguably riskier to the integrity of elections than the systems they replaced. The DHS has recently included election infrastructure under government facilities as a critical infrastructure sector. Under this designation, the EAC has developed an organization and standards for protecting and mitigating the risks to the election infrastructure. The EAC needs to use its authority to reduce the risks inherent in the current generation of voting technology. Finally, it is recommended the election infrastructure be promoted out from under government facilities to its own critical infrastructure sector, that state and local governments implement the EAC guidelines and that future systems be developed following a set of recommended principles and in concordance with these principles, direct recording type voting systems be phased out.

Privacy in the Age of Big Data

Zhuo Shan

Written: December 2017
Published: May 2018

Abstract: This paper discusses the various elements surrounding the topic of privacy, particularly in relation to the ever-expanding field of "big data. Part one presents a high-level examination of various techniques used to collect users' data, including an assessment of the definition of personally identifiable information and how corporations obtain it. Part two examines the risks of big data to both enterprises and individuals; part three looks at the applicable government regulations and laws; and the final part provides some risk mitigation recommendations.

Introduction

The age of big data is upon us. With the increasing amount of people, devices and services that are connected to the Internet, new data are generated every second from social media, email, search queries and online transactions. As the data mining and analytics technologies advance from the increase in computing power and storage capacity, data have become a new source of economic and social value. [1] Big data technology creates a new raw material for production that drives innovation, efficiency and growth. On the other hand, the extraordinary amount of data collected from users creates concern about privacy that can stir an ethical and legal backlash against the data industry. And the dilemma between big data and privacy will be an ongoing issue for both companies and individuals. We must work together to reconcile the tremendous social and economic benefits of big data with the risks exposed to the privacy of individuals.[2]

PII and Data Collection Techniques

Personally, Identifiable Information (PII) is any data that could potentially identify a specific individual.[3] With the rise of personalization and targeted services, linking data to personal identities has become a key component in many business models, such as online advertising and cloud computing. Therefore, PII has become an immensely valuable asset for corporations. Companies have developed and adopted various techniques to associate anonymous data with specific individuals, which fundamentally undermines Internet anonymization and individual's online privacy. Some commonly used techniques will be examined below.

One of the most common ways to collect user's identifiable personal information is to let them provide themselves. And self-uploaded information can be easily obtained by social media companies and online services providers. User profiles and posts contain personal information, such as birthday, gender, education, family members, etc. By looking at user's content, information about demographics, interests, behaviors and locations can be drawn. [4] Then, companies can create a comprehensive data profile of a user with specific personal details, which can enhance the accuracy of targeted advertisements. Search Engine Companies, such as Google can obtain information from user's search histories; email inbox and cloud drive to target users with personalized advertisements. [5]

Another commonly used technique to track users are Web Cookies. Cookies are small text files that websites place on a user's computer to store certain information about how they use the site. The abilities of Cookies include logging in to sites and delivering personalized content.[6] Cookies not only save login information on a website, they can also track the users across multiple sites and obtain information. Information is linked to users' identities by identifying their accounts. One of the most commonly used cookies across advertising platforms is Facebook Pixel. It has the ability to track users' behavior when they visit their website again, which would help measure the effectiveness of advertisement. [7]

Most people are aware of the existence of the Web Cookie and its ability. People can simply disable Cookies in their browsers. However, privacy is not guaranteed. Websites can use a technique known as Canvas fingerprinting to identify the users. And it is nearly impossible to prevent it because every device behaves in a subtly different way when websites interact with it. Therefore, third parties can tell when the same device is visiting their websites. [8] Many websites, such as Whitehouse.gov, use this technique to identify users who disable Cookies.[9]

There are many other unique and rarely discussed ways to track users who are browsing websites. One of them I would like to mention is Behavior Analysis. It detects user's physical behavior, such as how user types or clicks, to identify user.

Besides all the techniques used by websites to identify users, there is a much easier way to collect PII -- hiring a data broker. A professional data broker will collect various kinds of personal information of identifiable individuals and sell them to whoever is buying. Companies are buying those profiles because there is certain information they cannot easily obtain online. And data brokers will collect public information such as newspaper subscriptions, financial profile. They can gain insights about your personal life. Once your information is collected, data broker will sell them to buyers, such as your insurance companies, employers or your bank. [10]

Risks and Concerns

Big data poses big risks to both enterprises and individuals. The collecting and analyzing huge amount of personal data implicate growing concerns about privacy invasion, discrimination, information security and government surveillance. This part will examine the risks presented by big data from both enterprise and individual standpoint.

ENTERPRISE RISKS

There are serious and potentially catastrophic operational risks for enterprises. First and foremost, information security risk should be treated with great caution. In the past years, there were numerous data breaches happened to companies with sensitive information. In 2013, retail giant Target was hacked and more than 41 million of company's customer payment records were stolen. [11] In 2013, 3 billion Yahoo users' accounts were hacked. [12] Companies with huge amount of personal data have become the biggest targets for cyber criminals. Because of the information security risk, there is also potential legal/liability risk. As we know, not a single firewall or security measure could completely eliminate the possibility of a breach. After the recent cyberbreach,

Equifax was hit with at least 23 class-action lawsuits.[13] Therefore, companies have to take in the measure of potential lawsuits after the breach.

In addition, there is also risk of inappropriate business practice, such as invasion of privacy. Because all the private information is completely accessible to service providers due to privacy policy, there is little to no guarantee that companies would be held accountable when they use users' data inappropriately. As a result, companies are more inclined to utilize data with little caution. As reported, Uber CEO Travis Kalanick let his party attendees see all of the Ubers in a city using Uber's "God View" as a party trick.[14] Also, there is the potential of illegal government surveillance. After Snowden incidence, Snowden leaked that NSA was illegally obtaining users' data from companies, such as Google. [15]

Moreover, the ethical concern of discrimination arises because of the increasing usage of automated decision-making process. In a story from New York Times, it is uncovered that Target assigns a "pregnancy predication score" to customers based on purchase habits.[16] Companies use predictive analysis to automatically split users into categories in order to simplify decision-making process. However, it is problematic and unethical to group people by sensitive information, especially in an equal-opportunity process, such as hiring.

Moreover, failing to mitigate and manage operational risks mentioned above, companies would most likely suffer from reputational loss. Customers would definitely not provide any personal information to a company they find untrustworthy. Without user's trust, any big data companies would deem to fall.

The risks of big data to individuals can mostly boil down to the invasion of privacy. And the severity of risk exposed to individuals is closely related to the enterprises' ability of managing risks. If individual's data was stolen due to a security breach, identity theft could have a direct impact on one's daily life. There could also be engineered scam based on individual's personal information.

Government Regulations

Currently, there is no single national law in the U.S. regulating the collection, use and sharing of personal information.[17] There are federal and state laws and regulations that apply to certain types of personal information, such as health information. [18] The FTC and White House both released report on Big Data to provide guidance about Bid Data practices. [19]

There is regulation in other countries regarding the practices of Big Data. One of the most notable regulations is EU's General Data Protection Regulation (GDPR), which will go into effect on May 25, 2018.[20] It strengthens and unifies data protection for all people within the EU. And it also addresses the export of personal data outside the EU. This regulation will greatly protect the privacy of EU citizens and residents. There are several key points of GDPR. It gives individual total control over his/her personal data. Individuals will be able to request and remove any personal information stored in the database from any companies operating in EU. It also allows EU citizens and residents to deny the use of their personal information as easily as possible. GDPR also requires companies to provide notification within 72 hours if a data breach occurs. In addition, the fines for violating the regulation are exceptionally high, which could be as much as 4% of companies' preceding years profits worldwide.[21] This regulation as a whole does ensure the online privacy of EU citizens and residences. And it is a great example for the U.S government.

Recommendations

In this part of the article, I will present my recommendations regarding the risks discussed above. I will discuss recommendations for both enterprise and individuals.

RECOMMENDATIONS FOR ENTERPRISE

The first and most necessary action for any enterprise with sensitive data is to enhance information security measures. Companies should go beyond compliance, such as PCI DSS (Payment Card Industry Data Security Standard). Compliance does not equal security.[22] Companies should also have an assumption of breach, which means breaches are bound to happen, they are just a matter of time. [23] It is necessary to implement Data Loss Prevention (DLP) technology to monitor and detect potential data breach. After implementing the best information security measures, companies should develop and adopt a recovery plan and follow it if the breach happens.

In addition to information security, companies need to focus on reputation. In order to achieve and maintain positive reputation, companies should start with reducing inappropriate business practices and adopting a transparent business model. Even though there is no law and regulation regarding the use of personal data in the U.S.[24], companies can use EU's GDPR as a reference. The right to access one's personal information is one of the fundamental principles of privacy, which is underutilized in the U.S.[25] Allowing users to access their data will empower both users' understanding of their data and their trusts in the companies. Moreover, developing and adopting an ethical code of conduct regarding the use of users' data can convey organization's mission, values, and principles to the public, which will provide a positive image for the company.

RECOMMENDATIONS FOR INDIVIDUALS

People have different tolerance for risks and different values regarding privacy. Someone values convenience over privacy, and vice versa. However, how companies utilize your data might changes the minds of many people. Companies will use privacy policy as a tool to dig deeper into users' privacy. [26] And there is no way to prevent companies from using that data once you agree to the privacy policy. All the free services are not actually free. We are sacrificing our privacy to access those services. And the real customers who are paying for the services and buying our privacy are advertisers. Companies, like Google and Facebook, are only using the data collected from us to appeal to their real customers. In other words, if you are not paying for it, you are the product.

In order to protect our online privacy, I suggest using privacy tools when browsing online. Privacy tools, such as TOR and VPN, will hide IP addresses and prevent any identification tracking. [27]Encryption, such as OpenPGP, is also a great way to hide your personal information from being accessed.

In the future, when encountering any new service, it is important to make sure that the organization values your privacy and regards keeping your information safe as a mission.

Conclusion

With incredible growth of data technology and increasing use of data, researchers, businesses and individuals are all trying to find a balance point between convenience and privacy. This article has suggested the direction for changes for both enterprises and individuals in the age of Big Data. If organizations ensure the safety of users' personal data and provide users with the access to their personal information, big data will empower everyone and continue to improve society in many ways. In addition, transparency under an ethical code of conduct will motivate users to participate in achieving a greater future of big data.

Risks of Fake News to the American Democracy

Lukas Guericke

Written: December 2017
Published: July 2018

Abstract: This paper examines the toxic spread of "fake news" into the landscape of legitimate news organizations, and the rising tide of associated risks to government, news organizations, and ultimately each individual citizen. "Fake News" is not simply an inconvenience or insult; it is a threat to the access of U.S. citizens to accurate information, and the fundamental protections a free and independent press provides to a democratic society.

Introduction

Fake news is defined by the *Cambridge English Dictionary* as "false stories that appear to be news, spread on the Internet or using other media, usually created to influence political views or as a joke."[1] While the concept of fake news has been prominent in news stories recently, particularly after the U.S. presidential election in 2016, it is not a new problem. Since the invention of the printing press, "fake news" has been used for oppression, to spread propaganda, and for political disruption. Up until the penetration of the Internet into almost every household, newspapers were the golden standard for journalism. To print a newspaper, one would have to have funding, a printing press, multiple reporters, and other aspects of a functional newspaper. Now, anyone with a connection to the Internet anyone can be a "journalist," either generating "news" or sharing other unverified/untrustworthy "news" through social media.

With the rise of social media, news stories spread much more quickly than before; there is less time spent on verification and corroboration. These conditions are key to understanding the context of the modern concept of fake news.

Fake news has taken on two forms. The first is the distribution of fake news through social media and untrustworthy sources; the second is politicians using the exclamation of "fake news" to discredit the media, regardless of the accuracy of a story. Both of these forms carry an immense amount of risk to the American voter as well as to the fundamentals of the U.S. government, in addition to the risks to the freedom of the press.

Fake News in the 2016 U.S. Presidential Election

Fake news was a controversial topic during the 2016 U.S. Presidential Election. Some of the most popular storylines during the election were fake news. For example, the story that the Pope endorsed Trump for president was shared almost a million times on social median giant Facebook.[2] Fake news increasingly appeared in the months leading up to the election. Using data from Facebook, news organization *Buzzfeed* found that the amount of fake news being interacted with on Facebook exceeded the amount of news from 19 major news outlets by August 2016.[3] This is concerning considering 67 percent of Americans say they get at least some of their news on social media.[4] Where does this fake news come from? It comes from people trying to make money from pay per click ads[5] and the evidence is overwhelming that people within Russia used fake social media accounts to distribute fake news.[6]

For-profit fake news presents risks to the governments and the media. Writers of fake news can make up to $10,000 month from AdSense, a Google service that pays popular hosts to display ads, making it a common way to make money in some of the world's most impoverished countries.[7] For example, in the small town of Veles, Macedonia young tech-savvy entrepreneurs are making a small fortune off American gullibility.[8] The profiteering off deception of Americans is a risk to the government in the way that it creates a legal, regulatory risk, and a hazard risk. From the perspective of the government, legal risk and regulatory risk is one in the same. Fake news is a complicated risk as the U.S. Constitution has the First Amendment, which guarantees the right to free speech and freedom of the press.[9] To regulate fake news, the government would have to fight in the courts against the First Amendment. In the past, there have been very few exceptions to the first amendment. In fact, a California Senator tried to create a new law that would ban fake news.[10] However, this bill was flawed and found to be directly in violation of the First Amendment, so the bill never even went to committee.[11] The U.S. government (federal, state and local) and the Justice Department will have to find a way to manage the legal risk of government entities acting to infringe on the First Amendment by harshly regulating the press and free speech.

Another risk that for-profit fake news poses to the government is a hazard risk. Hazard risks are the risks that "pose a level of threat to life, health, property, or the environment."[12] Fake news is a hazard risk to the government because of fake news inciting violence towards citizens and government employees alike. For example, the day before the 2016 presidential election, November 6th, there was an article posted on Reddit claiming that an associate of presidential candidate Hillary Clinton was involved in a child sex ring, supposedly run out of a pizzeria in Washington DC.[13] On December 4th, an enraged man drove to the pizzeria with an assault rifle and fired shots inside the restaurant; he told police that he believed the story he read on Reddit.[14] Luckily no one was hurt, but this serves as evidences that there are people who believe fake news stories and react violently. The government needs to be aware of viral fake news stories spreading and make sure that potential targets of violence are secured.

For-profit fake news creates a market risk for the mainstream media. News networks primarily make their money through advertisement sales, just like fake news websites do. This creates a market risk because fake news websites are competing with legitimate news sites for user clicks and attention. In addition, fake news websites have no overhead and can tailor their content to figure what could be interesting to viewers. News networks have to hire journalists who work very hard to find, investigate, validate, and report on interesting stories that may not have the viral capabilities as a fake news story. However, there are two sides to the market risk associated with fake news and the mainstream news media. One side is that news networks revenues will go down from fewer ad sales and more competition from fake news outlets. The other side is that people flip and turn away from social media and other known venues for fake news and start getting their news from reputable news networks.

Russian Involvement in the 2016 Presidential Election

The full extent to which Russia interfered with the 2016 elections remains unknown, but the U.S. Intelligence Community concluded, with high confidence, that the Russian government engaged in electoral interference during the 2016 U.S. presidential election.[15] In Senate judiciary committee hearings lawyers from Facebook said that they believe 120 Fake Russian-backed pages crafted 80,000 posts that were seen by 29 million Americans directly but many more by users sharing, liking, and following the posts. [16] In addition, Twitter has found 2,752 accounts linked to Russian operatives.[17] These fake news outlets spread stories such as Hillary Clinton being sick, that she was a criminal, people close to her were mysteriously dying, and that Obama had a secret army.[18] The extent of the influence on American voters is still being assessed. Interference such as this one in a major election poses a huge risk to the U.S. government, voters, and social media sites.

Interference in another sovereign state's election is a type of external fraud. In this case, Russian actors used Twitter and Facebook to try to influence voters to push the candidates that they favored. This affects both voters and the government. Russian actors undermined the sovereignty of the U.S and interfered with U.S. citizens' confidence having fair and free elections. The government and voters risk voters losing faith in the electoral system because of the Russian interference.

Social media sites, by testifying on public record, take on a huge reputational, regulatory, and financial risk. The reputational risk stems from the negative press they have to endure by admitting that Russian actors were allowed to buy ads on their sites. Many people may blame a lack of vetting of ad buyers and negligence for the spread of fake news. In addition, since social media platforms are a popular way to spread fake news, people may discontinue use if they want to stay away from fake news. The regulatory risks are that the government tries to restrict ad sales on fake news and tries to limit the fake accounts that propagate fake news. Currently, the U.S. Senate is discussing a bill, called the Honest Ads Act, which would require disclosure of the buyer of political advertisements similar to the regulations on television and radio advertisements.[19] While industry leaders do not think that this bill goes far enough, they view it as a necessary first step. Adam Sharp, the former head of news, government, and elections for Twitter, said, "While the bill would curb law-abiding actors, any regulatory regime remains vulnerable to those who deliberately mask their identities. Don't expect to see 'Paid for by Vladimir Putin' volunteered anytime soon."[20] However, this shows that the government is working on reregulating advertisements on social media sites. Bills such as this one could create a slippery slope for regulations on advertisements. This poses a financial risk to social media outlets because this could hurt their advertisement sales, which is their primary source of revenue.[21]

Fake News as an Attack on Mainstream Media

Recently, the use of the term "fake news" has evolved from a term used to describe news that is intentionally fake to a term used by politicians and right-wing media outlets to discredit credible news organizations. President Donald Trump has called many well-respected and reputable news sources such as CNN, *The New York Times*, *The Washington*

Post, and others "fake news."[22] Right-wing news sources such as *Infowars* have also labeled many mainstream news sources as "fake news."[23] It is unclear as to why Trump has gone after the mainstream media outlets. Rupert Cornwell, a writer for the British newspaper the *Independent,* theorizes, "Now Trump's tirades against the media are in large measure a deliberate distraction. He knows they are red meat for his base that lapped them the attacks during the campaign. He knows they divert attention from his unmet policy promises, the Russian imbroglio and other matters of genuine national concern."[24] CNN's Chris Cillizza has a different theory. He claims "Because Trump doesn't like what the media writes about him. That's what he means when he uses the word "fake" -- and he uses it a lot. 'Fake' for Trump is rightly translated as 'not fawning.'"[25] In either theory, there are massive risks involved. By discrediting the media by calling them "fake news" presents a risk to the media, the government, and voters.

RISKS TO THE MEDIA

Being labeled "fake news" by one of the most powerful people in the world presents a reputational and financial risk to credible and legitimate news organizations. This risk, however, can be positive or negative. On one side, the ratings for news agencies have not been higher. On the other side, the confidence in the mainstream media is at an all-time low. For example, CNN has the most watched 3rd quarter in history in 2017[26], while also having the lowest credibility scores according to a poll by Morning Consult/Politico.[27][28] Increased ratings mean more advertisement revenue and low credibility mean less respect for the quality of content and the journalistic art. It is unclear how low credibility and trustworthiness will impact the balance sheet in the long run but this type of reputational risk need to be taken into account by risk managers.

RISKS TO THE GOVERNMENT

Discrediting credible new organizations by labeling reported news stories as "fake news" creates risk for all levels of the U.S. government. The relationship between the government and the media is very important. The media relies on the government for sources of information and the government relies on the media to distribute its message to the voters. In a sense, the media is a middleman between the government and the voters. When that relationship between the middleman and the source is strained, there are risks involved to the supplier. The media has the power to spread a message to voters. This is evidenced by polls that show that Americans trust Trump less than major news networks.[29] Trump's approval rating is lower than any other modern president at this point in office.[30] The government's reputation is seriously at risk and it starts by disrupting the relationship between the government and the place where most Americans go to get their information about the government.[31] In addition, by attacking free speech the President is empowering some of the US's enemies to brush of their own criticisms as fake news. An article by Politico shows how the use of "fake news" to discredit the media and deflect criticism has spread to some of the world's most authoritarian and oppressive regimes.[32] For example, Syrian President Bashar Assad brushed off an Amnesty International report that 13,00 people had been killed at one of his military prisons by claiming "you can forge anything these days, we are living in a fake news era". Additionally, a state official in Myanmar said, "there is no such thing as

Rohingya. It is fake news" when referring to the ethnic group that has been systematically killed and displaced by the government of Myanmar.[33],[34] By calling the credible new outlooks "fake news," the President has given authoritarian leaders and enemies of the U.S. a platform to deflect criticism and tighten their control without any checks or balances.

RISKS TO VOTERS

When the government and the media are at odds, the voters are exposed to the most risk. Voters are at a risk of not having their voice heard because of the noise that a battle between the media and the president creates. This is a major legal risk that dates back to the creation of the United States. The US Declaration of Independence states "Governments are instituted among Men, deriving their powers from the consent of the governed."[35] This means that the government only has power when the voters give it power and if voters have a 59 percent disapproval rating of the President then their voices are not being heard.[36] If voters are not being heard by the government, so much of what the government does for voters is at risk. These include important elements of people's lives such as social security, Medicare and Medicaid, the economy and jobs, human rights, education, the climate, and others.

Recommendations

It is apparent that fake news has many risks to the media, the government, and to voters. How does one stop the misinformation from spreading? How does a government regulate the media in a way that does not conflict with the First Amendment? How do credible new outlets fight back against being called fake news by the president? The answers to these questions are not simple. That is part of the risk involved with fake news. Since its practically impossible to stop the spread of fake news, the best option is to educate people about its existence and its impact and to teach people strategies of detection and refutation. In the upcoming election in Italy, the government is worried that fake news will be a factor. To get ahead of this issue the government has urged social media sites to step in. Facebook plans to team up with the Italian government and other web giants to teach students across 8,000 high schools how to spot fake news.[37] The efficacy of a program like this one is yet to be seen. However, the concept sounds promising. In addition, if social media sites such as Facebook lead the charge in the education of fake news, this mitigates some of the risks of fake news to Facebook and certainly helps with reputational risk.

Credible news sources must also be agents for spotting and refuting fake news. This starts with not reporting fake news. Recently, *ABC News* suspended a chief investigative reporter Brian Ross for errors made during his reporting on the guilty plea of former National Security Advisor Michael Flynn.[38] ABC issued a lengthy apology and correction but situations like this one give critics of mainstream media more ammunition for their attacks. The next step in the media's role in combating fake news is to create fact-checking divisions that add to the work of fact-checking organizations such as Snopes.com and Politifact. These two recommendations for the media should help people understand what is factual and what is not.

Lastly, each individual American citizen (and voter) is the most critical player in the battle against fake news. The first recommendation is to have a shared cultural value of wanting to know the truth. The Oxford English Dictionary's word of 2016 was "post-truth."[39] Post-truth means "relating to or denoting circumstances in which objective facts are less influential in shaping public opinion than appeals to emotion and personal belief."[40] Voters can combat this post-truth era by knowing their own biases and trying to remain objective when looking at an issue and demanding to know the facts. Another recommendation for citizens to increasingly practice applying critical thought when reading the news, and learn how to not click on, share, comment on, or "like" fake news. If the fake news is not interacted with, then there is no money to be made and the spread is limited. Individuals need to look for corroborate news stories and allow time for refutation, and confirm the credibility of the source. In addition to corroboration, voters need to allow time for refutation before making a decision on what the truth is. Refutation of a fake news story can often take much longer than the creation. This type of cautious skepticism is valuable for combating the risks of fake news tampering with elections as well as the use of the term "fake news" to discredit the media and deflect criticisms.

Conclusion

Fake news during elections and when used as a tool to discredit the media has many risks to the government, voters, and mainstream media. These include hazard risk from people acting because of a fake news story they saw, market risks because of the undermining of journalism, and legal risk for figuring out how to regulate fake news. However, the greatest risk of all is the risk of misinformation. There is not a time in history where misinformation is able to spread as fast or effectively as it can right now. This risk of misinformation has great power. It can help authoritarian leaders stay in power and undercut what voters think of as the truth. The solution to the risk of misinformation is unclear and untested. That is the risk climate we live in today. We are trying to find out how to manage risks at a scale that we have never seen before. That is where education is so important. We need to have the population educated about how this misinformation can spread and to make sure people have strategies with which to identify and refute misinformation. We cannot stop people from spreading fake news nor cannot we stop people from using the expression of "fake news" to deflect criticisms. We as consumers have to be vigilant about if we are being fed misinformation and what to do about it.

SECTION THREE

Incident Management and Response

PAPER	AUTHOR
Effective Global Incident Response	Bruno Langevin
Empowering Students to Prevent School Shootings	Phoebe Keleman
The Black Swan by the Festival	Emily Ye
The Worst Sexual Abuse Scandal in Athletics	Malory Rose

Effective Global Incident Response

Bruno Langevin

Written: November 2017
Published: January 2018

Abstract: This paper discusses some of the critical elements of our increasingly global corporate community, and the additional complexities of incident management across global geographies and cultures. In response to these complexities, the author identifies how companies can better prepare for and manage risk programs at the international level, which require additional awareness and adjustments in order to be successful.

Introduction

Managing risk, more than ever it seems, is about proper response to outside incidents that may affect any of the four pillars that constitute the foundational support structure of a company: people, processes, assets and reputation.

These areas are complex in nature, and too often the leadership is not truly prepared to respond to an incident, mainly because budget has a tendency to be allocated to what's impacting the daily success (and bottom line) of a company, not towards intangible, possibly far-stretched scenarios that might never occur. Who likes paying the premiums for insurance anyway?

To this initial duality of concerns between the day-to-day mission of the leadership and the planning visions from the risk management office, one must face the additional complexity of dealing with incidents occurring in other countries from the headquarters location, especially if it might impact one of the foundational support structures mentioned above. Many elements that we are taking for granted as part of a local "in-country" response can suddenly become a barrier overseas, and we will examine some of these elements in more detail in this research note.

The Fluid Definition of an Incident

Questions about the definition of an incident are always asked by fellow employees who are getting involved in risk management for the first time. "How can you tell it's an incident that needs attention?" or "Why do I have to declare this event as an incident anyway?" These are basically requests for a threshold definition. The one I've been using successfully for years is that an incident is "an unplanned event of a catastrophic nature." The two key ingredients, being unplanned and catastrophic, are working well when the audience comes from a similar background, although even the use of the word "incident" versus "disaster" can be discussed ad-nauseam between specialists. I personally prefer to avoid talking about disaster until the incident if over, in order to keep the emotional part of the equation aside during the critical response period.

But what is "catastrophic" for one region might not be so in another. I learned it the hard way when recently setting up an automatic alert notification system for earthquakes in Japan. During the first week our test group received notifications upon notifications, because earthquakes are basically daily events in that part of the world. At the end of the week, my Japanese counterpart told me very politely and directly (as only Japanese natives can do simultaneously) that I should change the Ritcher scale threshold to 5.0 and higher.

My North American definition of a catastrophic earthquake was obviously different than the Japanese one, and the risk response plan had to be adapted for that region. As importantly, the perception must be addressed at the leadership level also unless you want to be called at 5:30am by your CEO, asking "What are we doing about the 4.0 earthquake in Tokyo?" and having to politely and directly (without the flair of native Japanese) say that it is not an incident but simply a normal event in that region.

Centralized Versus Decentralized Authority

In North America we are used to the concept of a decentralized authority where, in theory, we assume that important decisions can be made by a manager down the chain of command within an impacted division or department during an incident. We might even say that we are talking about delegation of authority here, but that would be a wrong assumption. In all my years I think I saw just once a true delegation of authority, as the day-to-day reality is that C-level executives want to be part of the action: it is in their nature as they are problem solvers by definition. A classic example would be in the wording of notification messages during the early phase of an incident. One would think that a pre-defined message would go on within the next three minutes of an incident, but often the reality is that the executive will be changing the wording as part of a back-and-forth exchange with the notification manager, which can take hours before everyone is satisfied and the "push" button is pressed. The lack of delegation authority is a direct component of a centralized model which roots from having a small organization with few hierarchies of management. Companies that grow from national to international levels will often keep that model (and perception) because they are used to it, and they are not realizing that although the rest of the company might function in a decentralized model, the reaction during an incident almost invariably goes back to a centralized one. That might work if the whole company is located within a small time zone span and/or within the same cultural background, but it is quite another story otherwise.

For international companies, a decentralized authority to manage incidents must be in place with full support from the executives. Such an approach can be built in a "follow the sun" model with regional managers covering roughly an eight-hour time zone span, such as Seattle, New Delhi and Munich, for example. Each focal region would then interact and manage regions/countries within that eight-hour time zone span, and establish the communication flow accordingly. Executives in the headquarters will then be at the receiving end of the communications path, and would need to be active in the decision-making process only after the initial response (i.e. insuring people safety, stabilizing assets and processes) is completed. Full support means that an executive will not step into the response activity unless requested by the regional managers, leaving managers with the actual authority to respond initially to the incident.

Cultural Impact On Decentralized Authority

Once these initial steps are in place and the leadership team fully on board with the decentralized approach, the next hurdle to overcome is the culture barrier. For many cultures in Europe, and for almost all of Asia, the notion of following the hierarchy and fear of doing something that might not be approved by their managers is a serious impediment to a speedy decentralized approach. It has nothing to do with the actual capability of people being able to take ownership of the situation (quite the opposite as these cultures are often very creative), but simply that they are used to having their managers in the loop for every major decision.

One way to address this dilemma is to have sessions where everyone is present to review the communication flow and for managers to confirm their approvals on subordinates' actions in time of crisis. For example, going through the steps around an earthquake response plan, where some predefined messages could be sent directly to employees without having to be reviewed, would be a good way to "loosen up" this fear of feeling that their managers would be out of the loop. After doing this exercise, I've always had positive feedback on both the employee and the manager side, as they see the value on the response time (quicker) without a detriment on the escalation side ("who told you to send it?").

This of course is valid for the initial response phase of a crisis, where timing is more important than precision. Mitigation, recovery and return to operations are phases where inputs and decisions are required by the executives, but by making clear that the initial response is a very different phase where the regional team is in control and not the headquarters, an efficient crisis response process will emerge where potentially dangerous delays can be avoided.

Conclusion

Preparing for and managing a risk program at the international level cannot be done with a one-size-fits-all model, but many of the underlying aspects such as a true decentralized authority that is well understood and clearly supported can go a long way toward simplifying the program and ultimately making the initial response to an out-of-control crisis more streamlined and with less unacceptable delay than what we sadly see too often still today.

Empowering Students to Prevent School Shootings

Phoebe Keleman

Written: May 2018
Published: June 2019

Abstract: This paper discusses the uniquely American epidemic of gun violence – specifically mass shootings – currently occurring in schools. The author believes that regardless of the cause, a new approach needs to be taken for risk mitigation and prevention within the current context. The recommendations include suggestions for how students can work together with their teachers and administrators to help prevent school shootings.

Introduction

America is on track to set a horrific new record. While mass shootings in schools during the entirety of the 20th Century took the lives of fifty-five people, sixty-six adolescents and adults have been killed in the mere 18 years since the turn of the 21st Century.[1] If shootings continue at the same rate, without further escalation, more people will be killed by mass shootings in schools during this century than the total *wounded* during shootings in the 1900s. Media outlets, government officials, and various online communities are fond of attributing this rise to a myriad of causes; most recently, a Representative from Tennessee declared that pornography is the source of gun violence in schools, without any clear explanation of how it contributes.[2] Regardless of what is considered the root cause of these attacks, it is clear that a new approach must be taken to prevent and mitigate the risks posed by school shootings. Flipping the traditional emergency operations planning process on end, and empowering students to take the lead in preparing for an emergency, may be the coming generation's best chance for survival.

Introducing the concept of an emergency situation to students is one that needs to be handled carefully. A balance must be struck in order to make children aware and prepared for risks without scaring them and causing emotional damage.[3] The numbers show that children under 14 are most likely to be attacked by an adult who has gained access to their school campus,[4] as was the case in the devastating Sandy Hook Elementary School shootings in 2012. Accordingly, young students are most likely to be drilled in lockdown procedures, learning how to be silent and hide, closely following their teacher's instructions, as early as ages four or five.[5] This is arguably the most we can expect of such a young age group.

What, however, could be done differently once the switch flips in middle school and it becomes twice as likely that a shooter will be another student rather than an adult?[6] The current guide regarding preparation of Emergency Plans in schools highlights the need for superintendents and first responders to create the plans for prevention, protection, litigation, response, and recovery, with student and parent advisors mentioned only briefly as a part of the planning team.[7] It is interesting to note that this guide is produced not by the Federal Emergency Management Agency, the agency tasked with building a culture of resiliency in the U.S., but by the Department of Education. All of the suggestions regarding active shooter situations focus on responding to known threats, response during a crisis, and how to help the community recover following an event. Prevention is defined as "the capabilities necessary to avoid, deter, or stop an imminent crime or threatened or actual mass casualty incident."[8]

If the aftermath of the brutal school shootings in Parkland, Florida, in February of 2018 has shown America one thing, it is that the coming generation is prepared to do more than stand idly by and let the world fall apart around them. The survivors from Marjory Stoneman Douglas High School have been afforded a platform and started a movement that surpasses that of all previous tragedies.[9] Their resilience is reshaping how our nation views the voice of youth, and the planning for emergency operations needs to shift to reflect that change.

The basic structure necessary to make this change is already present. The business world has already created a solid framework for Enterprise Risk Management (ERM), consisting of risk identification, assessment, prioritization and planning, and monitoring.[10] Analogous phases are laid out in the Department of Education guide but with less simplicity; the plan calls for forming a collaborative planning team, understanding the situation (risk assessment), determining goals and objectives (prioritization), plan development (planning), plan preparation, review, and approval (planning again), and implementation and maintenance (monitoring).[11] ERM also calls for comprehensive buy-in from all levels in order for risk management plans to succeed.[12] This is the part that emergency planning at the school level currently lacks; there is already buy-in from the senior governing level (the superintendents and emergency management officials), but there is no emphasis placed on empowering students to be active participants in the planning process and, most crucially, in the risk identification process.

Three of the unifying traits historically associated with attackers are that they displayed concerning behaviors prior to their attack, had demonstrated issues dealing with loss or failure, and that they felt injured or bullied by their peers.[13] These are all indicators that fellow students are likely to recognize in their peers long before teachers and administrators might perceive them. And students, once they hit middle school, can no longer be sheltered from the reasons they practice lockdown and evacuation drills in their schools. They know, with certainty, that there are risks inherent with attending school every day, as barely a week goes by without reports of another school shooting. So how can students work together with their teachers and administrators to help prevent school shootings?

Let us begin by looking at risk assessment. One way for students to more fully participate, in a zero-tolerance setting, would be by informing upon their fellow students who they perceive as potential threats. Following a deadly shooting in Santa Fe, Texas Governor Greg Abbott has called for the adoption of the Telemedicine Wellness, Intervention, Triage, and Referral (TWITR) Project statewide.[14] Over the past four years, 41,807 students have been analyzed by the TWITR Project, 215 of which were identified as at-risk candidates; many of these were sent preemptively to juvenile detention centers, while others were sent to alternative high schools or put into inpatient care for mental health treatment.[15] This zero-tolerance approach to a perceived threat can be permanently damaging to youths, many of whom have committed no crimes, starting them down a spiraling path to incarceration and intolerance.[16] If students were encouraged to actively partake in this model, it might lead to a community rife with distrust and suspicion, one that is hardly conducive to education and growth.

A preferable alternative to increase risk assessment would be to adopt a support system for all students early on that could mitigate the potential for the underlying resentment and rage that often leads to school shootings. The Office of Special Education Program's Technical Assistance Center has put together extensive resources to help educators implement Schoolwide Positive Behavior Interventions and Supports (SW-PBIS), giving teachers a framework to encourage citizenship, respect, empathy, and understanding in their students.[17] While it would be beneficial for these techniques to be implemented even earlier, starting an open dialogue once students reach middle school about the importance of adopting these attitudes could create an opportunity for long-term behavioral change. If students were encouraged to have increased self-awareness of how their actions affect others, put into the harsh context of how past shootings have frequently been committed by those who felt isolated, it would afford them an opportunity to check their own behaviors in relation to their peers. Sugar coating that reality is no longer an option in the face of the school shooting epidemic; the days of bullies and mean girls need to fade into history.

Once students are encouraged to have increased awareness of how their behaviors can mitigate potential risk, they need to be empowered to be active participants in the prioritization and planning phases of risk management, as well as crisis response. The Department of Homeland Security's official recommendations during an active shooter scenario are to first attempt to run, next try to hide, and fight only if absolutely necessary.[18] In contrast, the ALICE Training Institute, one of the preeminent organizations offering in-school training for faculty and students to prepare for active shooter response, recognizes the danger in hiding; students who shelter or hide in place are frequently injured during an emergency, while those who make every attempt to distance themselves from an attack are often able to escape, especially since there is generally just a single shooter.[19] While potentially frightening, frank, open, and serious discussions in classrooms between students and their teachers about how they would respond to an active shooter situation could spell the difference between life and death. Instead of blindly following the instructions of an instructor who is likely just as scared as they are, they'll have a plan in mind that they're able to follow.

Arguments can be made against this level of planning that open discussion would give potential shooters increased knowledge of how their peers would respond in an attack, making it easier for them to target their victims. A counter-argument would point out that students already know how their peers will react. They've been training alongside them since elementary school in lockdowns and fire drills. They know where the exits are, and where everyone is meant to meet once they've exited the building. Once the fire alarm was pulled at Marjory Stoneman Douglas High, gunman Nikolas Cruz was able to slip away with the rest of the students, hidden in plain sight, and evade capture for a full hour following his murderous rampage.[20] The students who died on the third floor of the besieged building might have been saved had they not attempted to get through locked doors and instead raced away from Cruz and toward the exits.[21] Cruz having knowledge of their planned behavior would have had no effect on that outcome.

The final place to engage students—implementation and maintenance, or monitoring—is perhaps the one where we've already seen the most hopeful change. The members of iGen graduating this year grew up in both the post-Columbine and post-9/11 era. The possibility of being shot at school has been a known risk their entire lives, rather than an extreme rarity as experienced by older Millennials and GenXers. Implementation and monitoring, for them, will likely mean bringing about major change. The #NeverAgain movement spurred by Parkland has inspired dozens of other groups of high school students nationwide to stand up and be heard, striving to implement change in gun control laws.[22] They believe that they have the ear of their politicians—and any politician who isn't listening should take notice, as this generation is much more engaged and ready to vote than the generations that came before.[23] They are ready to vote like their lives depend on it, and the lives of future generations.

Eliminating the threat of school shootings in America is a goal that will likely take multiple lifetimes to achieve. Engaging those most affected by this threat – the children and young adults whose lives are constantly at risk – may be one of the most effective ways to prevent school shootings from happening. We need to help students have a heightened understanding and awareness of what the root causes of many school shootings have been, so they can respond with greater empathy to their peers. We need to listen to their ideas on how to reduce the impacts of attacks, inviting them to be active participants in preparing for emergencies on their campuses rather than passively following directions. Finally, and foremost, we need to support them as they find their voices and work to create change in our society. Their passion and presence in the democratic process will likely be the only thing that can change school shootings from a reality of everyday life to another ugly, but closed, chapter in our history books.

The Black Swan by the Festival

Emily Ye

Written: November 2017
Published: June 2018

Abstract: This paper discusses the operational risks revealed by the outlier event of the Las Vegas shooting in October 2017 where 58 people were killed and more than 500 people were injured. Black swan events - an extreme outlier that is almost impossible to prepare for – such as this shooting reveal their unique risks typically only after the event has happened. The Las Vegas shooting has resulted in discussions on event, public-space, and hotel security; this paper identifies some possible recommendations in order to address these risks.

Introduction

In the old days, machines were simple, individual objects and fields remained separate, and problems were trivial. As technology advanced, today's society has become a place where "the tools we use are complex, and breakdowns can be catastrophic, with far-reaching consequences… we must be constantly aware of the likelihood of malfunctions and errors."[1] When planning for any project, especially ones with large scales, it is now vital for enterprises to consider potential hazards and perform risk management. Not only does that help enterprises to fully understand their projects, clarify the priorities, and mitigate some risks, it also prepares enterprises to react to and resolve issues in the shortest time possible. However, it is tremendously challenging, even for the most sophisticated and detailed risk management plan, to cover every possibility, such as the black swan events – events that are unexpected due to the lack of indications in the past of their possibilities, involve extreme impacts, but become explainable after their occurrences.[2] One such event is an incident that took place in Las Vegas, Nevada on October 1, 2017.

On the last night of the Route 91 Harvest Festival, a mass shooting event occurred in Las Vegas, now commonly referred to as the Las Vegas shooting. The Route 91 Harvest Festival, also known as "the neon sleepover," is a 3-day open-air country music festival across a 15-acre concrete lot, where people gather to listen to various singers' live concerts, many of which are big names. It has been held annually for the past 4 years, only selling three-day passes and provides no parking space. The festival's safety regulations allow fans to bring beach chairs, binoculars, and motorized scooters, but banned stuffed animals, drones, selfie-sticks, and weapons. Security guards are also on site to ensure fans' and performers' safety.[3] Despite these efforts to keep the festival safe, tragedy occurred. On the last day of this festival during country music singer Jason Aldean's performance, a shooter fired shots into the concert venue for 10 to 15 minutes from the 32nd floor of the Mandalay Bay hotel across the street, approximately 1,000 feet away. It is believed that he fired from both rooms of the two-room suite he stayed in, in order to get different angles. The police quickly identified the shooter's location, and busted into the room after confirming that there were no other shooters at other locations. Upon entering, they discovered that the shooter had killed himself; beside his body, police found 23 guns and evidence of a carefully planned attack in the room. The significance of this event is that out of the 22,000 concert-goers, 58 were killed and more than 500 were injured, making this event the deadliest mass shooting in modern American history.[4] It also raised awareness in areas and aspects that were previously disregarded, revolving around how the shooting could be carried out.

The CEO of the security company that employed about 200 people to work security for the music festival mentioned his "company works with law enforcement and runs active shooter drills… [but] there's 'nothing you can do' when someone is shooting from another building above the venue."[5] This reveals how unexpected it was and the reason behind the event's physical security control failure, further proving that "the world has become more populated by those who want to exploit those [security] gaps, including those living among us – and who, in the United States, can easily obtain military-grade weapons."[6] This black swan event - an extreme outlier that is almost impossible to prepare for – reveals the exposure to multiple risks the enterprise MGM Resorts International, the owner of the Mandalay Bay hotel, where the shooter stayed, and the hotel itself. The first of which is operational risk of types physical security, disaster recovery, and external. However, the risk of encountering unforeseen attack that the security people and machines are not trained or designed for always exists, so it should have been included as a part of risk planning. The Las Vegas shooting led to reflection on hotel security as well, since most hotels in the U.S. do not have metal detectors, which enables anyone to bring firearms into the hotels easily.[7] As for preparation after a disaster, on the other hand, especially after unforeseen disasters like this one, recovery plans should have been created beforehand and available if one were to happen in order to guarantee business continuity in the quickest time possible. The recovery stage for Las Vegas, according to the country's emergency manager, will "be a very, very long process,"[8] which is not exceedingly problematic for a city. Nevertheless, for the Mandalay Bay Hotel, the longer it takes to recover, the greater the loss and the harder it is to pick the business back up. The last type of operational risk is external, which is only referring to terrorism for this topic. The day after the tragedy, ISIS claimed that the shooter was a soldier of theirs, but gave no evidence for the claim. The FBI dismissed the claim due to the lack of evidence suggesting connection between the shooter and any international terrorist group, as well as the trend of apparent false-claims of responsibility ISIS had been making.[9] Nevertheless, that does not verify that the shooter had no affiliation with ISIS, and given that the attack was planned with the involvement of so many firearms, it is not impossible that the shooter received support from and acted on behave of a terrorist group, perhaps ISIS or others.

Another risk exposed is conduct risk. One of the major questions raised revolving around the Las Vegas shooting is on how the shooter managed to keep the maid service from noticing anything. The shooter brought a substantial amount of firearms into the hotel. If he had taken several trips, carrying a portion of the firearms each time in a bag without any bellmen's help, it would explain why no one was suspicious when he brought weapons in. However, he had to keep and store all of them in his room for multiple days.[10] How was he able to hide them so well? Although the shooting incident is still under investigation, a possibility would be that he received help from an employee of the hotel, intentionally or unintentionally, by providing him information on the locations of discrete areas, showing him ways and places for cover-up, or other similar means. If the shooter was under the cover of an insider, it would be reasonable that he could stay undiscovered for such a long time. Regardless of whether the helper supported the shooter knowingly or unknowingly, it would have been misconduct.

One other risk is the third-party risk. MGM is the owner of the Las Vegas village, where the concert took place, but it was neither the organizer nor the promoter of the concert.[11] However, that does not prevent MGM from getting the blame. Even though the specific type of the mass shooting was unexpected, to the victims, it simply seemed like the organizers were not prepared – they did not have a plan and took a long time to respond, which was probably why there were so many casualties. As the owner of the space, MGM might have needed to contribute to only a small portion of concert planning, but it would end up getting nontrivial, if not equal impact from the shooting. It is presumed that MGM had built partnership with the organizers through contract for using the space, and thus they would share assessment program on the event operation and security, as well as the responsibility. Therefore, severe incidents like this one would not only affect the third parties, the organizers, but also MGM.

Lastly, as the owner of the concert space as well as the owner of the shooter's accommodation and shooting site, MGM faces apparent reputation, legal, and regulatory risks. Mandalay Bay Hotel quickly installed permanent, 24-hour security at elevator banks after the tragedy, checking every guest's room key in order to "boost its security image to attract more customers," but it inevitably experienced a spike in cancellations,[12] since it already earned itself a bad reputation on security. This situation is just like what

Benjamin Franklin had stated, "It takes many good deeds to build a good reputation, and only one bad one to lose it."[13] Moreover, the change in security rule raises the expense for labor and may cause customers to feel irritated, who can further affect its business and market, a regulatory risk it cannot disregard. Mandalay Bay Hotel's average room price[14] and MGM's stock price, because of the shooting, also fell significantly.[15] Mandalay Bay has not yet decided on what to do with the room the shooter stayed in and opened fire from,[16] but it is obvious that their final decision will further influence its reputation, for better or worse. Both elements challenge MGM's and Mandalay Bay Hotel's "focus on positive interactions with stakeholders" and how well they "know their customers, align company goals with customer needs and act to ensure a distinctively different experience for customers."[17] These will determine their direction of reputation gain and loss in the future. At the same time, many lawsuits are being filed against the hotel, but "one would have to show that the hotel had knowledge about this of some sort and they disregarded it" in order to sue the hotel successfully."[18] While it is unlikely that Mandalay Bay Hotel and MGM will have major losses legally, the possibility exists, and how they treat these legal issues will have an impact on their reputation as well. The vulnerabilities contained within these risks, along with the risks presented previously, exist not only in the Las Vegas Shooting and MGM particularly, but also in the sector. All the enterprises hosting or around any concert, any mass gathering, face the same risks and hazards. This is why risk management is significant, as enterprises can learn from each other and build safer environment through indirect collaboration.

A government regulation that should have prevented the event from happening is the gun regulation. While it is legal to bear arms in the U.S., regulations enforce precautions and background checks. These processes should have, or at least should supposedly avoid putting weapons into the wrong hands, but the shooter purchased from several Nevada gun shops, where the workers "have maintained that the gunman passed all necessary background checks," and the general manager of a gun store the shooter shopped in claimed that the shooter "never gave any indication or reason to believe he was unstable or unfit at any time." The businesses indicated that they took all precautions and sold firearms legally to the shooter just like to every other customer. However, Nevada has some of the most relaxed gun laws. Owners are not required to have licenses, nor do they have to register their weapons, and are not limited to possessing a certain number of firearms either.[19] Moreover, bump stocks, gun accessories that enabled the shooter to fire rapidly, "were originally created ostensibly to make it easier for people with disabilities to shoot," and although it is yet unsure, the bump stock maker that sold the part to the shooter is suspected to have geared its marketing to regular gun owners who wished to construct near-fully automatic weapons.[20] These are most likely the reasons why the regulations failed to prevent the event from happening. The use of background check on the shooter was next to nothing, as there were no restrictions at all following the check. Anyone who had never had a bad record can easily inflict harm on others at anytime, once they have developed malicious intents. In order to reduce the risk around such an event recurring, I would propose Nevada to implement stricter gun control regulations. This is not only for keeping

181

firearms away from potential criminals at the time of purchase, but also for preventing people who have gradually turned to be hateful towards the society and other people from causing harm, or in other words, prevent potential criminals in the future.

One other recommendation I would suggest is to host mass gatherings indoors. The main issue with the Las Vegas Shooting is that no one thought and prepared for active shooting from above the ground, at a place outside of the concert venue. Despite of the amount of security effort put into the festival, "mirroring the mainstream adoption of previously unheard-of safety precautions at airports around the country…[using] bomb-sniffing dogs, body scanners, and high-definition closed circuit cameras," the effort could not be applied to the shooter, as he stayed out of the realm. The shooter utilized the advantage of keeping "well outside the usual security perimeter of pat-downs and metal detectors… [and choosing] an open-air target that is by definition vulnerable from a high elevation." [21] Even though arranging events indoors cannot guarantee protection against black swan events, and it can be difficult to achieve for certain events that are outdoors by nature, it can force attackers to have to go through the security systems. This may successfully intimidate and stop some of them, and it would decrease the exposure of outdoor events to unknown factors.

Finally, increasing hotel security and planning for aerial assault would also be effective on decreasing the risk of having this kind of event reoccurring. It is certainly extremely challenging for hotels to install measures to scan through or check each customer's suitcase, but it is important for hotels to find a way to raise their security level during special times. It could be done through checking baggage, being more aware of customers and regular individuals going in and out of hotel, or using security cameras on more than just catching cheating gamblers. As in the situation mentioned above, "the key is creating security environments that make it difficult to carry out attacks and thus deter people from trying."[22] Other than security from the hotel side, organizers for major events should also include aerial assault planning for both mitigation and contingency purposes. There is high likelihood that there will be "copycat killers" that try to use the same tactics and cause more "entertainment venues…[to] be transformed into killing grounds,"[23] so it is crucial to develop plans for this type of mass shooting as soon as possible. In fact, Las Vegas is already doing so for its recent annual weekend marathon, by "posting snipers," adding "some counter-sniper surveillance posts along the route," and circling the police helicopter throughout the marathon. It was "the first large-scale outdoor event since…[the] country music festival,"[24] but it evidently learned from the festival, and made noticeable changes and security measures. Las Vegas had taken its first step in restoring people's confidence in the city; surely, MGM will soon forge ahead on repairing its name, and redeeming its customers' sense of security and faith in the Mandalay Bay Hotel.

The Worst Sexual Abuse Scandal in Athletics

Malory Rose

Written: May 2018
Published: May 2019

Abstract: This paper discusses how Dr. Larry Nassar was able to sexually abuse hundreds of underage athletes for over twenty years while under the failed oversight of two organizations – United States of America Gymnastics (USAG) and Michigan State University (MSU). The safety and risk mitigation systems – and the individuals who were responsible for implementing them - failed these athletes. There are lessons to be learned in order to prevent similar abuse from happening in the future.

When medals and money matter more than stopping the worse sexual predator in sports of all time, two organizations – United States of America Gymnastics (USAG) and Michigan State University (MSU) – failed to protect the athletes in their charge. The history of sexual predators in sports did not begin with Dr. Larry Nassar nor will it end with him.

Organizational risk mitigation must be implemented at all levels of sports to prevent the Larry Nassars of the world from having access to children. To clearly understand how this abuse happened, the first area to examine is how the USAG and MSU looked the other way when a sexual predator, Dr. Larry Nassar, was abusing female athletes. It is important to evaluate the organizational structures that failed to stop this individual from continuing to abuse girls. Investigating when the abuse first began and determining why no one stopped him could help mitigate this kind of chronic abuse from occurring again in the future. Finally, the abuser himself must be evaluated - and how he came to have unfettered access to young athletes with little to no oversight.

Clearly, those responsible for the safety of these athletes failed profoundly. Sponsorships, medals and reputation were protected as were coaches, medical professionals, and the organization as a whole, but not the athletes. Understanding the history of sexual predators in sports and the way they groom their victims provides the information necessary to unravel Nassar's deception, as well as the enablers who willingly or unwillingly either looked the other way or simply did not see the crimes.

Youth sports has a history of sexual perpetration. The Crimes Against Children Research Center reports, "one in five girls and one in 20 boys is a victim of child sexual abuse."[1] These figures are startling, but these conniving individuals find great success with children in sports as the parents are not always watching. Schools have extensive background checks, but youth sports often have very little safeguards in place. Many children are groomed by these pedophiles and the role of the coach presents a perfect authoritarian environment for both coaches and surrounding staff to groom these young victims. According to Deborah Serani, Psy.D., "Studies report about 7 percent of athletes (both minors and young adults) are victims of sexual assault - with elite athletes having higher rates of sexual assault than lower-level athletes."[2] Coaches, trainers, athletic directors, and physical therapists are often in positions of power and authority, which can lead to implementation of grooming techniques to target young athletes.

Serani outlines important points that bring to light the potential risk of sexual abuse by these individuals.[3] First, when there are loose guidelines with unstructured or unsupervised practices, the risk of sexual exploitation is the greatest. Youth athletics provides the environment for risk situations to be established, thereby enabling sexual predators to groom and manipulate their potential victims such as on the playing fields, in the locker rooms, and in the coach's home or car. Serani reports that "passive attitudes, non-intervention, denial and/or silence by people in position of power in sports culture increases the psychological harm of sex abuse for the athlete."[4] As will become evident, this passive attitude, non-intervention and the denial or silencing of those in power was exactly what allowed this predator to continue his behavior for so long.

What organizations allowed this predator to sexually abuse these girls?

The greatest sexual abuse scandal occurred at two organizations - USAG and MSU - for 20 years. USA Gymnastics was founded in 1963 and has grown to a membership of 148,000 athletes that train at over 3,000 USAG member clubs.[5] MSU is a part of the 62 Division I women's gymnastics programs which each provide 12 head count scholarships.[6] The vast majority of gymnasts who go on to compete in the NCAA rise through the USAG program.

It is interesting that both of these organizations have policies that ensure athletes are not using sports enhancing drugs through routine drug testing. Yet, there were no policies that were in place to protect athletes from sexual abuse. Instead, the organizations protected the physician over the athletes, then proceeded with cover ups and failed to report to law enforcement.

The structure of both of these organizations should have had risk mitigation procedures and policies in place that protected the athletes from sexual abuse. At each NCAA university there are compliance officers who handle sex abuse allegations.[7] Unfortunately, MSU failed to report any abuse to higher authorities. USAG simply did not have any formalized structure or oversight for the medical treatment of the athletes on the National Team. These individuals traveled to the Karolyi Ranch in Texas one week per month for intense training, competition and selection camps.[8] Their medical care was under the direction of Dr. Larry Nassar.[9]

Who was this monster?

Dr. Larry Nassar was the team physician for USAG's national team and the MSU athletic department. In 1978, Nassar first started working with gymnasts as a student athletic trainer at a Michigan high school. By 1985 he received his kinesiology degree from University of Michigan. He joined USAG national team medical staff as an Athletic Trainer in 1986. He then pursued his medical degree at Michigan State University in 1993 where he obtained his osteopathic medical degree. Nassar completed a family practice residency and was appointed National Medical Coordinator for USAG 1996. By 1997, he completed his sports medicine fellowship and became a team physician and assistant professor at MSU.[10] His training as a Doctor of Osteopathy involved learning intrarectal manipulation and intravaginal manual treatment techniques for pelvic floor muscular dysfunction and other pelvic disorders. Those who potentially allowed Dr. Nassar to sexually abuse these athletes were coaches of club, collegiate and elite level gymnasts at both USAG and MSU. Additionally, medical professionals including the Dean of the College of Osteopathy at MSU as well as athletic trainers, seemed to fail to report the abuse when informed by the athletes. Parents had left their children to be treated by Dr. Nassar, and some parents were even in the room during procedures.[11] "Were these enablers complicit or simply conned by a master manipulator?"[12]

When did the abuse first begin?

The first occurrence of abuse goes all the way back to 1994 at which time a gymnast, who later became an Olympic medalist, alleged that Nassar sexually abused her over six years according to a lawsuit that she filed in 2016.[13] The first report to others at MSU was in 1997 by Larissa Boyce when she was 16 years old. She reported to the head coach of the MSU gymnastic team, Kathy Klages, about feeling uncomfortable with digital penetration, but her concerns were dismissed.[14]

Then in 1998 a softball player for MSU reported to multiple athletic trainers (AT), as well as the head AT, that she was sexually assaulted with digital penetration. They told her that she did not understand the medical procedure.[15] According to an ESPN article by John Barr, the abuse continued unchecked at MSU until the spring of 2014.[16] The dean of Michigan State's College of Osteopathic Medicine, Dr. William Strampel, was notified at home that a student had accused Nassar of having massaged her breasts and vaginal area at a clinic appointment with Nassar to evaluate her hip injury.[17] The woman reported that she "felt violated."[18] According to Barr, "Strampel told the detectives that he suspended Nassar from seeing patients indefinitely the following afternoon, and he let law enforcement and the school's Title IX office take over from there."[19] Once the Title IX office cleared Nassar, Strampel thought the situation was resolved. Unfortunately, this individual, who could have put a stop Dr. Nassar's behavior, was guilty of similar behavior as well. It was later discovered that Dr. Strampel was arrested for sexual harassment of a medical student at MSU.[20] Thus, it is not surprising that Dr. Strampel never reported any of the sexual abuse allegations to Dr. Nassar's immediate supervisor nor to the USAG.

Nassar was allowed to return to work after the suspension with the requirement that his hands were to be gloved and an attendant be in the room during any procedures.[21] Unfortunately, Dr. Nassar's immediate supervisor had no knowledge of the allegations or the basic requirements to which Nassar was required to adhere.[22] After being cleared of this first official incident, Dr. Nassar was able to continue his abuse under the guise of performing a medical procedure.[23] Could it be that USAG did not take due diligence to properly vet Dr. Nassar because he was on staff at MSU? USAG allowed Dr. Nassar to have access to the athletes with no attendant and no other adult present. He was able to continue grooming these athletes, who were under tremendous stress and strict diets related to their athletic performance. Nassar become the "good cop" in a sea of extremely stressful training situations. He took advantage of this setting by bringing snacks to their rooms where he would perform his special "medical procedure."[24]

In September 2016, in an Indianapolis Star report, "gymnast Rachael Denhollander and an anonymous former Olympic medalist publicly accused Nassar of sexual abuse."[25] This was coupled with the coach of national team gymnast Maggie Nichols overhearing Maggie describe her uncomfortableness with Nassar's digital penetration while she was receiving medical treatment at the national training camp.[26] Only after this was reported by Maggie's coach to the USAG was an independent investigation initiated, and nearly seven weeks later the FBI was notified.[27] It is fortunate that on the day that the FBI went to Nassar's house, the trash had not been picked up on time; the FBI found a computer in the garbage from which tens of thousands of images of child pornography were discovered.[28] No longer did Nassar's "treatment" seem to be a legitimate medical procedure. Rather, it appeared to be sexual misconduct. The athletes finally had a chance to be taken seriously.

How did the organizational risk management structure fail?

MSU did not establish appropriate oversight from the top. Dr. Strampel, the dean of the Osteopathic College, did not alert Dr. Nassar's immediate supervisor to inform about the stipulations that were put in place to insure no abuse or allegations of abuse by Nassar could continue after the 2014 incident. There was no communication with USAG that an investigation was underway at MSU and that Dr. Nassar had been temporarily suspended. In the late 1990's, despite many individuals reporting the sexual abuse nature of Nassar's treatments, neither the head gymnastic coaches nor the trainers ever went to law enforcement. Michigan law does not require mandatory reporting for coaches, and the reporting laws in various states are inconsistent.[29] It was not until 2014 that an MSU official in their Title IX department was contacted and then followed up by contacting law enforcement.[30]

The USAG association failed to have a female attendant present for all medical examinations and treatment performed by Dr. Nassar.[31] There was no oversite board or system in place to evaluate medical documentation of the above referenced treatment, nor were they further reviewed by an independent board. Since most of these athletes were minors, there was no informed consent signed by the patient's parents or guardians discussing and consenting to the evaluation and treatment parameters.[32]

Organizational risk management failures included internal fraud when Dr. Nassar's associate removed patient files from the MSU sports medicine clinic.[33] There were regulatory noncompliance risk management failures that primarily consisted of Nassar's failure to follow standard medical practices of informed consent, parent notification of procedures to be performed, and use of gloved hands for procedures involving touching of sensitive areas as well as for intravaginal and intrarectal penetration. Physical security risk management failure included no oversight to protect underage athletes while training at the Karolyi Ranch.[34] The fact that Nassar was able to treat the girls in their cabins with no supervision[35] is not only a risk to physical security but is also a system failure. Gross misconduct by Nassar included having no attendant when performing examinations and treatments, no informed consent for either of these, and often no use of gloves on his hand. Conduct risk occurred when MSU gymnastics head coach Kathie Klages failed to alert authorities when she was approached by gymnasts of their concerns of sexual abuse[36] despite the fact that Michigan law does not delineate coaches among those designated as mandatory reporters.[37] National legislation should be developed to include all individuals who are in contact with youth sports to be required to be mandatory reporters.

Why did it go on so long and no one addressed or fixed the problem?

Three major factors which allowed the sexual abuse to continue.

1) No one oversaw Dr. Larry Nassar at MSU nor clearly at USAG, and no medical records were generated at USAG nor reviewed at MSU. There was no requirement for the presence of a female attendant nor glove usage with digital penetration of the vagina or rectum.

2) Legitimate intravaginal and intrarectal manual therapies do exist for pelvic floor dysfunction. As a result, Nassar was able to ward off attacks for quite some time because he was able to disguise his sexual abuse as being a legitimate medical procedure.

3) It seems that USAG was more interested in medals and the money from sponsors to the extent that they were willing to ignore the numerous complaints of sexual abuse and defer contacting law enforcement. One wonders if Nassar's computer (which contained child pornography) had never been discovered in the trash by the FBI, then would these victims have ever been believed.

How has this lack of risk management affected these two organizations?

USAG has lost the majority of their sponsors and is now embroiled in multiple lawsuits. It is uncertain if they will survive this scandal. Their entire board was required to resign, and new management has been put in place. The National Team has no direction nor central training facility. They have adopted SAFESPORT oversight procedures, but much more has to be implemented for trust and sponsors to be restored. MSU has already settled a law suit that will provide $500 million to those abused by Larry Nassar.[38]

Where do we go from here?

NCAA Sports: Jackie Mynarski is the Associate Athletic Director of Compliance at the University of Washington, reports there is a well-established process in place for an athlete to report sexual abuse.[39] As stated on the UW website, "Title IX protects people's access to educational programs from discrimination based on sex. Sexual harassment can be a form of discrimination prohibited by Title IX".[40] According to Amanda Paye, Office of Risk Management, the University of Washington Police Department (UWPD) and UWPD Victim Advocate are the two law enforcement avenues for reporting sexual abuse.[41] All personnel are required to mandatorily report sexual abuse allegations. Athletes can first contact Jackie Mynarski, who then alerts the Title IX department, which in turn contacts the UW police.[42] University of Washington students are fortunate to have a strong oversight, but apparently MSU previously did not. It is important to develop national laws that mandate all individuals who are in contact with young athletes be required to report sexual abuse. There should be no gray area.

USAG: Develop a board consisting of the following individuals: physicians among the following specialties – one from physical medicine, one from general practice, an AT, a PT, two lay people and one athlete. This board would select the national medical coordinator for USAG and approve all support medical staff. The medical board should have oversight on the policies and procedures for the healthcare needs of the athletes.[43] SAFESPORT should be implemented as an integral part of risk mitigation procedures for USAG. SAFESPORT is the policing body of the US Olympic Committee with the following statement: "Our mission is to make athlete well-being the centerpiece of our nation's sports culture".[44] Their website further states, "All athletes deserve to participate in sports free from bullying, hazing, sexual misconduct or any form of emotional or physical abuse".[45]

The gymnasts and their parents should be provided with a workshop to discuss the chain of command for reporting abuse with a system in place that protects their child's privacy and physical, emotional and mental wellbeing. The workshop should educate them in what is required of medical personnel regarding informed consent, what is sexual misconduct or abuse versus what is a true medical treatment. All minor aged athletes should have any medical procedures cleared through their parents/guardians unless there is a life threating situation where they must be transported for emergency situations. Workshops should also be provided for coaches to understand the parameters necessary for creating a safe sport environment and how to detect grooming from a sexual predator.

Sponsorships, medals and reputation were protected as were coaches, medical professionals and the organizations, but not the athletes. These young athletes were victimized by Dr. Nassar, and they were also victimized by the very organizations that were supposed to protect them. Dr. Nassar is in prison for the remainder of his life, but there could be others lurking. Parents must be vigilant and not worry about speaking up about abuse. They should not be threatened that their child will not make the team; not playing may hurt, but sexual abuse will scar their child for life. Speak up!

SECTION FOUR

Targeted Organizational Risks

PAPER	AUTHOR
#DeleteUber	Lee Segal
Evaluating the Risks to the National Football League	Lukas Guericke
Operational Risk Challenges for the CDC	Elizabeth Crooks
Risks within Tesla, Inc.	Blake Franzen
The State Department's Leadership Vacuum	Elizabeth Crooks
Understanding SEC's Inadequate Internal Controls	Miranda Lin

#DeleteUber

Lee Segal

Written: March 2018
Published: February 2019

Abstract: This paper discusses how the disruptive and once innovation company Uber has continued its downward spiral, with a growing number of stories emerging of executives making unethical decisions that will have lasting consequences for the company's reputation and bottom-line. Incidents run the gauntlet from practicing unethical methods of gathering data on competitors; a toxic internal culture that has resulted in numerous sexual harassment and discrimination cases; patterns of exploiting employees; and compromising private customer data access; and failure to secure sensitive private information. Despite leadership changes, Uber has a long way to go to demonstrate they have successfully implemented meaningful and lasting cultural and administrative changes.

In 2010, a revolutionary application came out allowing users to reserve a car – a taxi of sorts - via a smartphone application. No longer did people have to wait outside in extreme weather, fighting others to hail a cab, unsure when one would arrive. Understanding this unfulfilled need and leveraging mobile smartphone and geolocation technology maturity, two innovators created a service that enables users to order a car service based on their exact location.[1] The application has many useful features including informing the rider of expected arrival time, showing the price before the car is called, tracking the driver on a map, and the capability of contacting the driver if the rider forgets any of their belongings in the vehicle. This innovative service is

Uber, which quickly became extremely popular: instead of saying "let me hail a taxi," the new phrase is "let's call an Uber." The founder of Uber identified an unfulfilled need and developed a new business model that opened up a brand-new market—the ability to call cars, and eventually food, to their front door in real-time, at any time and from anywhere with just the touch of a button. The idea was gold. Nevertheless, a lack of ethics and morals led the company to turmoil in 2014; since 2014, Uber has been hit with many allegations placing its ethics into question.[2] However, the data breach revealed in November 2017 plunged Uber's reputation to rock bottom. The once-innovative company is now plagued by scandals and eroding customer trust.

Uber dealt with another security and reputation risk long before this data breach occurred. To fully understand Uber as a corporation and understand why this particular data breach enraged both customers and governments, it is essential to analyze Uber's past mistakes. In 2014, Uber was accused of targeting their competitor, Lyft, by booking thousands of fake rides in an effort to cut into Lyft's profits and services.[3] In that same year, Uber was also accused of having a "God View" which allowed Uber employees (managers and executives) to use the information Uber collected from customers—such as their location—unethically.[4] Employees allegedly used the "God View" to impress and entertain friends and associates, demonstrating a blatant misuse of privileged access to private customer data. This specific incident raised privacy concerns and demonstrated a fundamental lack of enforced policies and procedures related to authorization controls and access to customer data. Then in 2015, Uber revealed they had suffered a data breach that affected roughly 50,000 drivers.[5]

They concealed this breach for over a year and were fined twenty thousand dollars in New York.[6] Many Uber drivers started protesting, claiming Uber did not care for them. Uber even tried to keep them as contractors to avoid having to pay them employee benefits, and so they could keep cutting their wages, making it hard to make a living, and never told them that their personal information was stolen. More recently, in 2017, accusations of sexual harassment and discrimination toward females in the workplace arose within Uber.[7] Google also sued Uber, accusing them of stealing Google's technology for a self-driving car.[8] The list continues in March of 2017, when Travis Kalanick (at-the-time-CEO of Uber) was caught on camera yelling at his Uber driver after his driver complained about the difficulty of making a living with the company's declining rates.[9] Then in April, news leaked that Uber had a secret program called "Hell" that allowed the company to spy on its rival Lyft to uncover drivers who work for both companies.[10] They used this application to help steer drivers who worked for both companies away from the competitor. In June, an Uber executive obtained the medical records of a woman who was allegedly raped by an Uber driver just to cast doubt onto the rape victim. Uber fired the executive once the press got word of this incident, and the woman later sued the company for violating her privacy rights and defaming her.[11]

These are just the highlights of the allegations against the corporation's corrupt culture, abuse of power, and their lack of security measures and controls. These security breaches and allegations perfectly frame the tone Uber's chief executive officer (CEO) set for the corporation—it has been led without integrity, transparency, good ethics, or honesty. One of the responsibilities of the CEO is to lead the company in the manner expected of the employee to mimic. Analyzing all the actions Uber has taken in the last year, it is clear that the CEO has failed to set an ethical and just tone for his company. These examples prove that the majority of the executives are only concerned with selfish motives such as making money for their corporation, no matter the cost. In fact, the recent data breach—the focus of this paper—further backs Uber's reputation as a corrupt corporation focused on profits at the expense of ethical business practices.

The most recent data breach, and arguably, "Uber's lowest point," was just announced in November 2017.[12] Uber announced that in October of 2016, they had a data breach that affected over 57 million riders and drivers. *Bloomberg Technology* provides a detailed explanation of the hack: two attackers gained access to Uber's private GitHub repository (a digital directory/storage space) where their software engineers shared and updated code. The hackers succeeded in breaking into the repository because of a failure to implement internal controls and security measures. The hackers found login credentials to Uber's Amazon services account; on this account, the hackers found an archive of riders' and drivers' information including email addresses, full names, and phone numbers.[13] Alongside that information, they found up to sixty thousand driver's license numbers. The attackers blackmailed Uber and demanded one hundred thousand dollars.[14] The executives of Uber immediately agreed on the condition of having all stolen information and any evidence of the hack deleted. They even went through the extra effort of tracking down the hackers and making them sign a nondisclosure agreement to ensure they would not leak information about the hack.[15] In fact, Uber took a few actions to try and keep the hack hidden such as using their bug bounty program as a cover up for paying the ransom.[16] Uber has yet to make any apologies or take ownership for their actions even though they committed countless questionable actions. Uber's dealing with this breach further proves that their executives lack integrity, honesty, transparency, and respect when making decisions and representing the enterprise.

There are always consequences involved when a breach takes place; however, the potential consequences for Uber's customers, who remain oblivious of this breach, increased exponentially should the hackers decide to use the stolen information in the future. The 2016 data breach affected the entire user enterprise including the riders and drivers, Uber's corporate reputation, and Uber's executives. The biggest consequence of the data breach is that private information was stolen (names, email addresses, and phone numbers) from fifty-seven million riders and drivers, along with six-hundred thousand driver license numbers. One might question why the information the hackers stole is essential; however, this is the kind of information used to steal identities or commit social engineering attacks. What makes it even worse is that the users had no idea that their information was even stolen for over a year. In this case, or any case where your private information is stolen, ignorance is *not* bliss. Instead of immediately taking necessary steps to mitigate and protect themselves from a potential attack, the riders and drivers were left clueless and defenseless. Not only did Uber hide the attack from them for over a year, they still have not reached out to any affected riders, and have not communicated any plans to do so. The worst part is that Uber failed to even tell their drivers about their attack, which—after a 2014 ruling—are officially considered employees of the company.[17] Uber not only hid information from customers and the government, but also hid information from their own employees.

Even though none of Uber's information got stolen, they are not making it out of this breach unscathed. Uber is being put on blast from the media, multiple governments, their employees, customers, and other individuals. Uber dealt with reputation issues before the breach. But is safe to say that they have reached a new low. They are not only dealing with protests and strikes, but also countless legal suits. The two biggest suits include one with California and one with the FTC (Federal Trade Commission). In 2003, California mandated that businesses and state agencies are required to alert customers if their personal information is exposed in a security breach; since Uber hid this data breach from its customers, including the ones in California, it broke California's regulation.[18] Uber also broke Federal Trade Commission (FTC) policy by asking the Hackers to delete all forensic evidence of the data breach. A representative of the FTC stated, "Uber failed consumers in two key ways: First by misrepresenting the extent to which it monitored its employees' access to personal information about users and drivers, and second by misrepresenting that it took reasonable steps to secure that data." Most executives have worked in well-known companies for at least a decade; they should be familiar with the laws and protocols. Even if they were not, part of their job as leading a company is finding out what the regulation and protocols are in that area as part of decision-making processes. These actions prove that no matter what the executives were involved with in leading this incident, they knew they were committing illegal acts and decided to pursue them anyway. The crimes explained above are two prime examples of Uber executives prioritizing their company over following laws, regulations or corporate ethics.

Over the last couple of years, Uber's actions have concerned the population for many reasons. Uber has a huge issue with not adapting and learning from past mistakes; they would rather sweep issues under the rug than deal with them in an honest and transparent way. Uber also has huge security issues that have not been fixed. (Note: The new Uber CEO claims to be strengthening controls and security measures on their cloud storage services.) An example of Uber's serious security issues where executives failed to learn from past mistakes is the data breach that occurred in 2014. Uber only disclosed that there was a breach in 201, a whole year after the fact. The only difference is that in 2014 hackers stole less data. But the hackers still got away with personal data from roughly 10,000 Uber drivers. The attack vector used in both attacks is essentially the same; in 2014, the hackers broke into Uber's private Github repo after one of the engineers publicly posted the key to their GitHub. Through the repo they gained log-in information to an Amazon S3 Datastore which Uber used to store data in plain text.[19] The FTC recently settled their investigation into security and privacy complaints for the 2014 data breach; just this summer Uber agreed to 20 years of external audits and to abide by various conditions in the consent order.[20] According to TechCrunch, "the FTC consent order settling the 2014 and 2015 complaints prohibited Uber from misrepresenting how it protects the privacy, confidentiality, integrity, and authenticity of any personal information it handles and stores. However, before the ink could dry on that settlement, Uber revealed the 2016 data breach. The fact that Uber allowed both these attacks to happen in a span of a couple of year, raises a lot of questions about their security measures and the controls they have implemented. After the first attack Uber should have increased security, improved employee training, and added policies to prevent a data breach; or at least solve the vulnerability that had been breached once before. Clearly, they failed to increase security even slightly, not even patching up the vulnerability, which raises the question of whether security is even a priority for the corporation. Another concern is that Uber knew they were in violation of the settlement with the FTC while they were signing the contract with them, once again demonstrating Uber's lack of respect for laws, regulations, integrity, and honesty. They completely lied to the FTC and committed the same crime they committed two years prior. Repeatedly, Uber executives continue to lead the company with a tone of apathy for corporate ethics.

Not just individuals are outraged with Uber's actions. Governments are also taking a stand. Many governments—especially the UK—claim that Uber's behavior is reckless.[21] The governments are retaliating in response. First, the UK's digital minister, Matt Hancock, decided to create a new regulation. The new regulation "would oblige companies to report breaches 'likely to impact on data subjects to the information commissioner within 72 hours of becoming aware of it and in serious cases will also have to notify those affected by the breach'".[22] The US senate is also trying to pass a regulation that about data breaches that failed to pass in 2015. The bill "would make it a crime – punishable by up to five years in prison – for companies to knowingly conceal a breach of customer information."[23]   Hopefully this drastically bill will pass to emphasize to corporation like Uber that data breaches need to be told to the authorities immediately to mitigate the consequences of the breach. Some governments are even banning Uber completely, making it illegal for people to work for Uber and for the population to use Uber. Over 10 countries have already banned Uber, with more looking to follow suit.[24]

If you are currently or have ever been an Uber user, you should automatically assume that you have been infected. Uber has not informed users if they were affected by this hack and has not disclosed any plans to inform users; forcing them to trust that Uber successfully deleted the stolen data and implemented security measures to monitor the stolen data. This is extremely unfair considering that Uber has proven repeatedly to not prioritize security or care about their customers. However, there are a couple steps to try to protect personal information. First, change your password right now. Uber should have forced an automatic password reset. However, since they did not, you should immediately change it yourself. Next, delete all credit card information from the application, but do not delete the application itself. Disable anything that can gather information about you such as location services, credit card information, or any addresses you saved on the application. Keep the disabled application so you can monitor it and make sure there is no suspicious behavior occurring on your account. The third recommendation is to closely monitor your bank account. Uber claims that your social security number - if you are a driver - and credit card information were not stolen; however, as proven through their actions, they are not a reliable corporation.

Uber's board is taking some drastic steps to try to fix their reputation and past mistakes. The most essential step Uber took revolves around changing their leadership; with a change in leadership, a new culture can be fostered for the corporation, hopefully leading to a more transparent and ethical company.[25] Uber fired the two individuals in charge of leading the incident, replaced the CISO, and replaced the current CEO.[26] The new CEO, Dara Khosrowshahi, states that he "commit[s] on behalf of every Uber employee that [they] will learn from [their] mistakes." Uber promises to "[change] the way [they] do business, putting integrity at the core of every decision [they] make and working hard to earn the trust of [their] customers." CEO Dara has asked Matt Olsen, founder of a cybersecurity consulting firm and former general counsel of the National Security Agency and director of the National Counterterrorism Center, to help him think through how best to guide and structure Uber's security teams and processes going forward.[27] Dara also strengthened controls and implemented extra security measures to protect unauthorized access to their cloud data storage accounts.[28] These first two actions show that Dara is raising the priority of security in the company. With new leadership, Uber is taking steps to mitigate their mistakes taken in response to the 2016 data breach. First, they notified all the drivers with stolen driver's license numbers and are offering the infected drivers free credit monitoring and identity theft protection.[29] Even though Uber has still not notified the affected riders, they are monitoring all the affected accounts and have flagged them for additional fraud protection.[30] Uber already stated that they are increasing security measures and strengthening controls. However, another recommendation is to increase employee training. Clearly, Uber's software engineers need some extra guidance specifically on how to secure and share code uploaded to third-party vendor sites. Hopefully, Uber will continue taking steps towards more honorable actions and prioritization of both security and their customers over themselves.

The recklessness of Uber's actions raises concerns for federal, state, and local government agencies and consumers. Having access to so much personal data including location and credit card numbers proves to be a large security risk for both customers and employees. Uber's past actions are a clear indication that they care more about protecting their reputation and revenue over running the business in an ethical and transparent manner. Uber lied in the past about the protection they have for customer-data and allowed employees to access private data for personal use. They have been accused of having a rule-breaking culture, partaking in sexual assault, being unfair to their employees, breaking FTC regulations, breaking California state laws, and are involved in countless civil suites. Until recent leadership changes, Uber has proven itself as an untrustworthy enterprise that uses its power to take advantage of users and drivers and continuously prioritizes itself over others. Even though Uber made many changes and claim that they are "leading their company into a different direction,"[31] it is too soon to say if consumers and employees alike can trust these promises; first, the new leadership must demonstrate through actions that they are truly implementing a cultural and administrative change.

Evaluating the Risks to the National Football League

Lukas Guericke

Written: October 2017
Published: January 2019

Abstract: This paper discusses the various types of risks that the National Football League (NFL) faces, not only its unique risks to its players and fans, but those that stem from the vast number of employees who have built careers around the operations and broadcast of American football. The author evaluates the risk landscape, including the safety of players, the risks arising from player conduct, and the risks of cyber and physical attacks.

Introduction

The National Football League (NFL) is a cornerstone of American culture. Many Americans dedicate their entire Sundays to the sport. The NFL generated $13 Billion dollars in revenue in 2016.[1] Sunday Night Football, the NFL's flagship show, is the number one rated primetime show for six years running.[2] Due to the massive revenues and popularity, the NFL incurs massive risks as it tries to reach as many fans as possible. The risks outlined in this analysis are the risks to the level of play given the sharp decline in youth football participation due to the scare of brain trauma, the harm to the NFL brand from personal conduct of players and the NFL's handling of scandals, and finally the cyber and physical attacks on NFL stadiums and NFL players. These three specific risks can be categorized into strategic risks, reputational risk, and external risks.

Strategic Risk

A major strategic risk to the NFL is the decline of youth football participation. This is a risk since people tune in on Sundays to see some of the best athletes in the world compete in one of the world's most physical games. When the sport reduces the sample size of players playing at the youth level, it has negative effects on the level of play at the professional level. This could contribute to lower popularity and viewership. A major contributor to declining youth participation is the risk of major injury in football, specifically, injury to the brain. A recent study showed that for people who played tackle football before the age of 12 doubled the risk of problems with behavioral regulation, apathy, and executive functioning. More shockingly, the same subject group saw the risk of developing depression triple.[3] This research and others like it are affecting how parents feel about their kid playing football from a young age. A study by the PPRI showed that 31% of parents would not allow their child to play football.[4] In addition, this number increases to 41% of parents who have more education than a high school diploma.[5] Given these statistics, the NFL should look at youth participation in football as a major risk to its strategy that relies on talent from the youth through college levels of play. Not only does the NFL lose potential superstars who generate millions of dollars for the league, but also it loses tens of millions of dedicated fans who have been watching and playing the sport since a young age.

How can the NFL mitigate some of this risk? The NFL needs to make the game of football safer and prove to parents that there is no more risk of head injury than any other contact sport. The NFL has admitted to the risk of brain damage in football[6] and has funded a program called "Heads up Football." This program is intended to maximize youth player safety and has been implemented in more than 7000 youth and high school programs.[7]However, the results of this program are mixed. The NFL claims that according to a recent study that the "Heads Up" program has reduced the risk of concussion while a New York Times review of the study showed that it actually did not reduce the risk of concussion. [8] The "Heads Up" program is new so there may be more data that are conclusive over time but at this point, the program is not doing much to help with participation in youth football. In addition to youth programs, the NFL has invested $60 million dollars into research and development of helmets that reduce the risk of head injury. At this point, all the modern helmets are still in the development phase but have received positive feedback from both players and brain trauma experts.[9] One of the highest performing helmets is being developed by a Seattle company started by a brain trauma expert from the Seattle Children's Hospital who got the company off the ground with a grant from the University of Washington. However, there are experts who claim that technology will not solve the brain trauma problem. Dr. Robert Cantu, a prominent brain trauma specialist, claims that a better way to protect players is rule changes that restrict contact to the head and neck area.[10] Since 2002, the NFL has made 47 rule changes that do just that but experts say that it needs to go further.[11] Given all that the NFL has done to mitigate the risk of traumatic head injuries, there needs to be more money and more transparency about head injuries and the effectiveness of certain programs and technologies. The NFL needs to work harder to regulate their sport to show parents that their kid's brains will be ok if they let them play the game. Otherwise, the NFL risks a lot of talent and many lifelong fans.

Reputational Risk

A major reputational risk to the NFL has been the conduct of players that represent the league. Star running back Adrian Peterson was suspended a year when child abuse charges were filed, Ray Rice was suspended two games for video of him dragging his unconscious wife out of an elevator in Atlantic City and then indefinitely when another video was released that showed Rice punching his wife unconscious. Fallen star Colin Kaepernick in the 2017 season so far does not have a job because he knelt during the national anthem to highlight racial disparity in the United States. Currently, there is a massive legal battle going on over the suspension of star running back Ezequiel Elliott who allegedly committed acts of domestic against his girlfriend. The NFL in recent years has also been the source of a number of cheating scandals that include Deflategate, Bountygate, and Spygate all of which got massive media attention. The NFL a source of income of nearly 2000 players and hundreds of coaches who are constantly in the spotlight for what they do on and off the field. For example, there have been reports of low ticket sales in the NFL this season due in part by the National Anthem protest that was the controversy at the beginning of the 2017 NFL season.[12] This presents a huge amount of reputational risk to the NFL's brand because the NFL cannot control all of the people affiliated with it. Just as any company assumes the risk of the actions of the employee, the NFL risks its reputation with every player, coach, or team executive. Not only is the NFL critiqued on the actions of its players but also critiqued by fans and the media on how the scandals are handled. For example, the NFL's handling of the Ray Rice scandal related to domestic violence was heavily critiqued by the media and fans for its stance on domestic violence. Leading the critique was Hannah Storm, an anchor for ESPN, who called into question the integrity of the NFL for the initial minimal two game suspensions for Ray Rice.[13]

The NFL needs to accept the risk of a scandal and accept the risk that it will probably happen on a yearly basis. However, the NFL needs a better risk management plan when these events do happen. Insensitive handling of domestic violence and child abuse will lose the NFL viewership and revenue along the way. Roger Goodell, the commissioner of the NFL, currently is the person who decides what the punishment will be in accordance with the NFL's collective bargaining agreement. However, to direct the risk away from the NFL, the NFL could institute a policy in which they hire independent lawyers and investigators to handle scandals and deal punishments. This moves some of the risk away from the NFL since the NFL and Roger Goodell since they cannot be blamed for the punishment and handling of the case. Additionally, critics blast the NFL for responding to public relations disasters instead of showing initiative. For example, the NFL was criticized that they only suspended Ray Rice indefinitely once the second, more graphic, video was leaked. The facts of the case were the same before and after the video release, Ray Rice knocked out his wife on the elevator. However, the video attracted much more media attention and was more of a public relations disaster than the initial suspension. This forced Goodell to suspend Rice indefinitely. This raised the legitimate question: why wasn't Rice suspended indefinitely once the original facts were confirmed? To avoid such a criticism again, the NFL should get out in front of public relations issues by suspending players once they find out about the issue instead of tying the length of suspension to media attention.

External Risk

Average NFL attendance is 68,400.[14] A terrorist attack on one of these stadiums is a massive risk that the NFL needs to address. NFL games are especially at risk since football is such a cornerstone of American culture. An enemy of the United States could potentially find one of the 32 stadiums a compelling target given their value to Americans. After the Paris stadium attacks in 2015, the NFL has further increased their security measures. The NFL requires NFL franchises to have certain security elements such as metal detectors, no liquids, and clear bags. The NFL also has security protocols approved by the Department of Homeland Security.[15] The NFL works with teams to continuously update their security and risk protocols and often hires expensive security consultants to help with the work. In an article published in Risk Management Magazine, the chairmen of the 2012 Super Bowl Risk Management Committee claim that with an event such as the Super Bowl that the bottom line comes secondary to making sure the event goes off without a hitch and preparing for potential threats.[16]

Another type of risk that the NFL takes on is the risk of cyber attacks. These risks can come in two forms, hacking of player's social media accounts and private lives and hacking into increasingly connected stadiums. The threat of their social media accounts being hacked is a major risk players take on by having social media accounts. Laremy

Tunsil's scandal right before the 2016 NFL draft is an example of this. Tunsil was projected to be one of the first picks in the NFL draft until a video was released from his Twitter account showing him smoking marijuana out of a gas mask bong. In addition, his Instagram account was hacked and screenshots of text messages showing the Ole Miss coach and Tunsil exchanging messages about receiving money from the football program. These two posts made Tunsil fall in the draft to pick 13. Examples like these show just how much risk the NFL and players take on by having social media accounts and not employing better password management. To reduce the risk of cyber-attacks on players, the NFL could institute trainings on how to properly use social media and how to pick passwords that are harder to crack. In addition, these trainings should have players delete any posts or tweets that could be taken out of context and used against them by the media. Another recommendation is that players should have a public relations plan in case something from their past gets leaked.

The other type of cyber risk is the risk to stadiums. Stadiums are increasingly implementing Internet of Things technologies (IoT) to increase their customer service and streamline operations. However, these types of technologies have the risk of being hacked. For example, newly built Levi Stadium boasts 1200 public Wi-Fi access points that allow fans to order food and drinks to their seat.[17] This is a massive risk for the NFL to undertake since 70,000 fans are at risk for their credit card and other personal information to be hacked by a hacker connected to the same public network. The NFL and stadiums have to ensure that the technologies that they are installing are very difficult to hack and to set up protocols for when they are hacked. These technologies need to be rigorously tested before access to the public is allowed. Levi Stadium, which has wholly embraced the idea that it can better fan experience using IoT devices, spent the year before opening testing out the devices making sure that they are safe for fan use.[18] Other stadiums with smaller budgets or working with older technology may not have the same luxury and need to be very careful about which technologies they implement.

Conclusion

The NFL is the world's most profitable league, a cornerstone of American culture, and an employer of hundreds of thousands of journalists, medical professionals, and others who make their living on the game. With the profitability and the notoriety of the NFL, the league has to address the risk to the NFL brand, players, and fans. The safety of players, the conduct of players, and the risk of cyber and physical attacks need to be evaluated by NFL executives. To some extent the league office is addressing these risks, however, I believe that they can go further. The NFL needs to make the game safer for players, better get ahead of scandals and player misconduct, and make sure that players are notified of the risks of their social media being hacked as well as make sure that the IoT stadiums of the future are rigorously tested for hacking and other breaches. These risks, if not addressed, will negatively influence ratings and revenues as well as endanger players and fans.

Operational Risk Challenges for the CDC

Elizabeth Crooks

Written: April 2018
Published: April 2019

Abstract: This paper discusses the major operational risks facing the Centers for Disease Control and Prevention (CDC) – threats of funding cuts, and the impact of political appointments and whims. If the CDC is unable to fulfill its mandate - to protect America from health, safety and security threats, both foreign and in the U.S – the potential impacts are significant, and could span the globe.

Introduction

The Centers for Disease Control and Prevention (CDC) works as part of the U.S. Department of Health and Human Services (HHS) in order to "protect America from health, safety and security threats, both foreign and in the U.S."[1] The CDC's mandate has expanded from originally battling malaria to a mission that is much larger in scope, covering a wide swath of public health issues, from global pandemics to emergency preparedness. The CDC must effectively fulfill its mandate, "to increase the health security of our nation," while grappling with two major challenges – first, carrying out its duties in the face of budget cuts, and secondly, being subject to political appointments and political shifts.[2] Neither of these challenges is unique to the CDC, as they are faced by many government agencies and departments, but are particularly striking in light of the crucial public health work carried out by the CDC.

Reduced Funding

In 2018, the primary challenge faced by the CDC is the increased risk of reduced funding and the impact a reduced budget would have on both operations and the ability of the agency to fulfill its mandate. The Trump Administration's proposed budget for the CDC released in February 2018 cut the CDC's budget by approximately twelve percent. The proposed budget, while setting aside money for some new initiatives, would reduce and eliminate a variety of programs including ones that cover Global Health.[3] The potential decrease in funding not only increases risks to operations – having enough money and people to maintain its programs – but also raises the risk of CDC employees looking for or departing for other jobs. Additionally, other countries may choose to lower their funding commitments to Global Health initiatives, in reaction to the U.S. reducing its funding levels. In advance of Congress passing a budget, the CDC told employees that it would likely be "discontinuing work in 39 of 49 countries where its Center for Global Health helps prevent, detect and respond to dangerous infectious disease threats."[4]

Ending Global Health programs would decrease the resources and preparedness required to execute a fast and efficient response to a crisis like a global pandemic. In order to have a well-deployed response to an outbreak, the necessary resources and infrastructure must already exist. Budget cuts would be "undercutting the very same programs created in response to the lessons learned after the Ebola epidemic – programs that catch and halt infectious diseases early."[5] The CDC is meant to prepare the U.S. for the risks that come with external events like pandemics and other emergencies, something that cannot be done with a limited budget. Shuttering programs means that the next time the agency has to staff up to deal with a crisis, the staff in place would likely have less experience, and be less familiar with existing resources and procedures. Coordination across agencies and countries will be crucial for whenever the next deadly outbreak occurs; and many experts already agree, "that the world is not prepared for the next big pandemic."[6]

Political Appointment

The second major challenge for the CDC is the risks that arise when its mandate and staff become entangled by politics. This is most apparent in the position of the director of the CDC - the job is a politically appointed position. Political appointees must serve long enough to be effective, and high turnover can dramatically influence the performance of a government agency. While this is a common area of risk across many governmental bodies, the unique risk for the CDC is the fact that a political appointment can have consequences for global health. Changing leadership due to a change of parties can lead to internal instability, reduced strategic direction, and inefficient reprioritization of goals.

The risk of the CDC director being a political appointee manifested in the January 2018 resignation of CDC Director Brenda Fitzgerald, a Trump appointee. Fitzgerald had "complex financial interests" that posed ongoing conflicts of interests, notably "investments in companies directly related to Fitzgerald's work, including thousands of dollars in drug and insurance companies."[7] The required recusal would have limited her ability to complete all of her duties as the CDC Director - Fitzgerald's resignation came approximately six months after her appointment. The political nature of the appointment combined with the short tenure has increased the CDC's risk of experiencing operational failures within the agency. For example, CDC policy analysts were told not to use certain, core words like 'fetus' and 'transgender' in budget documents, creating ambiguity for employees and partner organizations.[8]

Additionally, the lack of consistent and constant leadership can lead to weakened internal controls. Internal controls that are facilitated from the top-down require a common understanding across the organization, for "[without] such an understanding, there can be significant control weaknesses."[9] All government agencies with political appointees have to contend with this problem - the degree to which the CDC is politicized changes over time and often depends upon administrative turnover.

Political Priorities

The CDC must not only deal with the challenges accompanying having a politically appointed leader at the helm, they must also deal with their funding being tied to political views and goals. When an administration that does not believe in foreign outreach and aid is in charge, efforts working with other countries and prioritizing problems that emphasize overall global health will suffer. This is very clearly seen in the budget priorities set by the Trump administration, although the proposed budget was overruled by Congress. The recently passed budget bill contains another example of the risks created by political decisions. For years, the CDC was not allowed to use funds designated for injury prevention to study gun violence per the Dickey Amendment.[10] The language in the recently passed budget bill gives the CDC the authority to conduct the research, but there is no institutional support beyond that. This is a notably politically polarized issue, and the CDC must tread carefully in order to do its work effectively, but also navigating the political demands imposed on it.

Going Forward

The potential impact of the CDC being unable to fulfill its mandate during the next health crisis is high, and potentially spans the globe. The CDC can try to maintain itself as a more independent, scientific agency, and look to other agencies for alternative approaches. A potential change would be adjusting the tenure of the CDC Director. In order to increase the distance from politics and maintain a level of independence, the duration of the CDC Director could be shifted to span presidential administrations, similar to the FBI Director who has a term of ten years. A longer timeframe would increase the stability of the agency, preventing leadership from changing with every presidential election. This would also increase the independence of the CDC, ideally reducing the impact of political agendas, and global partners working with the CDC would benefit from increased leadership continuity.

Body Text

Body Text

Risks within Tesla, Inc.

Blake Franzen

Written: March 2018
Published: March 2019

Abstract: This paper discusses the growing areas of risk within the progressive automaker industry, of which Tesla and Elon Musk have become synonymous household names. As Tesla has grown, production goals have increased, and their customer base expanded, numerous allegations and control failures within the company have increased the levels of risk within the company.

Tesla was founded in 2003 by Martin Eberhard along with several other engineers located in California. The original purpose of the company was to develop a high performance electric car that would dominate the already struggling industry, which included General Motor's EV1 that had just been recalled and destroyed. Tesla used the then-recent surge in the use of lithium-ion batteries to develop the Tesla Roadster, a vehicle rivaling many in the high-end sports car industry, built at a lower cost and higher-level of sustainability. To raise startup funds, Tesla pursued Elon Musk for investment funding, as his success with PayPal and SpaceX had earned him a prominent reputation in Silicon Valley. Initially, Elon Musk joined Tesla as chairman of the executive board; he took over as Tesla's Chief Executive Officer in 2008.[1] In the subsequent ten years, Tesla skyrocketed to the forefront of the automotive technology industry and independent automaker market. As their prominence has risen, the company has been scrutinized in more detail across the various parts of the organization. Tesla has experienced control failures due to processes, systems, and external events; they will likely face increasing risks in the future as well.

In the three years between 2014 and 2017, Tesla accumulated financial losses of over $3.9 billion.[2] Over 75 percent of these losses came from operational expenses, more than half of which is from the 2017 fiscal year. Despite Tesla's failure to turn a profit over the last 15 years, the net worth of the company surpassed Ford, which has been around for nearly 12 decades. This raises the question of why Tesla - which fails repeatedly to be a profitable business - is still able to operate. The continuing success of Tesla is mostly due to their investors and consumer perception of the company; Tesla investors believe they will receive a return on their investments based on the anticipated future of the car industry.

The Tesla golden ticket to the future of the automobile industry is the Model 3, a low-cost, mass-produced electric car that has a production goal of 500,000 of in 2018.[3] To give some perspective, Tesla has managed to make an average of 20,000 vehicles in the last three years.[4] Given this challenging task, there have been some issues surrounding the controls put in place by the company to achieve this goal. In April 2018, production was halted at Gigafactory 1 (where the Model 3 is manufactured) for several days. This is the second time in the past two months production has been halted at Gigafactory 1.[5] The reason for the halt, according to Elon Musk, was to fix the manufacturing process, which relies heavily on automation. Elon Musk said he had underestimated the importance of humans in the process.[6] Production rates for the Model 3 have failed to reach the projected goal of 5,000 cars per week and instead have barely reached 2,500.[7] As a response to these shortcomings, Musk sent out an email in which he stated that the factories producing vehicles had been modified in such a way that would ensure that they could raise production rates up to 6,000 a week. This promise puts Tesla in an extremely risky position should they fail to meet this goal.

Building off their factory complications, the California Division of Occupational Safety and Health (Cal/OSHA) currently has two open investigations into the operations of these factories. The investigations pertain to workplace safety; one is regarding a worker breaking their jaw at the Fremont factory, and the other is about reporting workplace injuries.[8] The second investigation emerged from claims that Tesla had incorrectly reported workplace injuries as personal medical issues, therefore resulting in workers being uncompensated for recovery costs and other medical finances. In addition to these investigations, a complaint was sent to the National Labor Relations Board (NLRB) for workplace violations relating to these instances, as well as Tesla allegedly not allowing workers to openly discuss unionizing to the point that employees were being interrogated and threatened with termination.[9] All these claims come at a time when Tesla is aiming to ramp up production by numbers not seen before and indicate increased risk to the future success of the company. An official hearing for the complaints mentioned is scheduled for June 2018.

Tesla's issues with workplace safety, specifically the issues reported in the NLRB complaint, double as a process and system error. Currently, the company has added a third shift to all factories to ramp up production for the Model 3.[10] This increase in productivity is a substantial risk because it adds the possibility of future incidents like those already reported. Thus, it would be in the best interest for the company to review bottleneck points within the factory that could greatly contribute to the safety concerns addressed in complaints to mitigate them. Additionally, it may be wise to institute preventative and corrective controls in the form of policies that address issues within the workplace, such as the ones recently brought up by employees. Most of all, it is important that Tesla actively participate in discourse with its staff because these issues have been reported for several years which clearly shows that the quality upon which the factory operates must be improved.

In respect to the factory shutdowns, it is important that the company analyze how its competitors do business. Early on, Musk stated that he wanted to disrupt the automotive industry with sustainable and well-built vehicles. In doing so, he automated a substantial portion of the building process that proved to be a mistake. It would be worthwhile to note that other automakers have been in business for over a century and have decades to determine the best way to produce a car. Therefore, it would be beneficial for Tesla to assess their current manufacturing system and possibly employ similar concepts seen elsewhere within places companies like Toyota, Nissan, or Ford to ensure that they meet their production goals. Moreover, the future of the company hinges on its ability to mass produce the Model 3 because many other automakers such as Chevrolet and Kia have already manufactured electric cars that compete heavily with the Tesla models, at a much lower cost. If Tesla wants to disrupt the industry, it will have to meet the demand it already has and compete with these well-established companies.

Moving on, over the past three years there have been increasing amounts of fatal crashes involving Tesla cars. Of these, there have been roughly four that claim their "autopilot" feature was activated during the incident. The most recent of these crashes was a month ago in California.[11] The driver had their hands of the wheel as the car crashed and was given audio/visual warnings six seconds before crashing into a barrier. The autopilot feature in these vehicles has been a very touchy subject recently therefore making it important to know how it functions. Many believe that it serves as an alternative to a human controlling the vehicle but its purpose is to analyze moving objects to assess their risk to the vehicle and avoid situations that result in collisions. Currently, it is unable to analyze stationary objects and therefore will not issue commands if one obstructs the view of the vehicle resulting in the fatalities discussed above.[12] Assessing the risks involved with having an autopilot feature greatly factors into the success of the company.

Tesla's autopilot feature and the issues surrounding it have been a centerpiece within the media in the past few years. This poses a significant risk to their automated systems. The future of such features will rely heavily on their ability to adapt to the growing demand for products with this level of sophistication. Consequently, it would be beneficial for Tesla to investigate technologies such as Lidar, which can map its surroundings more efficiently or increasing the number of sensors on its vehicles to reduce the fatalities that clearly present a risk to consumers. Additionally, with respect to the most recent crash, the driver was warned multiple times before the collision occurred so a possible corrective control for that could be instituting a software change within the autopilot that can stop the vehicle if an operator of the vehicle fails to recognize dangers ahead. Beyond this, much of the risk involved falls in the hands of drivers being more aware of the limitations and warnings of current automotive technology.

For Tesla, 2018 has been and will likely continue to be a trying year given the risks and issues thrown their way. It is imperative that they come out the end of this year with a better understanding of how to reduce their current risks and shortcomings, without reducing innovation. Innovative technology will always have problems and it is our job to ensure we do the most to mitigate those issues.

The State Department's Leadership Vacuum

Elizabeth Crooks

Written: February 2018
Published: November 2018

Abstract: This research note discusses the implications of President Donald Trump and Secretary of State Rex Tillerson's key goals of reducing the size of the State Department. The resulting organizational and operational changes have both created a leadership vacuum and greatly increased the risks associated with potential process and control failures.

Introduction

The U.S. Department of State ("State Department") fulfills a variety of important functions related to our relationships with foreign nations. The State Department negotiates treaties and other agreements with other countries, advises the U.S. President, and is home to the country's diplomatic corps. These diplomats ensure that risks related to foreign relations are understood and mitigated to the best of their abilities.[1] The tenure of Secretary of State Rex Tillerson, the former Chief Executive Officer of ExxonMobil appointed by President Trump effective February 1, 2017, has been tumultuous in his first year for many reasons. Changes instituted by Secretary Tillerson at the State Department have created a leadership vacuum, and greatly increased the potential for process and control failures. By November 2017, over 60 percent of the State Department's top-ranking career diplomats (people who have spent their lives working in the State Department) had resigned.[2] The number of people who took the Foreign

Service exam, the main requirement to become a foreign service officer, dropped by more than half between 2016 and 2017.[3]

The lack of senior leaders makes decision-making both slow and difficult; high management turnover is also associated with declining morale. Due to the structural changes – hiring freezes, caps on the number of promotions, closing entire sections of the Department, and supporting budget cuts – Secretary Tillerson has implemented across the agency, there are higher risks of organizational instability and operational ineffectiveness in fulfilling its critical functions. Additionally, the potential for information systems control failures has increased due to the planned 'redesign' of the department's information technology system.

Organizational Changes

Secretary Tillerson's proposed organizational changes have been fairly well documented, such as recommending a decrease in the budget of the State Department by more than a third, cutting more than a thousand jobs, and reshuffling structures within existing bureaus and offices across the agency. One of the largest changes that Secretary Tillerson has focused a great deal of energy on is the reorganization plan of the State Department, which, according to former Secretary of State Madeleine Albright, "nobody seems to understand."[4] Tillerson has both changed the organizational structure and how policies are generated within the various bureaus of the department. For example, the former Office of the Cybersecurity Coordinator went from its own entity (under President Obama) to "consolidated and wrapped into the Bureau of Economic

Affairs' Office of International Communications and Information Policy"[5] and is now reportedly being merged into a hybrid "Bureau for Cyberspace and the Digital Economy." This rapid shifting of divisions has created potential control failures, as goals may conflict, processes may be unclear under new directions and outlook, and stability and communication may erode across the Department. In another example, the duties of special envoys to Pakistan and Afghanistan have simply been "returned to the South and Central Asia Bureau"[6] which creates the potential for failures in communication and understanding, when countries do not have dedicated foreign policy channels through which to ask questions, and for our diplomats to explain U.S. policies.

The reorganization has affected process controls explicitly in the way that policy is now drafted and there is the potential for failure if the appropriate experts are not being consulted in diplomatic processes. The State Department's Policy Planning Staff, which was first "created in 1947 by legendary diplomat George Kennan...supposed to be an independent source of analysis and often acts as a secondary opinion on policy for the secretary,"[7] has dramatically expanded in power. Secretary Tillerson is relying on the twenty-five person office "as the principle vehicle for day-to-day decision-making"[8] which has left other bureaus feeling shut out of the process, with the Policy Planning Staff closed off and unaccepting of new and interesting ideas.[9] These changes have created incompatible goals, where career diplomats are not able to utilize the controls in the shape of the traditional policy-making process, historically in place, and are running up against Secretary Tillerson's desire for a streamlined organization with fewer people and layers. This potential control failure around the policy process and communication gives a much greater likelihood of information failing to reach the appropriate decision-maker.

Information Technology Systems

The systems that Secretary Tillerson has identified for an upgrade are ones crucial to how the employees of the State Department function, namely, how they communicate with one another (via email) and how they manage the crucial information necessary to facilitate the workings of the foreign service (databases). The details of the upcoming changes to the information technology of the State Department are not currently public, although they are "expected to include switching State's email and related technologies to cloud-based services; a plan to merge databases; and helping diplomats overseas be more efficient."[10] Ostensibly, these changes are an opportunity for the federal agency to become more effective. However, if these directives are not meticulously planned in advance, there is large potential for operational risk failures. System outages during the migration of email servers to the cloud could result in disruption and even chaos, if at a fragile diplomatic moment. Merging databases (which would need to take into account system compatibility, types of data, what needs to be moved and what does not) could result in employees unable to access crucial information or are no longer able to find what they need quickly as a result. Procedures will need to be updated, as will staff training, and failure to do so will put the department operating below its ideal capacity. Green categorizes failures like these as "creating operational disruptions and impairment of the organization's value streams, diminishing efficiency and reducing capacity."[11]

Risk Mitigation

The best path for mitigating the potential control failures that exist as a result of the organizational restructuring is a clear delineation of departments. That means a structure that reflects the priorities the State Department has to balance, in order to fulfill our diplomatic obligations around the world. In order to mitigate the potential control failure of information not being communicated properly, there needs to be less uncertainty about organization of the department as a whole, how affairs are being handled and who is responsible for what duties. Included in this would be the appropriate staffing of bureaus within the department, as many leadership roles are currently empty, with vacant ambassadorships and "seven of the nine top jobs at the department will be empty" with the departure of another senior career official earlier this month.[12] Even the senior official who was in charge of the overhaul and redesign of the department stepped down in November of 2017, after "three months in the position" due to "strong differences over the redesign itself and the parameters for implementing it."[13]

Mitigation for the potential control failure in the information technology system of the State Department would be ensuring that the continuity plan covers the possibility of failure and options for an event like something breaking while everything is being moved to the cloud, or something being deleted from a database while maintenance occurs. Continuity plans are there to help ensure "that operations can be efficiently and effectively in the event of an event such as a power outage, flood, or fire."[14] Losing access to email or databases during system overhauls could be just as disabling as an outage due to an external event. There should be backups in place to failover and tests ahead of time, in addition to meticulous planning, in order to reduce the possibility of a failure to the furthest extent possible. If there is effective preparation ahead of time, the organization will be far more resilient and less prone to control failures in this area.[15]

The potential control failures outlined here are by no means the only ones facing Secretary Tillerson's State Department, especially as external event risks make up a large part of the State Department's responsibilities. Reducing the risk and mitigating these potential control failures would go a long way to ensure ability of the State Department to function well in a time of uncertainty, both at home and abroad.

Understanding SEC's Inadequate Internal Controls

Miranda Lin

Written: October 2017
Published: February 2018

Abstract: This paper discusses recent risk-related incidents at the U.S. Securities and Exchange Commission (SEC), and the apparent lack of adequate internal controls enforced within the organization. The author identifies some of the possible improvements to be made to the SEC's internal controls environment regarding their people, process, and systems.

Introduction

The U.S. Securities and Exchange Commission (SEC)'s mission is to "protect investors, maintain fair, orderly, and efficient markets, and facilitate capital information" by helping investors and the public understand publicly traded companies' past and current state, as well as directions for future development.[1] One of the most important platform the SEC uses to electronically collect data from companies is the Electronic Data Gathering Analysis and Retrieval (EDGAR) system, where companies send in information such as their income statements, and EDGAR performs "automated collection, validation, indexing, acceptance, and forwarding of submissions."[2] Containing such valuable data, EDGAR is a target for hackers by nature. On September 20 2017, the SEC disclosed through a public statement by its chairman Jay Clayton that a breach on EDGAR occurred sometime in 2016. Though detected in 2016, Clayton claimed that they did not conclude until

August of 2017 that the "software vulnerability in [their] test filing component of [their] EDGAR system...was exploited and resulted in access to nonpublic information," which "may have provided the basis for illicit gain through trading."[3] The SEC provided very limited information regarding the breach, leaving out details such as the exact month and date of breach and possible suspects, but there is something we do know: there are numerous improvements to be made to the SEC's internal controls environment regarding their people, process, and systems.

SEC Internal Controls Environment

This is not the first time the SEC has experienced problems with protecting sensitive data, and the likelihood future security complications based on their current state seems high. Vulnerabilities exist due to negligent behavior of select employees as well as seemingly weak risk management culture. For example, in 2014 it was discovered that some of the Commission's employees lost their laptops, which "may have contained nonpublic information." Additionally, there were situations where SEC employees "sent nonpublic information through non-secure personal email accounts."[4] Based on these incidents, it is reasonable to conclude that within the SEC there is insufficient attention paid to the principle of due care: "the conduct that a reasonable person will exercise in a particular situation in looking out for the protection of things or the safety of others."[5] To encourage employees to practice due care and to strengthen their risk management culture, the SEC needs to re-evaluate the "degree to which it is instilling risk management behaviors into its culture...and how thoroughly it is practiced at all levels of the organization."[6]

If the SEC's leaders can "embrace and demonstrate appropriate enterprise risk management behaviors," the trickle-down effect will allow its employees to follow the tone, thus encouraging employees to act in accordance to best practices.[7]

On the other hand, the SEC's process and procedural controls are also inadequate. For instance, though the SEC developed information security policies, they do not appear to fully adhere to these policies. The U.S. Government Accountability Office (GAO)'s assessment conducted on the SEC in 2016 revealed that the SEC's disaster recovery plans were not "fully reviewed, completed, or up-to-date."[8] Additionally, in the report published on July 27 2017, the GAO stated that the SEC did not update their "network diagrams and asset inventories...to...reflect [their] current operating environment."[9] This raise questions as to whether the SEC can fully account for the risks inherent to their organization if they do not have a complete picture of their technology environment to aid in the process. Evidently, the Commission does not have enough oversight over their policies to ensure that their information security plans are updated. To achieve this and to develop defined processes for the organization to follow, the SEC should utilize the RACI model (responsibility assignment matrix) to identify who is responsible for updating security plans, who is accountable for oversight and approval of plans, who to consult with over concerns, and lastly, who communicates out these plans and to whom. At the minimum, these security plans should be reviewed and updated annually. Plans and policies are only useful if they are current and complete; the process of completing and updating security plans can only be accomplished with sufficient controls in place.

Regarding the SEC's technological systems, opportunities exist as well for improvement. The risks associated with a weak technical infrastructure "is relative based on the domain in which it is operated and the jurisdiction in which it thrives."[10] In the SEC's domain, privacy is at the greatest risk, yet the GAO reported in both 2016 and 2017 that the SEC failed to "encrypt sensitive information while in transmission" as well as had "confidential information stored on servers."[11] Considering that data encryption is one of the most standard best practices for protecting data, the SEC's insufficiency in this area cannot be tolerated. Besides encryption, the agency also has issues with authentication and authorization, for it did not "consistently identify and authenticate users" and "authorize access to resources."[12] To address the issue of authentication, the Commission needs to ensure that multi-factor authentication is in place. Adding an extra layer of identity verification will certainly reduce the likelihood of unauthorized access to the most confidential databases. As for the issue of authorization, the SEC needs to act in accordance with the principle of least privilege to guarantee that "only the minimum necessary rights [will] be assigned to a subject" for "access to a resource."[13] Not only does applying the principle of least privilege prevent unauthorized personnel from accessing sensitive data they do not need, it also ensures that authorized personnel only have access to the data for as long as their work requires.

Further problems involving the agency's data infrastructure exist. The GAO discovered that "13 of 42 user accounts reviewed had the same default password in the three key financial systems' servers" and that the SEC "did not disable these 13 active user accounts although they had never been used." In addition, the SEC did not consistently "protect its network boundaries from possible intrusions."[14] With fragile network boundaries, weak authentication for user accounts, combined with unencrypted data, the SEC's environment is welcoming to both internal and external hackers alike. Essentially, the door is wide open to everyone. Another issue common across the public sector is the use of outdated software, and the SEC is not excluded. They use some software programs that are no longer supported by the vendor, meaning that the vendor has also stopped releasing regular patches to bugs in the system.[15] With financial systems being such a significant part of its operations, it is surprising that the SEC has not yet addressed the risks of unpatched software and in fact continues to use it. The numerous inadequacies in their infrastructure as described can be attributed in part to the lack of directive and automated control activities; thus, it is essential that the Commission creates procedures for upgrading outdated software and securing network boundaries, such as adding additional layers of firewalls if possible. An IT configuration standard for strong passwords and strong encryption of data is also necessary. Ultimately, these controls should be automated, where data encryption occurs automatically across all servers. Regarding passwords, users should be forced by the system to change the default password immediately after their account is issued, and should be forced to change their passwords periodically as well. Likewise, automatic system alerts should be configured to inform managers of user accounts that contain no activity for a reasonable period, so they can be checked, altered, or removed if no longer in use.

Recommendations

Externally, the SEC has voiced to provide "cybersecurity guidance to help...market participants protect their customers from cyber threats", but internally, the agency themselves could use some cybersecurity guidance.[16] There are reasonable information security improvements to be made. First, to keep the U.S.'s publicly traded companies' data secure in their database; the SEC needs to follow through with the enforcement of their own security policies. This means ensuring security policies & procedures, disaster recovery plans, network diagrams, and asset inventories are all complete and up to date. To do so, the agency needs stronger oversight over their projects. In particular, the SEC should use the RACI model to define and clarify all parties involved in each program, project, and plan. A re-examination of the technological systems also needs to be completed with stronger authentication, authorization, and encryption in mind. Specific directive and automated controls the SEC should review in their infrastructure include setting procedures for outdated software, establishing guidelines for stronger network boundaries, requiring strong, complex passwords on user accounts, leveraging the principle of least privilege for these accounts, implementing multi-factor authentication for confidential databases, and encrypting all information in servers. Lastly, the risk management culture throughout the SEC needs to be strengthened. The necessary culture change must come from the top; leading by example facilitates the improvement of employee behavior and adherence to internal controls. Employees often emulate the actions of leaders, and by doing so, the SEC could reduce and prevent situations such as negligently sending sensitive information over unsecured personal emails. With a strengthened risk management culture, behaviors that illustrate due care can and will be instilled into the agency. The SEC's important role as a watchdog over U.S. corporations is legitimate, but to support this role and set an example, they need to improve their own internal controls first. The agency receives and stores a significant amount of corporate information every year, and it is expected of them to implement strong controls to secure this confidential data and prevent unauthorized access and illicit use. By thoroughly re-examining their current situation and both identifying and managing risks, the SEC can reduce the likelihood of incidents like the 2016 EDGAR breach.

REFERENCES

Arrayent's Inherent Risks

[1] "Company Overview of Arrayent, Inc." *Bloomberg.* N.D. Accessed Nov. 2017 <www.bloomberg.com>.

[2] "Managing the Risk of IoT: Regulations, Frameworks, Security, Risk, and Analytics." *ISACA Journal,* 2017, pp. 19-16.

[3] Carlson, Eric L. "Phishing for Elderly Victims: As the Elderly Migrate to the Internet Fraudulent Schemes Targeting Them Follow." *The Elder Law Journal.* 2006.

[4] Searle, Annie. "Enterprise Risk Management." Informatics 312, Autumn 2017, Week #3A Slideshow, p. 7.

[5] "IoT Services Platform." *Prodea.* Accessed Nov. 2017 <www.prodea.com>.

Life-Critical Applications and Serverless Computing

[1] "Critical Infrastructure Sectors." U.S. Department of Homeland Security. 11 July 2017. Accessed Mar. 2018 <www.dhs.gov>.

[2] "Emergency Services Sector." U.S. Department of Homeland Security. 26 January 2018. Accessed Mar. 2018 <www.dhs.gov>.

[3] "911 Master PSAP Registry." Federal Communications Commission. 1 March 2018. Accessed Mar. 2018 <www.fcc.gov>.

[4] "E9-1-1 Public Safety Answering Points." Connecticut Department of Emergency Services and Public Protection. 1 August 2016. Accessed Mar. 2018 <www.ct.gov>.

[5] "History of 911." Industry Council for Emergency Response Technologies. n.d. Accessed Mar. 2018 <www.theindustrycouncil.org>.

[6] "2017 Key Enacted 911 Legislation." National Conference of State Legislatures. 22 January 2018. Accessed Mar. 2018 <www.ncsl.org>.

[7] "History of 911."

[8] *Ibid.*

[9] "Emergency Services Sector Cybersecurity Initiative." US Department of Homeland Security. 20 June 2017. Accessed Mar. 2018 <www.dhs.gov>.

[10] "Cyber Risks to Next Generation 911." US Department of Homeland Security. n.d. Accessed Mar. 2018 <www.911.gov>.

[11] "Policy Statement and Notice of Proposed Rulemaking In the Matters of 911 Governance and Accountability Improving 911 Reliability." Federal Communications Commission. 21 Nov. 2014. Accessed 5 March 2018.
<apps.fcc.gov>.

[12] Stephens, Joe, and Flaherty, Mary Pat. "Federal lawmakers call for stemming failures of 911 services." *The Washington Post.* 4 December 2012. Accessed Mar. 2018 <www.washingtonpost.com>.

[13] "NENA Next Generation 9-1-1 Security (NG-SEC) Information Document." National Emergency Number Association (NENA). 8 December 2016. Accessed Mar. 2018 <c.ymcdn.com>.

[14] "NENA Security for Next-Generation 9-1-1 Standard (NG-SEC)." National Emergency Number Association (NENA). 6 Feb. 2010. Accessed Mar. 2018 <c.ymcdn.com>.

[15] "Next Generation 9-1-1 Security (NG-SEC) Audit Checklist." National Emergency Number Association (NENA). 14 December 2011. <c.ymcdn.com>.

[16] "NENA Resource, Hazard and Vulnerability Analysis Information Document." National Emergency Number Association (NENA). 10 September 2016. Accessed Mar. 2018 <c.ymcdn.com>.

[17] "NENA Communications Center/PSAP Disaster and Contingency Plans Model Recommendation." National Emergency Number Association (NENA). 12 Nov. 2015. Accessed Mar. 2018 <c.ymcdn.com>.

[18] "Next Generation 911 (NG911) Standards Identification and Review." 911.Gov. March 2016. Accessed Mar. 2018 <www.911.gov>.

[19] "Emergency Services Sector Profile." US Department of Homeland Security. Nov. 2017. Accessed Mar. 2018 <www.dhs.gov>.

[20] Burgess, Matt. "What is the Internet of Things? WIRED explains." *Wired.* 16 Feb. 2018. Accessed Mar. 2018 <www.wired.co.uk>.

[21] "Public Safety Digital Transformation: The Internet of Things (IoT) and Emergency Services." European Emergency Number Association. 3 March 2016. Accessed Mar. 2018 <www.eena.org>.

[22] "Strategic Principles for Securing the Internet of Things (IoT)." US Department of Homeland Security. 15 Nov. 2016. Accessed Mar. 2018 <www.dhs.gov>.

[23] Boyd, Mark. "What Serverless and the Internet of Things Can Learn from Each Other." *The New Stack.* 4 May 2017. Accessed Mar. 2018 <thenewstack.io>.

[24] Butler, Brandon. "Serverless explainer: The next generation of cloud infrastructure." *Network World.* 3 April 2017. Accessed Mar. 2018 <www.networkworld.com>.

[25] "Serverless Computing and Applications." Amazon Web Services, Inc. n.d. Accessed Mar. 2018 <aws.amazon.com/serverless/>.

[26] Pariseau, Beth. "Serverless computing supporters ponder NoOps." *TechTarget*. 31 May 2016. Accessed Mar. 2018 <searchitoperations.techtarget.com>.

[27] Boyd, Mark. "The Road to NoOps: Serverless Computing is Quickly Gaining Momentum." *The New Stack*. 18 May 2016. Accessed Mar. 2018 <thenewstack.io>.

[28] Boeckman, Matthew. "Ops, DevOps, NoOps and AWS Lambda." 24 April 2015. Accessed Mar. 2018 <www.slideshare.net>.

[29] Duff, Steven. "When should I use AWS Lambda versus Amazon EC2?" 30 June 2016. Accessed Mar. 2018 <cloudranger.com>.

[30] Asay, Matt. "Convenience, not cost, is driving serverless adoption among developers." *TechRepublic*. 8 January 2018. Accessed Mar. 2018 <www.techrepublic.com>.

[31] "Azure Functions." Microsoft. n.d. Accessed Mar. 2018 <azure.microsoft.com>.

[32] "Cloud Functions." Google. n.d. Accessed Mar. 2018 <cloud.google.com>

[33] "IBM Cloud Functions." IBM. n.d. Accessed Mar. 2018 <www.ibm.com>.

[34] Hecht, Lawrence. "AWS Lambda Still Towers Over the Competition, but for How Much Longer?" The New Stack. 9 December 2017. Accessed Mar. 2018 <thenewstack.io>.

[35] "AWS Lambda." Amazon Web Services. n.d. Accessed Mar. 2018 <aws.amazon.com>.

[36] "Netflix & AWS Lambda Case Study." Amazon Web Services. n.d. Accessed Mar. 2018 <aws.amazon.com>.

[37] Asay, Matt. "Serverless architecture is the future, but we're not getting rid of containers just yet." *TechRepublic*. 11 January 2018. Accessed Mar. 2018 <www.techrepublic.com>.

[38] Butler, Brandon. "What is Amazon cloud's Lambda and why is it a big deal?" NetworkWorld. n.d. Accessed Mar. 2018 <www.networkworld.com>.

[39] Lardinois, Frederic. "AWS Greengrass brings Lambda to IoT devices." *TechCrunch*. 30 Nov. 2016. Accessed Mar. 2018 <techcrunch.com>.

[40] Foye, Brendon. "Base2Services deploys serverless computing on AWS for Victorian emergency services app." *CRN Australia*. 9 March 2017. Accessed Mar. 2018 <www.crn.com.au>.

[41] "Agero Works to Improve Driver Safety Using Amazon Web Services." Agero, Inc. 6 December 2016. Accessed Mar. 2018 <www.agero.com>.

[42] "What Is AWS Lambda?" Amazon Web Services, Inc. n.d. Accessed Mar. 2018 <docs.aws.amazon.com>.

[43] Foye, Brendon.

[44] Hatt, Nick. "AWS Lambda has been HIPAA Eligible for a Month, and it's Awesome." Redox, Inc. 28 Nov. 2017. Accessed Mar. 2018 <www.redoxengine.com>.

[45] Proffitt, Chris. "DPS: Cyberattack on city's communication system." *The Indy Channel.* 20 January 2015. Accessed Mar. 2018 <www.theindychannel.com>.

[46] Guri, Mordechai, Mirsky, Yisroel, and Elovici, Yuval. "9-1-1 DDoS: Threat, Analysis and Mitigation." Ben-Gurion University of the Negev. N.d. Accessed Mar. 2018 <arxiv.org>.

[47] Stone, Adam. "Emergency Agencies Prepare for Cyberbreaches to 911 Systems." *Government Technology.* 21 January 2014. Accessed Mar. 2018 <www.govtech.com>.

[48] "IAM Best Practices." Amazon Web Services, Inc. n.d. Accessed Mar. 2018 <docs.aws.amazon.com>.

[49] Venezia, Paul. "Murder in the Amazon cloud." *Info World.* 23 June 2014. Accessed Mar. 2018 <www.infoworld.com>.

[50] Bright, Peter. "Anonymous speaks: the inside story of the HBGary hack." *ArsTechnica.* 15 Feb. 2011. Accessed Mar. 2018 <arstechnica.com>.

[51] Criddle, Linda. "What is Social Engineering?" Webroot. n.d. Accessed Mar. 2018 <www.webroot.com>

[52] "What is social engineering?" Symantec Corporation. n.d. Accessed Mar. 2018 <us.norton.com>.

[53] Jones, Rich. "Gone in 60 Milliseconds: Intrusion and Exfiltration in Server-less Architectures." 28 December 2016. Accessed Mar. 2018 <media.ccc.de>.

[54] Frank, Blair Hanley. "AWS' Serverless Application Repository compounds its early advantage." *VentureBeat.* 21 Feb. 2018. Accessed Mar. 2018 <venturebeat.com>.

[55] "AWS Serverless Application Repository." Amazon Web Services, Inc. n.d. Accessed Mar. 2018 <aws.amazon.com>.

[56] Screenshot dated March 15th, 2018, showing a GitHub link as the sole means of viewing source code: <drive.google.com>.

[57] "Shared Responsibility Model." Amazon Web Services, Inc. n.d. Accessed Mar. 2018 <aws.amazon.com>

[58] "Multi-Factor Authentication." Amazon Web Services, Inc. n.d. Accessed Mar. 2018 <aws.amazon.com>.

[59] "IAM Best Practices."

[60] "System and Organization Controls 3 (SOC 3) Report." Amazon Web Services, Inc. 26 October 2017. Accessed Mar. 2018 <d1.awsstatic.com>.

[61] "System and Organization Controls 3 (SOC 3) Report."

[62] Hagopian, Matt. "Effective Emergency Response in AWS: LiveSafe." 27 Nov. 2017. Accessed Mar. 2018 <www.slideshare.net/AmazonWebServices/wps204effective-emergency-response-in-awspdf>.

[63] Brown, Jennings. "Facebook Expands Self-Harm Prevention Program That Monitors Users' 'Thoughts of Suicide.'" *Gizmodo*. 27 Nov. 2017. Accessed Mar. 2018 <gizmodo.com>.

[64] Ingram, Mathew. "Twitter Is Now Trying to Detect and Curb Abuse in Real Time." *Fortune*. 1 March 2017. Accessed Mar. 2018 <fortune.com>.

[65] Widner, Kasumi, and Busselle, Chris. "UPDATE: Helping Human Trafficking and Modern Day Slavery Victims Around the World." 12 January 2015. Accessed Mar. 2018 <publicpolicy.googleblog.com>.

[66] "AWS Certification." Amazon Web Services, Inc. n.d. Accessed Mar. 2018 <aws.amazon.com>.

[67] "App Review." Apple, Inc. n.d. Accessed Mar. 2018 <developer.apple.com>.

[68] "Tone at the Top and Third Party Risk." Ponemon Institute and Shared Assessments. May 2016.

[69] Banjo, Shelly. "After public outrage over worker treatment, Amazon's hiring a director of social responsibility." *Quartz*. 9 September 2015. Accessed Mar. 2018 <qz.com>.

[70] "Form 10-K 2018." Amazon.com, Inc. 1 Feb. 2018. Accessed Mar. 2018 <www.sec.gov>.

[71] "Leadership Principles." Amazon.com, Inc. n.d. Accessed Mar. 2018 <www.amazon.jobs/principles>.

[72] Sons, Susan, Jackson, Craig, and Russell, Scott. "Chapter 7: Proportionality." O'Reilly. October 2017. Accessed Mar. 2018 <www.safaribooksonline.com>.

Risks with BYOD in Government Agencies

[1] Ogie, Robert. "Bring Your Own Device: An Overview of Risk Assessment." EEE Consumer Electronics Magazine. Jan. 2016. Accessed Jun 2017 <www.ieeexplore.ieee.org>.

[2] *2016 Annual Report.* Cisco. Nov. 2016. Accessed Jun. 2017 <www.cisco.com>.

[3] "Feds: You Have a BYOD Program Whether You Like it or Not." *2015 Lookout State of Federal BYOD Report.* Lookout. Jun. 2015. Accessed Jun. 2016 <info.lookout.com>.

[4] Federal Chief Information Officers Council (CIO Council). *Bring Your Own Device: A Toolkit To Support Federal Agencies Implementing Bring Your Own Device (BYOD) Programs.* Accessed Jun. 2017 <www.cio.gov>;

Joanne E. Hale, "BYOD Policy Release." Office of Information Technology, State of Alabama. June 2016. Accessed Jun. 2017 <www.oit.alabama.gov>.

[5] "3 Keys to Mastering BYOD - IAPP Academy Session." International Association of Privacy Professionals. 2 Oct. 2013. Accessed Jun. 2017 <www.iapp.org>;

"Staff Mobile Phone Policy Pilot Program." Financial Policy Office, Harvard University. 2014. Accessed Jun. 2017 <www.policies.fad.harvard.edu>;

James Sherer and Melinda McLellan. "Privacy, Security, and Practical Considerations for Developing or Enhancing a BYOD Program." International Association of Privacy Professionals. 2015. Accessed Jun. 2017 <www.iapp.org>;

"IT Peers Share Advice on Effective 'Bring Your Own device'(BYOD) Strategies." Wisegate Community Viewpoints. Mar. 2017. Accessed Jun. 2017 < www.wisegateit.com>.

[6] "IBM: Sorry, Siri. You're Not Welcome Here." *InformationWeek*, Accessed <www.informationweek.com>.

Shadow IT and Organizational Risks

[1] "Shadow IT." Gartner. N.D. Accessed <www.gartner.com>.

[2] "FAQ: How Does Shadow IT Complicate Enterprise Regulatory Compliance?" *SearchCompliance.* Oct. 2012. Accessed <www.searchcloudcomputing.techtarget.com>.

[3] The Hidden Truth Behind Shadow IT: Six Trends Impacting Your Security Posture. Frost & Sullivan. Nov. 2013. Accessed <www.mcafee.com>.

[4] "Third Party Risk." Federal Deposit Insurance Corporation. Jun. 2013. Accessed <www.fdic.gov>.

[5] McCubbrey, Don. "What is Legal Risk?" *Boundless*. 2014. Accessed <www.boundless.com>.

[6] "Financial Risk." *Investopedia*. N.D. Accessed <www.investopedia.com>.

[7] "Reputational Risk." *Investopedia*. N.D. Accessed <www.investopedia.com>.

[8] Culey, Graham. "55 Percent of Net Users Use The Same Password For Most, If Not All, Websites. When Will They Learn?" *Naked Security*. 23 Apr. 2013. Accessed <www.nakedsecurity.sophos.com>.

[9] "The Hidden Truth Behind Shadow IT." McAfee. N.D. Accessed <www.mcafee.com>.

[10] Diana, Alison. "Bring Shadow IT Out of the Dark, Gartner Tells Tech." *EnterpriseTech*. 17 Jun. 2015. Accessed <www.enterprisetech.com>.

[11] Moyle, Ed. "5 Strategies to Combat Shadow IT." *SecurityCurrent*. 11 Sep. 2014. Accessed <www.securitycurrent.com>.

[12] The Hidden Truth Behind Shadow IT.

Smart Homes: Evaluating Risks and Being Smart

[1] "Technology Driving Innovation - The Internet of Things: The Next Mega-Trend." Goldman Sachs. N.D. Accessed 07 Dec. 2016 <www.goldmansachs.com>.

[2] "2015 State of the Smart Home Report." Icontrol Networks. Jun. 2015. Accessed 07 Dec. 2016 <www.icontrol.com>

[3] "A Guide to the Internet of Things Infographic." Intel. N.D. Accessed 07 Dec. 2016 <www.intel.com>.

[4] "2015 State of the Smart Home Report."

[5] Ibid.

[6] "Top 50 Home Automation Companies." Home Automation Info. N.D. Accessed 07 Dec. 2016 <www.homeautomationinfo.com>

[7] Smallwood, Philip. "Lighting, LEDs and Smart Lighting Market Overview." U.S. Department of Energy. Feb. 2016. Accessed 07 Dec. 2016 <www.energy.gov>

[8] Schroeder, Stan. "Smartphone-Controlled Light Bulb Raises $260,000 on Kickstarter." *Mashable.* 17 Sept. 2012. Accessed 07 Dec. 2016 <www.mashable.com>.

[9] Jing, Qi, Athanasios V. Vasilakos, Jiafu Wan, Jingwei Lu, and Dechao Qui. "Security of the Internet of Things: Perspectives and Challenges." SemanticScholar. Springer Science Business Media. 17 June 2014. Accessed 07 Dec. 2016 <www.pdfs.semanticscholar.org>.

[10] Ibid.

[11] Ibid.

[12] Kumar, Ajay. "Internet of Things (IOT): Seven Enterprise Risks to Consider." *TechTarget*, Mar. 2014. Accessed 07 Dec. 2016 <www.internetofthingsagenda.techtarget.com>.

[13] Prince, Brian. "Consumers Ready for Internet of Things, But Fear Data Privacy and Security Implications: Survey." *SecurityWeek.* 23 Jun. 2014. Accessed 07 Dec. 2016 <www.securityweek.com>.

[14] Stanislav, Mark, and Tod Beardsley. "Hacking IoT: A Case Study on Baby Monitor Exposures and Vulnerabilities." Rapid7. Sep. 2015. Accessed 07 Dec. 2016 <www.rapid7.com>.

[15] Storm, Darlene. "Of 10 IoT-connected Home Security Systems Tested, 100% Are Security Failures." *Computerworld.* 11 Feb. 2015. Accessed 07 Dec. 2016 <www.computerworld.com>.

[16] Jing, Qi.

[17] Storm, Darlene.

[18] Ibid.

[19] Weiner, Jonathan B. "The Regulation of Technology, and the Technology of Regulation." Duke University School of Law. 2004. Accessed 07 Dec. 2016 <www.scholarship.law.duke.edu>.

[20] Reidel, Daniel. "IoT Default Passwords: Just Don't Do It." Dark Reading. 13 Oct. 2016. Accessed 07 Dec. 2016 <www.darkreading.com>.

[21] Ragan, Steve. "Here Are the 61 Passwords That Powered the Mirai IoT Botnet." *CSO Online.* 03 Oct. 2016. Accessed 07 Dec. 2016 <www.csoonline.com>

[22] Reidel, Daniel.

[23] Ragan, Steve.

[24] Jing, Qi.

[25] Basenese, Louis. "Internet of Things: Five Barriers to Adoption." *Wall Street Daily.* 21 Dec. 2015. Accessed 07 Dec. 2016 <www.wallstreetdaily.com>.

[26] Price, Rob. "The Government Needs to Step in and save the Internet from Hacked Toasters." *Business Insider.* 25 Oct. 2016. Accessed 07 Dec. 2016 <www.businessinsider.com>.

[27] Ibid.

[28] Weiner, Jonathan B.

[29] Price, Rob.

[30] Basenese, Louis.

[31] Roe, David. "Top 5 Internet of Things Security Concerns." *CMS Wire.* 30 July 2014. Accessed 07 Dec. 2016 <www.cmswire.com>.

The Airline Industry's IoT Risks

[1] Mann, Jason. "The Internet of Things: Opportunities and Applications Across Industries." *International Institute for Analytics.* Dec. 2015. Accessed Nov. 2017 <www.sas.com>.

[2] Dalal, Raj. "Why The Aviation Industry Needs to Hurry Up With IoT Implementation." *Data Science Central.* 27 Oct. 2016. Accessed Nov <www.datasciencecentral.com>.

[3] "About Us." *Online Trust Alliance.* N.D. Accessed Oct. 2017 <www.otalliance.org>.

[4] Searle, Annie. "Enterprise Risk Management." Informatics 312. Information School, University of Washington, Week #3B Oct. 2017, Seattle, WA. Lecture Slides.

[5] Ibid.

[6] Ibid.

[7] Ibid.

[8] Ibid.

[9] Ibid.

[10] Ibid.

[11] "About Us." Tile Inc. N.D. Accessed Nov. 2017 <www.thetileapp.com>.

[12] Searle, Annie.

[13] "Tone at the Top and Third Party Risk." *Ponemon Institute.* 19 May 2016. Accessed Nov. 2017 <www.ponemon.org>.

[14] "About Us." Online Trust Alliance.

The Internet of Things: A Dark Precursor

[1] Turner, Vernon, Carrie Macgillivray, and Patrick Gorman. "Connecting the IoT: The Road to Success." IDC Corporate USA, Mar. 2017. Accessed Sep. 2017 <www.idc.com>.

[2] Osborne, Charlie. "Researchers Discover over 170 Million Exposed IoT Devices in Major U.S. Cities." *ZDNet.* 15 Feb. 2017. Accessed Sep. 2017 <www.zdnet.com>.

[3] "Mirai Botnet." New Jersey Cybersecurity & Communications Integration Cell. 28 Dec. 2016. Accessed Sep. 2017 <www.cyber.nj.gov>.

[4] Medical Device Security: An Industry Under Attack and Unprepared to Defend. Ponemon Institute. May 2017. Accessed Sep. 2017 <www.synopsys.com>.

[5] Velosa, Alfonso. "Competitive Landscape of IoT Platform Vendors." Gartner. 26 May 2017. Accessed Sep. 2017 <www.gartner.com>.

[6] Grisham, Preston. "U.S. Tech Industry Employment Surpasses 6.7 Million Workers." CompTIA. 29 Feb. 2016. Accessed Sep. 2017 <www.comptia.org>. 23 May 2017.

[7] Kushner, David. "The Real Story of Stuxnet." IEEE Spectrum. 26 Feb. 2013. Accessed Sep. 2017 <www.spectrum.ieee.org>.

[8] Kelley, Michael B. "The Stuxnet Attack On Iran's Nuclear Plant Was 'Far More Dangerous' Than Previously Thought." *Business Insider.* 20 Nov. 2013. Accessed Sep. 2017 <www.businessinsider.com>.

[9] *Budget of the U.S. Government Fiscal Year 2018.* Office of Management and Budget. Accessed Sep. 2017 <www.whitehouse.gov>.

[10] Petit, Jonathan. "How We Attacked Autonomous Cars at Security Innovation, Security Innovation." OnBoard Security. 4 Nov. 2015. Accessed Sep. 2017 <blog.onboardsecurity.com>.

[11] "Alert (ICS-ALERT-13-164-01): Medical Devices Hard-Coded Passwords." Industrial Control Systems Cyber Emergency Response Team, U.S. Department of Homeland Security. 29 Oct. 2013. Accessed Sep. 2017 <www.ics-cert.us-cert.gov>.

An Open Letter to Librarians: Ethical Imperatives in Post-Truth America

[1] Barthel, Michael. "Newspapers Fact Sheet." Pew Research Center. 15 June 2016. Accessed Mar. 2017 <www.journalism.org>.

[2] Balkin, Jack. Digital Speech and Democratic Culture: A Theory of Freedom of Expression for the Information Society. NYU Law Review, 79(1). 2004.

[3] Regan, Tom. 2005. "Introduction to Moral Reasoning," *Information Ethics*. Accessed Mar. 2017 <tomregan.free.fr>.

[4] "News | Definition of News by Merriam Webster." Merriam-Webster. n.d. Accessed Mar. 2017 <www.merriam-webster.com>.

[5] Dowden, Bradley and Swartz, Norman. "Truth." The Internet Encyclopedia of Philosophy. n.d. Accessed Mar. 2017 <www.iep.utm.edu>.

[6] Floridi, Luciano. *Information: A Very Short Introduction*. Oxford University Press. 2010. Accessed Mar. 2017 <www.lustiag.pp.fi>.

[7] "Democracy Statement." American Library Association. n.d. Accessed Mar. 2017 <www.ala.org>.

[8] "Selection and Withdrawal of Materials." Seattle Public Library. n.d. Accessed Mar. 2017 <www.spl.org>

[9] "Code of Ethics of the American Library Association." American Library Association. n.d. Accessed Mar. 2017 <www.ala.org>.

[10] Horrigan, John. "Americans' Attitudes Towards Public Libraries." Pew Research Center. 9 Sep. 2016. Accessed Mar. 2017 <www.pewinternet.org>.

[11] "Framework for Information Literacy for Higher Education." Association of College & Research Libraries. 2 Feb. 2015. Accessed Mar. 2017 <www.ala.org>.

[12] Ibid.

[13] Barclay, Donald. "The Challenge Facing Libraries in an Era of Fake News." *The Conversation*. 5 January 2017. Accessed Mar. 2017 <www.usnews.com>.

[14] Zuckerberg, Mark. 18 Nov. 2016. In Facebook [User Page.] Accessed Mar. 2017 <www.facebook.com>.

[15] "Facebook – Resources." Facebook. n.d. Accessed Mar. 2017 <investor.fb.com>.

[16] "Fake News Challenge." Fake News Challenge. n.d. Accessed Mar. 2017 <www.fakenewschallenge.org>.

Facebook and Google Data, Privacy and Transparency

[1] "Google and Facebook Tighten Grip on US Digital Ad Market." *eMarketer*. Sep. 21 2017. Accessed Feb. 2018 <emarketer.com>.

[2] Garrahan, M. "Google and Facebook Dominance Forecast to Rise." *Financial Times*. Dec. 3 2017. Accessed Feb. 13 2018 <www.ft.com>.

[3] McCarthy, T. (2017, October 31). "Facebook, Google and Twitter grilled by Congress Over Russian Meddling – As It Happened." Oct. 31 2017. *The Guardian*. Accessed Feb. 13 2018. <www.theguardian.com>.

[4] Nahon, Karine and Hemsley, Jeff. *Going Viral.* Polity. Nov. 2013.

[5] Lemley, Mark. "Terms of Use." *Minnesota Law Review.* Dec. 22 2006. Accessed Feb. 2018 <www.minnesotalawreview.org>.

[6] *Form 10-K: For the Fiscal Year Ended December 31, 2017.* Facebook. Feb. 2018. Accessed Feb. 2018 <www.facebook.com>.

[7] *Form 10-K: For the Fiscal Year Ended December 31, 2017.* Alphabet. Feb. 2018. Accessed Feb. 2018 <www.abc.xyz>.

[8] Kaye, Barbara and Medoff, Norman. *Just a Click Away: Advertising on the Internet.* Allyn and Bacon. Nov. 2000.

[9] *Form 10-K,* Facebook.

[10] *Search Engine Market Share Worldwide.* StatCounter. N.D. Accessed Feb. 2018. <www.gs.statcounter.com>.

[11] Lessig, Lawrence. *Code v2.* Creative Commons Attribution-ShareAlike. Dec. 5 2006. Accessed Feb. 2018 <www.codev2.cc>.

[12] "Facebook Ad Targeting." Facebook. N.D. Accessed Feb. 2018 <www.facebook.com>.

[13] "Google Ads." Google. N.D. Accessed Feb. 2018 <www.google.com>.

[14] Form 10-K, Alphabet.

[15] *Form 10-K,* Facebook.

[16] Ibid.

[17] Birchler, Urs and Bütler, Monika. *Information Economics.* Routledge, Jul. 2007.

[18] Lemly, Mark.

[19] Ibid.

[20] "Facebook Terms." Facebook. Jan. 30 2015. Accessed Feb. 2018 <www.facebook.com>.

[21] "Google Privacy & Terms." Google. Oct. 25 2017. Accessed Feb. 2018 <www.google.com>.

[22] Justine Rapp, Ronald Paul Hill, Jeannie Gaines & R. Mark Wilson. "Advertising and Consumer Privacy: Old Practices and New Challenges." *Journal of Advertising Volume 38, 2009 Issue 4.* 2009.

[23] Richards, Jef I. "Legal Potholes on the Information Superhighway." *Journal of Public Policy & Marketing, Vol. 16, No. 2.* Sep. 1997.

[24] "EU GDPR Site Overview." EUGDPR.org. N.D. Accessed Feb. 2018 <www.edugdpr.org>.

[25] Jolly, Ieuan. "Data Protection in the United States: Overview." Loeb & Loeb LLP, Thomson Reuters. Jul. 2017. Accessed Feb. 2018 <www.content.next.westlaw.com>.

[26] Bennett, Steven C. "The Right to Be Forgotten: Reconciling EU and U.S. Perspectives." *Berkeley Journal of International Law Volume 30, Issue 1.* 2012. Accessed Feb. 2018 <www.scholarship.law.berkeley.edu>.

[27] Anderson, Horace E. "The Privacy Gambit: Toward a Game Theoretic Approach to International Data Protection." *Vanderbilt Journal of Entertainment and Technology Law Review.* Jan. 2006. Accessed Feb. 2018 <www.digitalcommons.pace.edu>.

[28] *Form 10-K*, Facebook.

[29] *Form 10-K*, Alphabet.

[30] "GDPR Regulation." EUGDPR.org. N.D. Accessed Feb. 2018 <ww.eugdpr.org>.

[31] Zittrain, Jonathan. "The Future of the Internet and How to Stop It." Yale University Press & Penguin UK. 2008. Accessed Feb. 2018 <nrs.harvard.edu>.

[32] "United States v. Microsoft Corp." SCOTUSBlog. 27 Feb. 2018. Accessed Mar. 2018 <www.scotusblog.com>.

[33] Albrecht, Jan Philipp."How the GDPR Will Change the World." *European Data Protection Law Review.* 2016. Accessed Feb. 2018 <www.lexxion.eu>.

[34] Bennett, Steven.

[35] Bamberger, Kenneth and Mulligan, Deirdre. "Privacy on the Book and on the Ground." *Berkeley Law Scholarship Review.* Jan. 2010. Accessed Feb. 2018 <www.scholarship.law.berkeley.edu>.

[36] Ibid.

[37] Morozov, E. (2013). To Save Everything, Click Here: The Folly of Technological Solutionism. New York: Public Affairs.

[38] Ibid.

[39] Bertot, John Carlo, Paul T. Jaeger and Justin M. Grimes. "Promoting Transparency And Accountability Through Icts, Social Media, And Collaborative Government." *Transforming Government: People, Process and Policy.* 2012.

[40] Ibid.

[41] Nahon and Hemsley.

[42] Vaccaro, Antonio, and Peter Madsen. "Corporate Dynamic Transparency: The New ICT-Driven Ethics?" *Ethics and Information Technology.* Apr. 3 2009.

[43] Ibid.

[44] "Facebook Transparency Report." Facebook. N.D. Accessed Feb. 2018 <www.transparency.facebook.com>.

45 "Google Transparency Report." Google. N.D. Accessed Feb. 2018 <transparencyreport.google.com>.

46 Stretch, Colin. "Global Government Requests Report." Aug. 27 2013. Accessed Feb. 2018 <www.newsroom.fb.com>.

47 "Google Transparency Report." Google.

48 "Explore Your Activity Log." Facebook. N.D. Accessed Mar. 2018 <www.facebook.com>.

49 "How Can I Download A Copy Of My Facebook Data?" Facebook. N.D. Accessed Mar. 2018 <www.facebook.com>.

50 "My Activity." Google. N.D. Accessed Mar. 2018 <myactivity.google.com>.

51 Kaptein, Muel and Schwartz, Mark S. "The Effectiveness of Business Codes: A Critical Examination of Existing Studies and the Development of an Integrated Research Model." Jan. 2008. *Journal of Business Ethics.*

52 Ibid.

53 "FAQs." Facebook Investor Relations. Accessed Mar. 2018 <investor.fb.com>.

54 "Facebook Code of Conduct." Facebook. N.D. Accessed Mar. 2018 <www.facebook.com>.

55 "Google: Our Company." Google. N.D. Accessed Feb. 2018 <www.google.com>.

56 "Google Code of Conduct." Alphabet, Inc. Oct. 12 2017. Accessed Feb. 2018 <www.abc.xyz>.

57 Nahon and Hemsley.

58 Birchler and Bütler.

59 Balkin, Jack. "Digital Speech and Democratic Culture: A Theory of Freedom of Expression for the Information Society." *New York University Law Review.* Apr. 2004. Accessed Feb. 2018 <www.nyulawreview.org>.

60 "Facebook Privacy," Facebook.

61 "Google Privacy & Terms," Google.

62 Porter, Eduardo. "Your Data Is Crucial to a Robotic Age. Shouldn't You Be Paid for It?" *New York Times.* 6 Mar. 2018. Accessed Mar. 2018 <www.nytimes.com>.

63 "Government, Regulation and the Social Safety Net." Pew Research Center. Oct. 5 2017. Accesses Mar. 2018 <www.people-press.org>.

Healthcare IT's Insider and Outsider Threats

[1] "Healthcare and Public Health Sector." *Department of Homeland Security.* 11 Jul 2017. Accessed May 2018. <www.dhs.gov>

[2] *Healthcare and Public Health Sector-Specific Plan.* Department of Homeland Security. May 2016. Accessed May 2018. <www.dhs.gov>

[3] *Ibid.*

[4] Black, Ryan. " March's Reported Data Breaches: Another 120,000 Patients at Risk (So Far)." *Healthcare Analytics News.* 2 Apr 2018. Accessed May 2018. <www.hcanews.com>

[5] *2018 Data Breach Investigations Report, 11th Edition.* Verizon. Apr 2018. Accessed May 2018. <www.verizonenterprise.com>.

[6] Jay, Jay. "Healthcare sector suffered more than half of all cyber-attacks in 2017." *SC Media.* 4 May 2018. Accessed May 2018. <www.scmagazineuk.com>

[7] *2018 Data Breach Investigations Report, 11th Edition.* Verizon. Apr 2018. Accessed May 2018. <www.verizonenterprise.com>

[8] *Ibid.*

[9] Donovan, Fred. "Most Healthcare Workers Admit to Non-Secure Healthcare Data Sharing." *Biscom.* 21 May 2018. Accessed May 2018. <www.biscom.com>.

[10] *Protenus Breach Barometer Report.* Protenus. 3 May 2018. Accessed May 2018. <protenus.com>

[11] Moeller, Robert. *COSO Enterprise Risk Management.* John Wiley & Sons, Inc. 2011, p. 11.

[12] *Ibid.*

[13] U.S. Department of Defense Inspector General. *Protection of Patient Health Information at Navy and Air Force Military Treatment Facilities.* 2 May 2018. Accessed May 2018. <media.defense.gov>

[14] *Ibid.*

[15] *Ibid.*

[16] The Office of Management and Budget. *Federal Cybersecurity Risk Determination Report and Action Plan.* May 2018. Accessed May 2018. <www.whitehouse.gov>

[17] DOD, *Protection of Patient Health Information at Navy and Air Force Military Treatment Facilities.*

[18] The Office of Management and Budget. *Federal Cybersecurity Risk Determination Report and Action Plan.* May 2018. Accessed May 2018. <www.whitehouse.gov>

[19] Moeller, Robert. *COSO Enterprise Risk Management.* John Wiley & Sons, Inc. 2011.

[20] Perlroth, Nicole and Sanger, David E. "White House Eliminates Cybersecurity Coordinator Role." *The New York Times.* 15 May 2018. Accessed May 2018. <www.nytimes.com>

[21] OMB, *Federal Cybersecurity Risk Determination Report and Action Plan.*

[22] Moeller, Robert.

[23] Dorch, Sheryl. " Merlin International & Ponemon Institute Cybersecurity Study Signals Dangerous Diagnosis for Healthcare Industry." *BusinessWire.* 12 Mar 2018. Accessed May 2018. <www.businesswire.com>

[24] *Ibid*

[25] Jay, Jay. "Healthcare sector suffered more than half of all cyber-attacks in 2017." *SC Media.* 4 May 2018. Accessed May 2018. <www.scmagazineuk.com>

[26] Davis, Jessica. "When medical devices get hacked, hospitals often don't know it." *Healthcare IT News.* 11 May 2018. Accessed May 2018. <www.healthcareitnews.com>

[27] Snell, Elizabeth. "How IoT Impacts Medical Device Cybersecurity Considerations." *Health IT Security.* 29 Nov 2017. Accessed May 2018. <healthitsecurity.com>

[28] *Ibid.*

[29] Warner, Mark, et al. *Internet of Things Cybersecurity Improvement Act of 2017. S. 1691.* U.S. Senate. 1 Aug 2017. Accessed May 2018. <www.congress.gov>.

[30] *Healthcare and Public Health Sector-Specific Plan.* Department of Homeland Security. May 2016. Accessed May 2018. <www.dhs.gov>

[31] Fox, Bill. "How to protect patient data that's being shared widely." *Health Data Management.* 25 May 2018. Accessed May 2018. <www.healthdatamanagement.com>.

[32] Osborne, Charlie. "US hospital pays $55,000 to hackers after ransomware attack." *ZDNet.* 17 Jan 2018. Accessed May 2018. <www.zdnet.com>.

[33] Ibid.

[34] *2018 Data Breach Investigations Report, 11th Edition.* Verizon. Apr 2018. Accessed May 2018. <www.verizonenterprise.com/verizon-insights-lab/dbir/>

[35] Healthcare Cybersecurity and Communications Integration Center. *Report on Ongoing SamSam Ransomware Campaigns.* 30 Mar 2018. Accessed May 2018. <www.aha.org>.

Information Security in the Rise of E-Commerce

[1] "Number of Active Amazon Customer Accounts Worldwide from 1st Quarter 2013 to 1st Quarter 2016". Statista. 2016. Accessed 28 Nov. 2017 <www.statista.com>.

[2] Jolly, Ieuan. "Data Protection in the United States: Overview". *Thomson Reuters*. 01 July 217. Accessed 20 Nov. 2017 <content.next.westlaw.com>.

[3] "Desktop Retail E-Commerce Sales in the United States from 2002 to 2016". Statista. 2016. Accessed 25 Nov. 2017 <www.statista.com>.

[4] Orendorff, Aaron. "Global Ecommerce Statistics [Infographic] and 10 International Growth Trends You Need to Know". Shopify Plus. 1 Sept. 2017. Accessed 24 Nov. 2017 <www.shopify.com >.

[5] "Connected Commerce is Creating Buyers Without Borders". Nielsen. 20 Jan. 2016. Accessed 30 Nov. 2017 <www.nielsen.com>.

[6] *2017 Q3 Cybercrime Report.* ThreatMetrix. 2017. Accessed 25 Nov. 2017 <www.threatmetrix.com>.

[7] Molitor, Kerri. "How to Protect Your E-commerce Site from Cyber Attacks". Liquid Web. n.d. Accessed 26 Nov. 2017 <www.liquidweb.com>.

[8] Stambor, Zak. "How much did Amazon's outage cost the online giant?" Digital Commerce 360. 11 Mar. 2016. Accessed 30 Nov. 2017 <www.digitalcommerce360.com>.

[9] "Cross-site Scripting (XSS) Attack". Acunetix. n.d. Accessed 25 Nov. 2017 <www.acunetix.com>.

[10] "Who We Are". eBay. n.d. Accessed 30 Nov. 2017 <www.ebayinc.com

[11] Finkle, Jim, et al. "EBay asks 145 million users to change passwords after cyber attack". Reuters. 21 May 2014. Accessed 19 Nov. 2017 <www.reuters.com>.

[12] Quittner, Jeremy. "How the Once Impregnable EBay Fell Victim to Hackers (And You Can too)". Inc. 30 May 2014. Accessed 30 Nov. 2017 <www.inc.com/jeremy-quittner/new-details-emerge-on-ebay-hack-attack.html>.

[13] "Amazon.com's Third Party Sellers Hit By Hackers". Fox Business. 10 Apr. 2017. Accessed 19 Nov. 2017 <www.foxbusiness.com>.

[14] "Managing Payment Security". PCI Security Standards Council. n.d. Accessed 25 Nov. 2017 <www.pcisecuritystandards.org

[15] "FTC Welcomes Revised OECD Guidelines for E-commerce". Federal Trade Commission. 4 Apr. 2016. Accessed 25 Nov. 2017 <www.ftc.gov>.

[16] *Electronic Commerce: Selling Internationally.* Federal Trade Commission. Mar 200. Accessed 25 Nov. 2017 <www.ftc.gov>.

[17] *Framework for Improving Critical Infrastructure Cybersecurity.* National Institute of Standards and Technology. 12 Feb. 2014. Accessed 25 Nov. 2017 <www.nist.gov>.

[18] *Tone at the Top and Third Party Risk.* Ponemon Institute LLC and Shared Assessments. May 2016. Accessed 31 Oct. 2017 <sharedassessments.org>.

[19] "65% of Top 100 Retail Domains are at Risk of Single DNS Provider Outages". DNS Made Easy. 16 Nov. 2016. Accessed 1 Dec. 2017 <social.dnsmadeeasy.com>.

[20] "ThreatMetrix Study Finds Nearly 40 Percent of Retail Organizations Have No Online Fraud Prevention". ThreatMetrix. 21 Mar. 2013. Accessed 25 Nov. 2017 <www.threatmetrix.com>.

Operational Risk Challenges to the U.S. Election Infrastructure

[1] Padgett, Tim. "Mob Scene in Miami." *Time Magazine.* 26 Nov. 2000. Accessed May 2018 <www.time.com>.

[2] "Bush v. Gore Law Case" *Encyclopaedia Britannica.* 16 Nov. 2017. Accessed May 2018 <www.britannica.com>.

[3] "Help America Vote Act." U.S. Election Assistance Commission. N.D. Accessed May 2018 <www.eac.gov>.

[4] "Critical Infrastructure Sectors." U.S. Department of Homeland Security. N.D. Accessed May 2018 <www.dhs.gov>.

[5] *Starting Point: U.S. Election Systems as Critical Infrastructure.* U.S. Election Assistance Commission. Jun. 2017. Accessed May 2018 <www.eac.gov>.

[6] "AB-182 California Voting Rights Act of 2001." California Legislative Information. 26 Jan. 2015. Accessed May 2018 <leginfo.legislature.ca.gov>.

[7] "Computer Technologists' Statement on Internet Voting." Verified Voting Foundation, Inc. Sep. 2012. Accessed May 2018 <www.verifiedvoting.org>.

[8] "Types of Voting Equipment." National Conference of State Legislatures. Apr. 2018. Accessed May 2018 <www.ncsl.org>.

[9] *Ibid.*

[10] "How the Vote Hacking Was Done at DefCon25." AlienVault. 1 Aug. 2017. Accessed May 2018 <www.alienvault.com>.

[11] Cohn, Jennifer. "What Is the Latest Threat To Democracy? Bar-Codes and Ballot Marking Devices A.K.A. 'Electronic Pencils.'" *Medium*. 6 Mar. 2018. Accessed May 2018 <www.medium.com>.

[12] "Computer Technologists' Statement on Internet Voting."

[13] Hasen, Richard L. "Scalia's Goal of Unwinding Voter Protection is Becoming a Reality." *Talking Points Memo*. 2 Apr. 2018. Accessed May 2018 <www.talkingpointsmemo.com>.

[14] Kurtz, David. "Watch This One Very Closely." *Talking Points Memo*. 31 May 2018. Accessed May 2018 <www.talkingpointsmemo.com>.

[15] *Government Facilities Sector-Specific Plan An Annex to the NIPP 2013*. U.S. Department of Homeland Security. 2015. Accessed May 2018 <www.dhs.gov>.

[16] Moeller, Robert R. *COSO Enterprise Risk Management: Understanding the New Integrated ERM Framework*. Wiley. Jul. 2007.

[17] "Computer Technologists' Statement on Internet Voting."

[18] Zetter, Kim. "The Myth of the Hacker-Proof Voting Machine." *The New York Times*. 21 Feb. 2018. Accessed May 2018 <www.nytimes.com>.

[19] Konst, Stefan. "Secure Log Files Based on Cryptographically Concatenated Entries." Institute of Theoretical Computer Science, *Technische Universität Braunschweig*. Aug. 2000. Accessed May 2018 <www.konst.de>.

[20] "Computer Technologists' Statement on Internet Voting."

[21] "ZT595 ATM Keypad, Encrypted Keypad." SZZT Electronics Co. N.D. Accessed May 2018 <www.szztelectronics.com>.

Privacy in the Age of Big Data

[1] Cukier, Kenneth. "Data, Data Everywhere." *The Economist*. 25 Feb. 2010. Accessed Dec. 2017 <www.economist.com>

[2] Tene, Omer & Jules Polonetsky. *Privacy in the Age of Big Data: A Time for Big Decisions*. 2012.

[3] Warren, Cory. "What is Personally Identifiable Information (PII)?" Life Lock. 6 Sep. 2017. Accessed Dec. 2017 <www.lifelock.com>.

[4] Matuga, Jim. "How does Facebook advertising work?" *The State Journal*. 4 Dec. 2017. Accessed Dec. 2017 <www.theet.com>.

[5] "We want you to understand what data we collect and use." Google. N.D. Accessed Dec. 2017 <privacy.google.com>.

[6] "How Cookies Track You on the Web." Inflection. Accessed Dec. 2017 <inflection.com>.

[7] Casandra Campbell. "Relax, advertising on Facebook Just Got a Lot Easier." *Shopify Blogs*. 15 Jan. 2016. Accessed Dec. 2017 <www.shopify.com>.

[8] Hill, Simon. "How much do online advertisers really know about you? We asked an expert." *Digital Trends*. 27 Jun. 2015. Accessed Dec. 2017 <www.digitaltrends.com>.

[9] Ibid.

[10] Naylor, Brian. "Firms are Buying, Sharing Your Online Info. What Can You Do About It?" *NPR*. 11 Jul. 2016. Accessed Dec. 2017 <www.npr.org>.

[11] McCoy, Kevin. "Target to pay $18.5M for 2013 data breach that affected 41 million consumers." *USA Today*. 23 May 2017. Accessed Dec. 2017 <www.usatoday.com>

[12] Selyukh, Alina. "Every Yahoo Account That Existed In Mid-2013 Was Likely Hacked." *NPR*, Oct.3, 2017. Accessed Dec. 2017 <www.npr.org>.

[13] McCoy, Kevin. "Equifax hit with at least 23 class-action lawsuits over massive cyberbreach." *USA Today*. 11 Sep. 2017. Accessed Dec. 2017 <www.usatoday.com>.

[14] Hill, Kashmir. "'God View': Uber Allegedly Stalked Users For Party-Goers' Viewing Plesure." *Forbes*. 3 Oct. 2014. Accessed Dec. 2017 <www.forbes.com>.

[15] "Snowden leaks: NSA 'hacked Google and Yahoo data links'." *BBC*. 13 Oct. 2013. Accessed Dec. 2017 <www.bbc.com>.

[16] Duhigg, Charles. "How Companies Learns Your Secrets." *New York Times*, Feb.16, 2012. Accessed Dec. 2017 <www.nytimes.com>.

[17] Greguras, Fred. "Legal Issues In Big Data: 2017." *Water Online*. 29 Jun. 2017. Accessed Dec. 2017 <www.wateronline.com>.

[18] Duhigg, Charles.

[19] "Big Data: A Tool for Inclusion or Exclusion? Understanding the Issues." Federal Trade Commission. Jan. 2016. Accessed <www.ftc.gov>.

[20] The EU General Data Protection Regulation (GDPR). ND. Accessed Dec. 2017 <eugdpr.org>.

[21] "Big Data: A Tool for Inclusion or Exclusion? Understanding the Issues."

[22] Treglia, Stephen. "Compliant does not equal protected: our false sense of security." CSO Online, Oct.22, 2015 Accessed Dec. 2017 <www.csoonline.com>.

[23] UW CISO Office, *Assumption of Breach*, UW CISO Office. Accessed Dec. 2017 <ciso.uw.edu>.

[24] Duhigg, Charles.

[25] Singer, Natasha. "Consumer Data, but Not for Consumers." *New York Times*. 21 Jul 2012. Accessed Dec. 2017 <www.nytimes.com>.

[26] "Google privacy changes 'in breach of EU law'." *BBC*. 8 Mar. 2012 Accessed Dec. 2017 <www.bbc.com>.

[27] "5 Ways to surf Internet without leaving a digital trace." *GIZBOT*. Nov.23, 2017. Accessed Dec. 2017 <www.gizbot.com>.

Risks of Fake News to the American Democracy

[1] "Definition of "fake news" - English Dictionary." Fake news Definition in the Cambridge English Dictionary. Accessed Dec. 2017 <dictionary.cambridge.org>.

[2] Ritchie, Hannah, and Special To CNBC.com. "Read all about it: The fakest news stories of 2016." *CNBC*. 30 Dec. 2016. Accessed Dec. 2017 <www.cnbc.com>.

[3] Silverman, Craig. "This Analysis Shows How Viral Fake Election News Stories Outperformed Real News On Facebook." *BuzzFeed*. 16 Nov. 2016. Accessed Dec. 2017 <www.buzzfeednews.com>.

[4] Shearer, Elisa, and Jeffrey Gottfried. "News Use Across Social Media Platforms 2017." *Pew Research Center's Journalism Project*. 7 Sep. 2017. Accessed Dec. 2017 <www.journalism.org>.

[5] Velshi, Ali. "How Fake News Makes Money." *NBC News*. 14 Jun. 2017. Accessed Dec. 2017 <www.nbcnews.com>.

[6] Timberg, Craig. "Russian propaganda effort helped spread 'fake news' during election, experts say." *The Washington Post*. 24 Nov. 2016. Accessed Dec. 2017 <www.washingtonpost.com>.

[7] Ohlheiser, Abby. "Analysis | This is how Facebook's fake-news writers make money." *The Washington Post*. 18 Nov. 2016. Accessed Dec. 2017 <www.washingtonpost.com>.

[8] "The Fake News Machine: Inside A Town Gearing Up For 2020. *CNN Money*. 13 Sep. 2017. Accessed Dec. 2017 <www.money.cnn.com>.

[9] "Constitute". *Constituteproject.Org*. 2017. Accessed Dec. 2017 <www.constituteproject.org>.

[10] Durden, Tyler. "California Senator Forced To Pull Bill Banning 'Fake News' After Realizing It's Idiotic". *ZeroHedge*. 31 Mar. 2017. Accessed Dec. 2017 <ww.zerohedge.com>.

[11] Ibid

[12] *Air Cadet Publication 5: Health, Safety & Environmental Protection*. Royal Air Force Air Cadets. Accessed Dec. 2017 <witneyaircadets.co.uk>.

[13] "FALSE: Comet Ping Pong Pizzeria Home To Child Abuse Ring Led By Hillary Clinton". 2016. *Snopes.Com*. Accessed Dec. 2017 <www.snopes.com/pizzagate-conspiracy/.

[14] Ibid

[15] Feldman, Brian. 2017. "DNI Report: High Confidence Russia Interfered With U.S. Election". *Select All*. Jan. 2017. Accessed Dec. 2017 <www.nymag.com>.

[16] Solon, Olivia, and Sabrina Siddiqui. 2017. "Russia-Backed Facebook Posts 'Reached 126M Americans' During US Election". *The Guardian*. 30. Oct. 2017. Accessed Dec. 2017 <www.theguardian.com>.

[17] Ibid

[18] "This Is How Russia Used Fake News On Facebook To Help Elect Donald Trump (VIDEO)". 7 Sep. 2017. *Huffpost*. Accessed Dec. 2017 <www.huffingtonpost.com>.

[19] "S.1989 - 115Th Congress (2017-2018): Honest Ads Act". U.S. 115th Congress. Accessed Dec. 2017 <www.congress.gov>.

[20] Sharp, Adam. "'Honest Ads' On Social Media One Step To An Honest Political System." *The Hill*. 31 Oct. 2017. Accessed Dec. 2017 <www.thehill.com>.

[21] Gadkari, Pia. "How Does Twitter Make Money?" *BBC News*. 7 Nov. 2013. Accessed Dec. 2017 <www.bbc.com>.

[22] Rosen, Christopher. "All The Times Donald Trump Has Called Something 'Fake News'". *Entertainment Weekly*. 27 Jun. 2017. Accessed Dec. 2017. <ew.com>

[23] "The Ultimate "Fake News" List". 2016. *Infowars*. Accessed December 10 2017. <www.infowars.com/the-ultimate-fake-news-list/.

[24] Cornwell, Rupert. " Donald Trump Can Criticise the 'Mainstream Media' All He Likes, the Press Will Continue To Do Its Job Brilliantly." *The Independent*. 18 Feb. 2017. Accessed Dec. 2017 <www.independent.co.uk>.

[25] Cillizza, Chris. "Trump's Chilling Escalation Of His Media War." *CNN*. 5 Oct. 2017. Accessed Dec. 2017 <www.cnn.com>.

[26] Ariens, Chris. "Q3 2017 Ratings: CNN Has Most-Watched Third Quarter Ever". *TVNewser*. 26 Sep. 2017. Accessed Dec. 2017 <www.adweek.com>.

[27] "National Tracking Poll Project 170701. July 07-09, 2017." *Morning Consult*. Jul. 2017. Accessed Dec. 2017 <www.morningconsult.com>.

[28] Marcin, Tim. "Voters consider CNN the least-credible major news outlet—but Trump is trusted even less." *Newsweek*. 12 Jul. 2017. Accessed Dec. 2018 <www.newsweek.com>.

[29] Ibid

[30] Ibid.

[31] Barthel, Michael. "Pathways to News." *Pew Research Center.* 7 Jul. 2016. Accessed Dec. 2017 <www.journalism.org>.

[32] Schwartz, Jason. "Trump's 'fake news' Mantra a Hit with Despots." *Politico.* 8 Dec. 2017. Accessed Dec. 2017 <www.politico.com>.

[33] Ibid

[34] "UN News - UN Report Details 'Devastating Cruelty' Against Rohingya Population In Myanmar's Rakhine Province." 3 Feb. 2017. *UN News Service Section.* Accessed Dec. 2017 <www.news.un.org>.

[35] "The Declaration Of Independence." Independence Hall Association. 1776. Accessed Dec. 2017 <www.ushistory.org>.

[36] Calfas, Jennifer. "President Trump's Approval Rating Is Lower Than Any Modern President". *Time.* 5 Nov. 2017. Accessed Dec. 2017 <www.time.com>.

[37] "Facebook To Help Italy Prevent Fake News Ahead Of 2018 Election". *The Week.* 27 Nov. 2017. Accessed Dec. 2017 <www.theweek.co.uk>.

[38] Littleton, Cynthia. "ABC News Suspends Investigative Reporter Brian Ross For Michael Flynn Error." *Variety.* 2 Dec. 2017. Accessed Dec. 2017 <www.variety.com>.

[39] "Word Of The Year 2016 Is... "Oxford Dictionaries. N.D. Accessed Dec. 2017 <www.langues.oup.com>.

[40] Ibid

Empowering Students to Prevent School Shootings

[1] Katsiyannis, A., Whitford, D., and Parks Ennis, R. "Historical Examination of United States Intentional Mass School Shootings in the 20th and 21st Centuries: Implications for Students, Schools, and Society." *Journal of Child & Family Studies.* 19 Apr. 2018.

[2] Stracqualursi, V. "Tennessee Lawmaker Says Pornography is a 'Root Cause' of School Shootings." *CNN Politics.* 30 May 2018. Accessed May 2018 <www.cnn.com>.

[3] Leefeldt, E. "Are active shooter drills too scary for children?" *CBS News.* 30 Nov 2017. Accessed May 2018 <www.cbsnews.com>.

[4] Katsiyannis, pg. 4.

[5] Leefeldt, pg. 3.

[6] Katsiyannis, pg. 4.

[7] *Guide for Developing High-Quality School Emergency Operations Plans.* U.S. Department of Education. 2013. Accessed May 2018 <rems.ed.gov>.

[8] *Ibid.*

[9] Wong, A. "The Parkland Students Aren't Going Away." *The Atlantic.* 24 Feb. 2018. Accessed May 2018 <www.theatlantic.com>.

[10] Moeller, R. *COSO Enterprise Risk Management.* Hoboken, New Jersey: John Wiley & Sons, Inc. 2007.

[11] *Guide for Developing High-Quality School Emergency Operations Plans.*

[12] Moeller, pg. 115.

[13] *Guide for Developing High-Quality School Emergency Operations Plans*, pg. 3.

[14] Sommerfeldt, C. "Texas Gov. Greg Abbott rolls out plan to arm teachers, beef up police presence in the wake of Santa Fe massacre." *New York Daily News.* 30 May 2018. Accessed May 2018 <www.nydailynews.com>.

[15] Martin, R., Parrott, S.M., Freeman, A. *Data Brief.* The TWITR Project. 30 Apr. 2018. Accessed May 2018 <www.twitrproject.org>.

[16] *Juvenile Justice.* Positive Behavioral Interventions & Supports. 2018 Accessed May 2018 <www.pbis.org>.

[17] *Classroom PBIS Practices.* Positive Behavioral Interventions & Supports. 2018. Accessed May 2018 <www.pbis.org>.

[18] "Active Shooter." Department of Homeland Security. N.D. Accessed May 2018 <www.ready.gov>.

[19] Crane, Greg. *How ALICE Training Made the Difference in Saving More Lives.* ALICE Training Institute. 17 Feb 2017. Accessed May 2018 <www.alicetraining.com>.

[20] Hobbs, S., Zhu, Y., and Chokey, A. "New details: How the Parkland School Shooting Unfolded." *Sun Sentinel.* 24 Apr 2018. Accessed May 2018 <www.sun-sentinel.com>.

[21] *Ibid.*

[22] Karlis, N. "Generation Z Finds Its Rebellious Spirit in Lobbying for Gun Reform." *Salon.* 5 May 2018. Accessed May 2018 <www.salon.com>.

[23] Peoples, S. and Swanson, E. "Poll: More Young People Say Politicians Care What They Think." *Associated Press.* 30 May 2018. Accessed May 2018 <www.apnews.com>.

The Black Swan by the Festival

[1] Bernstein, Peter L. *Against the Gods: The Remarkable Story of Risk.* Wiley and Sons. 1998.

[2] Taleb, Nassim Nicholas. "The Black Swan: The Impact of the Highly Improbable." Random House Trade Paperbacks. 2007.

[3] Ashley Hoffman, "The Route 91 Harvest Festival in Las Vegas Ended in a Mass Shooting. Here's What to Know About It." *Time Magazine*. 2 Oct. 2017. Accessed Nov. 2017 <www.time.com>.

[4] "How the Las Vegas Strip Shooting Unfolded." *The Washington Post*. 2 Oct. 2017. Accessed Nov. 2017 <www.washingtonpost.com>.

[5] LaVito, Angelica. "'There are Bodies Lying Everywhere': the Security CEO from the Doomed Vegas Concert Talks About Getting the Call." *CNBC*. 2 Oct. 2017. Accessed Nov. <www.cnbc.com>.

[6] Brill, Steven. "Is America Any Safer?" *The Atlantic*. Sep. 2016. Accessed Nov. 2017 <www.theatlantic.com>.

[7] Gaffey, Conor. "How did Las Vegas Shooter Stephen Paddock Get 23 Guns into His Mandalay Bay Hotel Room?" *Newsweek*. 3 Oct. 2017. Accessed Nov. 2017 <www.newsweek.com>.

[8] Wamsley, Laurel. "1 Week Later, Las Vegas Moves From Response to Recovery." *NPR*. 8 Oct. 2017. Accessed Nov. 2017 <www.npr.org>.

[9] Smith, Sephora. "Las Vegas Shooting: ISIS Claim of Responsibility is Sign of Desperation." *NBC News*. 3 Oct. 2017. Accessed Nov. 2017 <www.nbcnews.com>.

[10] Gaffey, Conor. "How Did Las Vegas Shooter Stephen Paddock Get 23 Guns into His Mandalay Bay Hotel Room?" *Newsweek*. 3 Nov. 2017 <www.newsweek.com>.

[11] Kennedy, Gerrick. "Site of Las Vegas Mass Shooting is Key Venue in Effort to Make the City a Live-music Destination." *Los Angeles Times*. 2 Oct. 2017. Accessed Nov. 2017 <www.latimes.com>.

[12] Woods, Amanda. "Mandalay Bay adds 24/7 Elevator Security after Gunman's Rampage." *New York Post*. 17 Nov. 2017. Accessed Nov. 2017 <www.nypost.com>.

[13] Eccles, Robert G., Scott C. Newquist, and Roland Schatz. "Reputation and its Risks." *Harvard Business Review*. Feb. 2007. Accessed Nov. 2017 <www.hbr.org>.

[14] Burke, Matt. "Hotel Room Price at Mandalay Bay after Las Vegas Shooting." *Metro*. 24 Oct. 2017. Accessed Nov. 2017 <www.metro.us>.

[15] Shen, Lucinda. "The Owner of Mandalay Bay Lost Almost a Billion Dollars in Value after the Las Vegas Shooting." *Yahoo Finance*. 2 Oct. 2017. Accessed Nov. 2017 <www.finance.yahoo.com>.

[16] "Mandalay Bay Weighs Fate of Vegas Gunman's Infamous Suite." *New York Post*. 10 Oct. 2017. Accessed Nov. 2017 <www.nypost.com>.

[17] "Board Oversight of Reputation Risk." *Board Perspectives: Risk Oversight - Issue 83*. 12 Sep. 2016. Protiviti. Accessed Nov. 2017 <www.protiviti.com>.

[18] Siegler, Kirk."Why It Will be Tough to Hold Hotel Legally Responsible for the Vegas Shooting." *National Public Radio*. 13 Oct. 2017. Accessed Nov. 2017 <www.npr.org>.

[19] Gaffey, Connor.

[20] "Lawsuits Filed Against Mandalay Bay, Concert Organizers, Bump Stock Sellers." *CBS News*. 15 Nov. 2017. Accessed Nov. 2017 <www.cbsnews.com>.

[21] Ugwu, Reggie and Joe Coscarelli. "In Las Vegas, Concert Security Met a New Threat: Aerial Assault." *The New York Times*. 3 Oct. 2017. Accessed Nov. 2017 <www.nytimes.com>.

[22] LaVito, Angelica. "'There are Bodies Lying Everywhere': the Security CEO from the Doomed Vegas Concert Talks About Getting the Call." *CNBC*. 2 Oct. 2017. Accessed Nov. 2017 <www.cnbc.com>.

[23] Barkas, Sherry, Benjamin Goad and Wyatt Buchanan. "Las Vegas shooting: Festival security can't stop every 'black swan event.'" *USA Today*. 4 Oct. 2017. Accessed Nov. 2017 <www.usatoday.com>.

[24] Cano, Regina Garcia. "Las Vegas is Surrounding Marathoners This Weekend With Snipers and Security Measures." *Business Insider*. 11 Nov. 2017. Accessed Nov. 2017 <www.businessinsider.com>.

The Worst Sexual Abuse Scandal in Athletics

[1] Engh, Fred. "Is a Sexual Predator Lurking on Your Kid's Team?" *The Huffington Post*. 1 June 2015. Accessed May 2018 <www.huffingtonpost.com>.

[2] Serani, Deborah. " Sexual Abuse in Sports." *Psychology Today*. 1 Dec. 2011. Accessed May 2018 <www.psychologytoday.com>.

[3] Ibid.

[4] Ibid.

[5] Taylor, Tom. "After the Larry Nassar Scandal. Where Does USA Gymnastics Go from Here?" *Sports Illustrated*. 7 Feb. 2018. Accessed May 2018 <www.si.com>.

[6] Ibid.

[7] Interview: Mynarski, Jackie. [Associate Athletic Director of Compliance at University of Washington.] Personal Interview. 28 May 2018.

[8] Tarrant, David & Terri Langford. "On Karolyi Ranch, Gymnasts with Olympic Dreams Endured 'Perfect Environment for Abuse." *Dallas News*. 23 Feb. 2018. Accessed May 2018 <www.dallasnews.com>.

[9] Ibid.

[10] Ibid.

[11] Barr, John & Dan Murphy. "Nassar Surrounded by Adults Who Enabled His Predatory Behavior." *ESPN*. 16 Jan. 2018. Accessed May 2018 <www.espn.com>.

[12] Ibid

[13] "Who Is Larry Nassar?"

[14] Ibid.

[15] Ibid.

[16] **Barr.**

[17] Barr, John & Dan Murphy.

[18] Ibid.

[19] Ibid.

[20] Madani, Doha. "Larry Nassar's Boss Accused of Assaulting Students in Practice Exam." *The Huffington Post*. 26 Apr. 2018. Accessed May 2018 <www.huffingtonpost.com>

[21] **Barr.**

[22] Ibid.

[23] Ibid.

[24] Tarrant, David & Terri Langford.

[25] Kwiatkowski, Marisa, et al. "How the USA Gymnastics Scandal Unfolded." *Indianapolis Star*. 22 Mar. 2017. Accessed May 2018 <www.indystar.com>.

[26] Barr, John & Dan Murphy.

[27] Ibid.

[28] Kwiatkowski.

[29] Barr, John & Dan Murphy.

[30] Ibid.

[31] Interview: Robinson, Kris, and Jeff Robinson. [Physical Therapist and past NCAA College Coach; and Past NCAA Junior Olympic Men's Coordinator and Present Head Gymnastic Coach at the Air Force Academy.] Telephone Interview. 25 May 2018.

[32] Ibid.

[33] Barr, John & Dan Murphy.

[34] Tarrant, David & Terri Langford.

[35] Ibid.

[36] "Who Is Larry Nassar?"

[37] Barr, John & Dan Murphy.

[38] "Who Is Larry Nassar?"

[39] Mynarski.

[40] "Title IX." University of Washington. N.D. Accessed May 2018 <www.washington.edu>.

[41] Ibid.

[42] Mynarski.

[43] Robinson, Kris, and Jeff Robinson.

[44] "Who We Are." U.S. Center for SafeSport. N.D. Accessed May 2018 <www.safesport.org>.

[45] Ibid.

#DeleteUber

[1] "Finding the Way Creating Possibilities for Riders, Drivers, and Cities." Uber, www.uber.com/our-story/.

[2] Balachandran, Manu. "A timeline of events that led to the downfall of Travis Kalanick at Uber." *Quartz India*. 21 Jun. 2017. Accessed Mar. 2018 <www.qz.com>.

[3] Levin, Sam. "Uber's Scandals, Blunders and PR Disasters: the Full List." The Guardian, Guardian News and Media, 27 June 2017, www.theguardian.com/technology/2017/jun/18/uber-travis-kalanick-scandal-pr-disaster-timeline.

[4] Ibid.

[5] Ibid.

[6] Ibid.

[7] Ibid.

[8] Ibid.

[9] Ibid.

[10] Ibid.

[11] Ibid.

[12] Isaac, Mike, et al. "Uber Hid 2016 Breach, Paying Hackers to Delete Stolen Data." *The New York Times*. 21 Nov. 2017. Accessed Mar. 2018 <www.nytimes.com>.

[13] Newcomer, Eric. "Uber Paid Hackers to Delete Stolen Data on 57 Million People." *Bloomberg*. 21 Nov. 2017. Accessed Mar. 2018 <www.bloomberg.com>.

[14] Ibid.

[15] Ibid.

[16] Isaac, Mike, et al.

[17] Hern, Alex. "Uber Driver Declared Employee as the Company Loses Another Ruling." *The Guardian*. 11 Sept. 2015. Accessed Mar. 2018 <www.theguardian.com>.

[18] "Data Security Breach Reporting." State of California - Department of Justice - Office of the Attorney General. 14 Sept. 2017. Accessed Mar. 2018 <www.oag.ca.gov>.

[19] Newcomer, Eric.

[20] "Uber Settles with FTC over Privacy and Data Security Promises." *Consumer Information*, U.S. Federal Trade Commission. 24 Aug. 2017. Accessed Mar. 2018 <www.consumer.ftc.gov>.

[21] Siddique, Haroon, and Shaun Walker. "Uber Hacking: Customers Not at Risk of Financial Crime, Says Minister." *The Guardian*. 23 Nov. 2017. Accessed Mar. 2018 <www.theguardian.com>.

[22] Ibid.

[23] Vaas, Lisa. "Proposed Law Would Jail Execs Who Fail to Report Data Breaches." *Naked Security*. 4 Dec. 2017. Accessed Mar. 2018 <www.nakedsecurity.sophos.com>.

[24] Rhodes, Anna. "Uber: Which Countries Have Banned the Controversial Taxi App." *The Independent*. 22 Sep. 2017. Accessed Mar. 2018 <www.independent.co.uk>.

[25] Khosrowshahi, Dara. "Uber Newsroom." Uber. 21 Nov. 2017. Accessed Mar. 2018 <www.uber.com>.

[26] Ibid.

[27] Ibid.

[28] Ibid.

[29] Ibid.

[30] Ibid..

[31] Ibid.

Evaluating the Risks to the National Football League

[1] Belzer, Jason. "Thanks To Roger Goodell, NFL Revenues Projected To Surpass $13 Billion In 2016." *Forbes*. 29 Feb. 2016. Accessed Oct. 2017 <www.forbes.com>.

[2] "NBC's 'Sunday Night Football' Is Primetime Television's No. 1 Show for Record Sixth Consecutive Year as TV Season Ends." *The Futon Critic*. 25 May 2017. Accessed Oct. 2017 <www.thefutoncritic.com>.

[3] Gregory, Sean. "Youth Football Linked To Brain Damage Later In Life." *Time*. 19 Sep. 2017. Accessed Oct. 2017 <www.time.com>.

[4] Cox, Daniel and Robert P. Jones. "Nearly One-Third of Americans Say They Would Not Let Their Son Play Football." *PRRI*. 28 Jan. 2016. Accessed Oct. 2017 <www.prri.org>.

[5] Ibid

[6] Bieler, Des. "In stunning admission, NFL official affirms link between football and CTE." Chicagotribune.com. March 15, 2016. Accessed Oct. 2017 <www.chicagotribune.com/sports/football/ct-nfl-exec-admits-to-cte-football-head-trauma-link-20160314-story.html.

[7] "HEADS UP FOOTBALL: SAFETY IN ACTION." USA Football. Accessed Oct. 2017 <usafootball.com/programs/heads-up-football/.

[8] Schwarz, Alan. "N.F.L.-Backed Youth Program Says It Reduced Concussions. The Data Disagrees." The New York Times. July 27, 2016. Accessed Oct. 2017 <www.nytimes.com/2016/07/28/sports/football/nfl-concussions-youth-program-heads-up-football.html?smid=tw-share&_r=0.

[9] "The Quest for a Better Football Helmet." SI.com. Accessed Oct. 2017 <www.si.com/mmqb/2017/05/31/nfl-quest-better-football-helmet.

[10] Ibid.

[11] Ibid.

[12] Berr, Jonathan. "NFL national anthem protest denting ticket sales." *CBS News*. 29 Sep. 2017. Accessed Oct. 2017 <www.cbsnews.com>.

[13] Johnson, Zach. "ESPN's Hannah Storm Questions the NFL's Integrity After Explaining Ray Rice Scandal to Her Kids." *E! News*. 15 Sep. 2014. Accessed Oct. 2017 <www.eonline.com>.

[14] "NFL Sees Small Regular-Season Attendance Decline; Titans, Rams Down Sharply At Home." *Sports Business Daily*. 5 Jan. 2016. Accessed Oct. 2017 <www.sportsbusinessdaily.com>.

[15] Florio, Mike. "NFL Statement on Stadium Security." *NBC Sports*. 14 Nov. 2015. Accessed Oct. 2017 <www.profootballtalk.nbcsports.com>.

[16] Saltsgaver, Mark and Steven Strammello. "ERM in the Red Zone: Lessons from the Super Bowl." *Risk Management*. 3 Jun. 2012. Accessed Oct. 2017 <www.rrmagazine.com>.

[17] "About Levi's® Stadium." Levi's® Stadium. N.D. Accessed Oct. 2017 <www.levisstadium.com>.

[18] Alex Koma "How Santa Clara uses IoT, open data to tackle NFL invasion." *StateScoop*. 16 Sep. 2015. Accessed Oct. 2017 <statescoop.com>.

Operational Risk Challenges for the CDC

[1] "Mission, Role and Pledge." Centers for Disease Control and Prevention. Apr 2014. Accessed Apr. 2018 <www.cdc.gov>.

[2] Ibid.

[3] Kwon, Diana. "Proposed Federal Budget Slashes Funds to EPA, CDC." *The Scientist*. 13 Feb 2018. Accessed Apr 2018 <www.the-scientist.com>.

[4] Drash, Wayne. "Cuts to CDC Epidemic Programs Will Endanger Americans, Former Chief Says." *CNN*. 5 Feb 2018. Accessed Apr. 2018 <www.cnn.com>.

[5] Yong, Ed. "The CDC Is About to Fall Off a Funding Cliff." *The Atlantic*. 2 Feb 2018. Accessed Apr 2018. <www.theatlantic.com>.

[6] Sun, Lena. "World Leaders Rehearse for a Pandemic That Will Come 'Sooner Than We Expect'." *Washington Post*. 24 Oct 2017. Accessed Apr. 2018 <www.washingtonpost.com>.

[7] Newkirk II, Vann R. "Is the CDC Losing Control?" *The Atlantic*. 3 Feb 2018. Accessed Apr. 2018 <www.theatlantic.com>.

[8] Elperin, Juliet, and Lena H. Sun. "CDC gets Lists of Forbidden Words: Fetus, Transgender, Diversity" *Washington Post*. 15 Dec. 2017. Accessed Apr. 2018 <www.washingtonpost.com>.

[9] Moeller, Robert R. *COSO Enterprise Risk Management*. John Wiley & Sons, Inc. 2011.

[10] Greenfieldboyce, Nell. "Spending Bill Lets CDC Study Gun Violence; but Researchers are Skeptical It Will Help." *NPR*. 23 Mar 2018. Accessed Apr. 2018 <www.npr.org>.

Risks within Tesla, Inc.

1 Baer, Drake. "The Making of Tesla: Invention, Betrayal, and The Birth Of The Roadster." *Business Insider*. 11 Nov. 2014. Accessed Apr. 2018 <www.businessinsider.com>.

2 *Form 10-K for the Fiscal Year Ended December 31, 2017: Tesla, Inc.* U.S. Securities and Exchange Commission. 22 Feb. 2018. Accessed Apr. 2018 <www.sec.gov>.

3 Lee, Timothy B. "How Tesla surpassed GM and Ford to Become America's Most Valuable Car Company." *Vox*. 10 Apr. 2017. Accessed Apr. 2018 <www.vox.com>.

4 "Number of Tesla Vehicles Delivered Worldwide From 2nd Quarter 2015 To 1st Quarter 2018 (In Units)." *Statistica*. Accessed Apr. 23 2018 <www.statistica.com>

5 Hull, Dana. "Model 3 Production Line Skids to a Halt for Tesla." *Bloomberg LP.* 20 Apr. 2018. Accessed Apr. 2018 <www.bloomberg.com>.

6 *Ibid.*

7 Field, Kyle. "Tesla Adds 3rd Shift To Model 3 Production In Push To 6,000 Vehicles/Week Run Rate." *Clean Technica.* 18 Apr. 2018. Accessed Apr. 2018 <www.cleantechnica.com>.

8 "Another Cal/OSHA Tesla Investigation After Factory Worker Breaks Jaw." *CBS Broadcasting Inc.* 20 Apr. 2018. Accessed Apr. 2018 <www.sanfrancisco.cbslocal.com>.

9 Felton, Ryan. "U.S. Labor Agency Files Amended Complaint Against Tesla For Alleged Worker Rights Violations." *Gizmodo Media Group.* 30 Mar. 2018. Accessed Apr. 2018 <www.jalopnik.com>.

10 Field, Kyle.

11 Wattles, Jackie. "Tesla Model X was in autopilot before fatal crash." *CNN.* 31 Mar. 2018. Accessed Apr. 2018 <www.money.cnn.com>.

12 Stewart. Jack. "Why Tesla's Autopilot Can't See A Stopped Firetruck." *Wired.* 15 Jan. 2018. Accessed Apr. 2018 <www.wired.com>.

The State Department's Leadership Vacuum

1 *FY 2018 State Department Budget Request.* U.S. Department of State. Jun. 2017. Accessed Feb. 2017 <www.state.gov>.

2 Stephenson, Barbara. "Time to Ask Why." American Foreign Service Association, *Foreign Service Journal.* Dec. 2017. Accessed Feb. 2018 <www.asfa.org>.

3 Ibid.

4 Bruzek, Alison & Meghna Chakrabarti. "Former Secretary of State Madeleine Albright on the State of Democracy." *WBUR Radio Boston.* 25 Jan. 2018. Accessed Feb. 2018 <www.wbur.org>.

5 Bing, Chris. "Tillerson Proposes New 'Cyber Bureau' at the State Department." *CyberScoop.* 7 Feb 2018. Accessed 7 Feb 2018. <www.cyberscoop.com>.

6 Toosi, Nahal.

7 Toosi, N. "Leaked Document Shows Tillerson Power Play." *Politico.* 26 Oct 2017. Accessed 7 Feb 2017 <www.politico.com>.

8 McKean, David. "Rex Tillerson Is Fiddling with PowerPoint as the World Burns." *Politico.* 26 Nov 2017. Accessed 7 Feb 2018. <www.politico.com>.

[9] Gramer, Robbie, Dan De Luce, and Colum Lynch. "How the Trump Administration Broke the State Department." *Foreign Policy.* 31 Jul 2017. Accessed 7 Feb 2018. <www.foreignpolicy.com>.

[10] Toosi, Nahal. "Tillerson Scales Back State Department Restructuring Plan." *Politico.* 7 Feb 2018. Accessed 7 Feb 2018. <www.politico.com>

[11] Green, Philip E.J. *Enterprise Risk Management: A Common Framework for the Entire Organization.* Elsevier. 2016, p. 60.

[12] Faries, Bill, and Mira Rojanaskul. "At Tillerson's State Department, Seven of the Nine Top Jobs Are Empty." *Bloomberg Politics.* 2 Feb 2018. Accessed 7 Feb 2018 <www.bloomberg.com>.

[13] Hudson, John. "Top Official in Charge of State Department Redesign Quits Job." *Buzzfeed News.* 28 Nov 2017. Accessed 7 Feb 2018. <www.buzzfeed.com>.

[14] Green, p. 102.

[15] Green, p. 73.

_____

Understanding SEC's Inadequate Internal Controls

[1] "What We Do." U.S. Securities and Exchange Commission. 10 Jun. 2013. Accessed Oct. 2017 <www.sec.gov>.

[2] "Everything EDGAR." U.S. Securities and Exchange Commission. 6 Jan. 2017. Accessed Oct. 2017 <www.sec.gov>.

[3] "Statement on Cybersecurity." U.S. Securities and Exchange Commission. 20 Sept. 2017. Accessed Oct. 2017 <www.sec.gov>.

[4] Isidore, Chris. "Why the SEC Hack is a Really Big Deal." *CNNMoney.* 21 Sept. 2017. Accessed Oct. 2017 <money.cnn.com>.

[5] Albin-Wurzer, Melissa, et al. "2014 Information Security and Privacy Report." UW Office of the Chief Information Security Officer. 2014. Accessed Oct. 2017 <ciso.uw.edu>.

[6] Coffin, Bill, et al. "The 2008 Financial Crisis: A Wakeup Call for Enterprise Risk Management." The Risk and Insurance Management Society. 2009. Accessed Sept. 2017 <www.rims.org>.

[7] Ibid.

[8] "Opportunities Exist for SEC to Improve its Controls Over Financial Systems and Data". U.S. Government Accountability Office. 28 Apr 2016. Accessed Oct. 2017 <www.gao.gov>.

[9] "SEC Improved Control of Financial Systems but Needs to Take Additional Actions." U.S. Government Accountability Office. 27 Jul 2017. Accessed Oct. 2017 <www.gao.gov>.

[10] Atluri, Indrajit. "Managing the Risk of IoT: Regulations, Frameworks, Security, Risk and Analytics". ISACA Journal, Volume 3. 2017. Accessed Oct. 2017.

[11] "SEC Improved Control of Financial Systems but Needs to Take Additional Actions."

[12] Ibid.

[13] Barnum, Sean, and Gegick, Michael. "Least Privilege". US-CERT. 10 May 2013. Accessed Oct. 2017 <www.us-cert.gov>.

[14] "SEC Improved Control of Financial Systems but Needs to Take Additional Actions."

[15] *Ibid.*

[16] "Cybersecurity, the SEC and You". U.S. Securities and Exchange Commission. 02 Oct. 2017. Accessed Oct. 2017 <www.sec.gov>.

www.ingramcontent.com/pod-product-compliance
Lightning Source LLC
Chambersburg PA
CBHW060543200326
41521CB00007B/467